Q & A SERIES
PUBLIC INTERNATIONAL LAW

Cavendish
Publishing
Limited

London • Sydney

TITLES IN THE Q&A SERIES

BUSINESS LAW
CIVIL LIBERTIES
COMMERCIAL LAW
COMPANY LAW
CONFLICT OF LAWS
CONSTITUTIONAL & ADMINISTRATIVE LAW
CONTRACT LAW
CRIMINAL LAW
EMPLOYMENT LAW
ENGLISH LEGAL SYSTEM
EQUITY & TRUSTS
EUROPEAN COMMUNITY LAW
EVIDENCE
FAMILY LAW
INTELLECTUAL PROPERTY LAW
INTERNATIONAL TRADE LAW
JURISPRUDENCE
LAND LAW
PUBLIC INTERNATIONAL LAW
REVENUE LAW
SUCCESSION, WILLS & PROBATE
TORTS LAW
'A' LEVEL LAW

Q & A SERIES
PUBLIC INTERNATIONAL LAW

Owain Blackwell
University of Buckingham
and
David Ong
University of Buckingham

Cavendish
Publishing
Limited

London • Sydney

First published in Great Britain 1998 by Cavendish Publishing Limited, The Glass House, Wharton Street, London WC1X 9PX.
Telephone: 0171-278 8000 Facsimile: 0171-278 8080
e-mail: info@cavendishpublishing.com
Visit our Home Page on http://www.cavendishpublishing.com

© Blackwell, O and Ong, D 1998

All rights reserved. No part of this publication may be reproduced, stored in a retrieval system, or transmitted, in any form or by any means, electronic, mechanical, photocopying, recording, scanning or otherwise, except under the terms of the Copyright Designs and Patents Act 1988 or under the terms of a licence issued by the Copyright Licensing Agency, 90 Tottenham Court Road, London W1P 9HE, UK, without the permission in writing of the publisher.

Blackwell, Owain
Public International Law – (Questions & Answers Series)
I. Title II. Series
341

ISBN 1 874241 37 6

Printed and bound in Great Britain

Preface

This book is intended for students of public international law who may feel that they have acquired a certain body of knowledge on the subject but are nevertheless unsure as to how they should go about applying this knowledge in an examination situation. It is at least arguable that the nature of public international law itself contributes to the anxiety that students often feel when approaching this subject from the perspective of preparing for an examination on it. Perhaps more than any other legal topic, public international law requires students to grapple with different subjects of the law (States), different sources of law (treaties, custom, general principles, etc) and different institutions (UN, ICJ, etc) which do not readily find their counterpart in national or domestic laws.

The study of public international law, therefore, requires students almost to have to begin anew in their understanding of this complex legal system, rather than being able to approach the subject merely in terms of the acquisition of a new body of rules to be applied to a special set of circumstances, as is usually the case in other areas of domestic law. The necessarily brief introduction to public international law that students usually obtain when the course is taught at the undergraduate level often has the consequence of enabling students to grasp the notion of public international law as a different system of law only towards the end of the course itself. This means that in the case of public international law, again arguably more so than in other areas of domestic law, the need to have a good understanding of nearly every aspect of this different system of law is imperative.

Another important aspect of the preparation for a public international law examination, that derives from the nature of the discipline itself, is the fact that, although questions may be posed on various different public international law topics, in reality they often raise or are concerned with rather basic issues in respect of the system of public international law itself. These are, for example, questions related to the applicable sources of international law in respect of an identified dispute, the rules governing the creation and recognition of States under international law, the rights and duties of States vis à vis other States and other different entities regulated under international law, the circumstances in which State responsibility arises, the methods of dispute settlement available under international law and the possibility of the individual and collective use of force by States following the breakdown of all possible means of peaceful dispute settlement under international law.

The factual information that is provided in a public international law examination, especially within the context of a problem question, is crucial in raising the basic issues or questions that need to be posed in attempting to answer the questions. These attempts at analysing the issues raised are often the major aim of the whole exercise, quite apart from whether the right answer is actually forthcoming from the given facts to hand. As with other subjects within an undergraduate law degree course, it is the application of a certain analytical technique or methodology within the public international law discipline that examiners are on the lookout for in the examination.

The above point is important to note as it forms the basic premise for a book such as the present one. In other words, students must approach this book from the perspective of having already acquired a certain amount of knowledge in the subject and needing only to sharpen their analytical skills in respect of the type of questions, either essay or problem, that may be posed in an examination on public international law. As we shall see, all the model answers provided in respect of the essay and problem questions on the various topics of public international law presuppose a working knowledge of the substantive rules on the topic, and attempt to build on this by the presentation of legal arguments employing a structured analysis of these rules. Reading the model answers under the relevant topic heading as an opportunity to receive some first hand knowledge of the substantive topic covered by that chapter of the book is, therefore, unlikely to be successful.

In the preparation of this book, the following breakdown in the individual chapters was observed: Owain Blackwell was responsible for writing the introduction and answers in Chapters 1–8, 13 and 14; whilst David Ong was responsible for writing the answers in Chapters 9–12.

Owain Blackwell
David Ong
April 1998

Contents

Preface — v
Table of Cases — ix
Table of Statutes — xv
Table of Conventions — xvii

1. The Nature of Public International Law — 1
2. Sources of International Law — 17
3. The Law of Treaties — 37
4. The Relationship between International and Municipal Law — 59
5. Personality and Recognition — 79
6. The Acquisition of Territory — 107
7. Jurisdiction — 131
8. Immunity from Jurisdiction — 157
9. The Law of the Sea — 179
10. State Responsibility — 205
11. International Environmental Law — 229
12. Human Rights — 271
13. Peaceful Settlement of Disputes — 291
14. Use of Force — 315

Index — 335

Table of Cases

A Ahlstrom Oy v Commission (the Wood Pulp Case) 4 CMLR 901 154
Advisory Opinion in Interpretation of Peace Treaties
  with Bulgaria, Hungary and Romania [1950] ICJ Rep 71 309
Advisory Opinion of the Continued Presence of South
  Africa in Namibia (South West Africa) [1971] ICJ Rep 321
Ahmed v Government of the Kingdom of Saudi Arabia
  [1996] 2 All ER 248 171
Aland Island Case (1920) 94
Alcom Ltd v Republic of Colombia [1984] 2 All ER 6 178
Ambatielos Arbitration Case (Greece v UK) (1956)
  12 RIAA 83; 23 ILR 306 .... 213, 215
Ambatielos Case [1948] ICJ Rep 28 47
Annette, The; The Dora [1919] P 105 82
Arango v Guzman Travel Advisors Corp (1980) 621 F 2d 1371 176
Arantzazu Mendi, The [1939] AC 256; ILR 60 85
Attorney General for Canada v Attorney General for
  Ontario [1937] AC 326 .... 69, 71
Attorney General of Israel v Adolf Eichmann (1961) 36 ILR 5 .... 137, 149
Attorney General's Reference (No 1 of 1982) [1983] 3 WLR 72 154

BP v Libya (1974) 53 ILR 329 .... 211, 216
Baccus SRL v Servico Nacional del Trigo [1956] 3 All ER 732 78
Bank of China v Wells Fargo Bank & Union Trust Co (1952)
  104 Fed Supp 59 87
Barbuit's Case (1737) Cas temp Talb 281 .... 63, 73–75
Barcelona Traction, Light and Power Co Case (Belgium v Spain)
  [1970] ICJ Rep 3 .... 24, 217
Blackmer v United States 284 US 421, 52 S Ct 252, 76 L Ed 375 136
Bleir v Uruguay (1982) 1 Selected Decisions HR Comm 109 .... 279, 288
Brazil-British Guiana Boundary Dispute 127
British Airways Board v Laker Airways Ltd [1983] 3 All ER 375 156
British Guinea v Venezuela Boundary Arbitration (1899–1900) 92 BFSP 160 127
British Nylon Spinners Ltd v Imperial Chemical Industries Ltd
  [1953] 1 Ch 19 154
Burkina Faso v Mali [1986] ICJ Rep 112

Carl Zeiss Stiftung v Rayner and Keeler Ltd (No 2) [1967] AC 853 .... 84, 85
Case Concerning questions of interpretation and application
  of the Montreal Convention arising out of the aerial incident
  at Lockerbie (Provisional Measures) [1992] ICJ Rep 3 313
Case of the Free Zones of Upper Savoy and Gex
  (1932) PCIJ Ser A/B, No 46 57
Certain Expenses of the United Nations (Advisory Opinion)
  [1962] ICJ Rep 151 321

Certain German Interests in Polish Upper Silesia Case
(1926) PCIJ Ser A, No 7 216
Chamizal Arbitration, The (1911) 5 AJIL 782 ....110, 123, 129
Chorzow Factory Case (Indemnity) (Merits) (1928)
PCIJ Ser A, No 17..51, 202, 210, 222
Chung Chi Cheung v R [1939] AC 160..64, 66, 75
City of Berne, The v Bank of England (1804) 9 Ves Jun 347....................................82
Clipperton Island Arbitration (France v Mexico)
(1931) 26 AJIL 390; (1932) 2 RIAA 1105..............................114, 115, 125, 127–29
Commissioners of Customs and Excise v Minister of
Industries and Military Manufacturing (1992) unreported,
see Fox (1994) 43 ICLQ 193 172
Competence of the General Assembly for the Admission of a State
to the United Nations [1950] ICJ Rep 4 45
Cook v United States (1933) 288 US 102 70
Cooper v Stuart (1889) 14 App Cas 286 109
Corfu Channel Case (Merits) (UK v Albania)
[1949] ICJ Rep 4..47, 240, 253,
254, 264, 332, 333
Cutting Case (1886) Moore D, Vol II 228 137

Deutsche Continental Gas-Gasellschaft v Polish State
(1929) 5 AD 11...90
DPP v Doot [1973] AC 807, HL 143

Eastern Carrying Insurance Co, The v The National Benefits
Life and Property Insurance Co Lts (1919) 35 TLR 292 83
Eastern Greenland Case (1933) PCIJ Rep Ser A, No 53 ....46, 125–28
Edye v Robinson (The Head Money Case) (1884)...70
Egypt v Gamal-Eldin [1996] 2 All ER 237...170
Ellerman Lines v Murray [1931] AC 126 68
Engelke v Musmann [1928] AC 433 ....75, 77

Fatemi v United States 192 At 2d 525 DC (1963); ILR 34....................................161
Filartiga v Peña-Irala (1980) 19 ILM 966 ....203, 273,
277, 288
Fisheries Jurisdiction Case (Merits) [1974] ICJ Rep..112
Flegenheimer Claim (1958) 25 ILR 91..210, 221, 282
Frisbie v Collins 342 US 519 (1952)..150

Gabcikovo-Nagymaros Project Case (Hungary v Slovakia)
[1997] ICJ Rep..243, 255
Gdynia Ameryka Linie v Boguslawski [1953] AC 70 ....104, 105

TABLE OF CASES

Grand Jure Subpoena Duces Tecum Addressed to Canadian
  International Paper Co, Re 72 F Supp 1013 (1947)..153
Gur Corp v Trust Bank of Africa Ltd [1987] QB 599, CA...............................88, 103
Gutierrez, Re 24 ILR 265..144
Haile Selassie v Cable and Wireless Ltd (No 2) [1939]
  1 Ch 182; ILR 94...86, 102, 103
Hartford Fire Insurance Co v California (1986)..154
Hesperides Hotels v Aegean Holidays Ltd [1978] 2 All ER 1168........................88
Hispano Americana Mercantil SA v Central Bank of Nigeria [1979]
  2 Lloyd's Rep 277 ....76, 158
Home Missionary Society Claim (US v Great Britain) (1920)
  6 RIAA 42 211

I Congreso Del Partido [1981] 3 WLR 328; [1978] 1 QB 500...................77, 158, 170
ICI v Commission [1972] ECR 619..154
IRC v Collco Dealings Ltd [1962] AC 1..69
Interhandel Case [1959] ICJ Rep 305
Island of Palmas Arbitration (Netherlands v US)
  (1928) 33 AJIL 875; 2 RIAA 829.......................................111, 114–16, 125–29, 133

Janes Claim (US v Mexico) (1926) 4 RIAA 82...227
Joyce v DPP [1946] AC 347 ....136, 138, 142
Jurisdiction of the Courts of Danzig (Danzig Railway Officials)
  Case (1928) PCIJ...98

Ker v Illinois 119 US 342 (1888)...150
Kuwait Airlines v Iraqi Airways [1995] 3 All ER 694 174–76

Lake Lanoux Arbitration (Spain v France) (1957) 24 ILR 101......................240, 254
Laker Airways Ltd v Department of Trade [1977] QB 643 69
Laker Airways Ltd v Sabena 731 F 2d 909 (1984)...154
Legal Consequences Case [1971] ICJ Rep 16..312
Legality of the Threat or Use of Nuclear Weapons Case [1996] ICJ Rep 41 326
Libyan Arab Jamahiriya v United Kingdom; Libyan Arab
  Jamahiriya v United States (1998) ICJ website:
  http:/wwwicj-cij.org..311, 313
Littrell v United States of America (No 2) [1994] 4 All ER 203....................170, 178
Lotus, The (1927) PCLJ Ser A, No 10..132, 137, 143, 151
Luther v Sagor [1921] 1 KB 456 83

Macarthys v Smith [1979] 1 WLR 1189; 3 All ER 325, CA......................................65
Maclaine Watson v Department of Trade and Industry [1989] Ch 72 ....66, 68
Mannington Mills v Congoleum Corp 595 F 2d 1287 (1979) 153

xi

Mavrommatis Palestine n Concessions (Jurisdiction) Case (1924)
PCIJ Ser A, No 2 99
Military and Paramilitary Activities in and against Nicaragua
(Merits) Case (Nicaragua v US) [1986] ICJ Rep 110 .... 54, 148, 150, 305,
322, 324, 330
Minquiers and Ecrehos [1953] ICJ Rep 47 .... 125, 127, 129
Mortensen v Peters (1906) 8 F 75
Murray v Parkes [1942] 2 KB 123 .... 82, 83

Naim Molvan (Owner of Motor Vessel Asya) v Attorney General
for Palestine [1948] AC 251 138
Namibia case [1971] ICJ Rep 68 321
Naulilaa Arbitration 2 RIAA 1011 (1928) 328
Neer Claim (US v Mexico) (1926) 4 RIAA 60 .... 220, 221
Nicaragua v United States (the Nuclear Weapons Case)
[1997] ICJ Rep 41 .... 25, 26, 31
Nikitschenkoff Case (1867) 165
North Sea Continental Shelf Case [1969] ICJ Rep 21, 28, 40, 56, 294
Norwegian Loans Case [1957] ICJ Rep 48, 302, 304, 305

Nottebohm case (Liechtenstein v Guatemala)
[1953] ICJ Rep 111 .... 138, 210, 215, 221, 282
Noyes Claim (US v Panama) (1933) 6 RIAA 308 .... 211, 227
Nuclear Test Cases (Australia v France and New Zealand v France)
(Merits) [1974] ICJ Rep 240, 241, 254

Panevezys v Saldutiskis (1939) PCIJ Ser A/B, No 76; 9 ILR 99
Paquete Habana, The 175 US 677 (1900) 10, 19
Parlement Belge, The [1874–80] All ER Rep 71
Philippine Admiral (Owners) v Wallem Shipping (Hong Kong)
Ltd [1976] 1 All ER 78 78
Pianka v The Queen [1929] AC 107, PC 140
Playa Largo (Owners of Cargo Lately Laden on Board) v I Congreso
de Partido (Owners) [1983] AC 244; [1981] 2 All ER 1064 175
Propend Finance Pty v Sing (1997), The Times, CA 178
Public Prosecutor v Antoni 32 ILR 140 144

Qatar v Bahrain (the Maritime Delimitation and Territorial
Questions Case) [1995] ICJ Rep 6 44

R v Anderson (1868) 11 Cox's CC 198 140
R v Horseferry Road Magistrates' Court ex p Bennett [1994]
1 AC 42, HL 149

TABLE OF CASES

R v Kelly [1982] AC 665 141
R v Keyn (The Franconia) (1876) 2 Ex D 63 ....62, 66, 75
R v Roques (1984) 26 AJIL xvii 164
R v Sansom [1991] 2 All ER 145, CA 135
R v Secretary of State for The Home Department ex p Bagga
    [1991]1 All ER 777 172
R v Secretary of State for The Home Office ex p Thrakar [1974] 78
R v Secretary of State for Transport ex p Factortame
    (Case 213/89) [1990] ECR I 2433; 1 AC 85 ....65, 71

Radwan v Radwan [1972] 3 All ER 967 160
Rahimtoola v Nizam of Hyderabad [1957] 3 All ER 441 78
Rankin v Iran (US v Iran) (1987) 17 Iran-USCTR 135 ....216, 220, 221
Reparation for Injuries suffered in the Service of the United Nations
    Case (Advisory Opinion) [1949] ICJ Rep 174 ....96, 286
Republic of Somalia v Woodhouse; Drake v Carey (Suisse) SA
    [1993] QB 54 ....86, 103
Rio Tinto Zinc v Westinghouse Electric Corp [1978] 2 WLR 81 155
Roberts Claim (US v Mexico) (1926) 4 RIAA 77 220
Rustomjee v The Queen (1876) 1 QBD 487 97

Salem Case (Egypt v US) (1932) 2 RIAA 1161 221
Saloman v Commissioners of Customs and Excise [1967] 2 QB 116 68
Schooner Exchange, The v McFaddon (1812) 11 US (7 Cranch) 116 ....138, 157
Sei Fujii v The State of California (1952) 38 Cal 2d 718 71
Sengupta v Republic of India [1983] ICR 221 171
Short v Iran (US v Iran) (1987) 16 Iran-US Claims
    Tribunal Rep (Iran-USCTR) 76 ....211, 221
South African Supreme Court in State v Ebrahim 31 ILM 888 (1992) 149
Southern Pacific Properties (Middle East) Ltd v Arab Republic
    of Egypt Case (1993) 32 ILM 933 212
Starrett Housing Corp v Iran (1983) 4 Iran-USCTR 122;
    (1984) ILM 1090 ....212, 216
Strassheim v Daly (1911) 141

Taylor v Barclay (1828) 2 Sim 213 82
Temple of Preah Vihear Case [1962] ICJ Rep 6 ....110, 114, 117, 126, 127
Thai-Europe Tapioca Service Ltd v Government of Pakistan
    [1975] 3 All ER 961 78
Timberlane Lumber Co v Bank of America 549 F 2d 597 (1976) 153, 154
Trail Smelter Arbitration (US v Canada) (1938–41)
    3 RIAA 1905 ....240–42, 253, 254, 264
Treacy v DPP [1971] AC 537 135

xiii

Trendtex Trading Corp v Central Bank of
  Nigeria [1977] QB 578; 1 All ER 881........................60, 61, 65, 66, 72, 75–78, 158
Triquet v Bath (1764) 3 Burr 1478; 1 Wm Bl 471 ....63, 73–75

Uganda (Holdings) Ltd v Government of Uganda [1979]
  1 Lloyd's Rep 481 ....76, 158
United Kingdom v Norway (the Anglo-Norwegian Fisheries Case)
  [1951] ICJ Rep 116..26, 30, 57, 112
United States Diplomatic and Consular Staff in Tehran Case
  (US v Iran) [1980] ICJ Rep 3 ....48, 162, 211, 227
United States ex rel Lujan v Gengler 510 F 2d 62 (1975) 148
United States v Aluminium Co of America 148 F 2d (1945).........................152, 153
United States v Alvarez-Machain [1992] 95 ILR 355...148
United States v American Tobacco 221 US 106 (1911)..152
United States v Belmont (1937) 301 US 324 71
United States v Imperial Chemical Industries (1949) 154
United States v Imperial Chemicals Ltd 105 F Supp 215 (1951)..........................153
United States v Noriega 746 F Supp 1506 (1990); 99 ILR 143.................................99
United States v Pizzarusso 388 Fed 2d 8 (2nd Cir 1968)......................................142
United States v Toscanino 500 Fed 2d 267 (1975) 148

Walker v Baird [1892] AC 491 68
West Rand Central Gold Mining Co v R [1905] 2 KB 407 ....10, 66, 75
Western Sahara Case [1975] ICJ Rep 12 ....93, 112, 114, 117, 128
Wildenhus's Case 120 US 1 (1887)..140

Yeager v Iran (US v Iran) (1987) Iran-USCTR 76..210, 216
Youmans Claim (US v Mexico) (1926) 4 RIAA 110 ....210, 228
Yunis v Yunis (1991) 30 ILM 403, US Ct App DC Circuit 137

TABLE OF STATUTES

Counterfeit Currency (Convention) Act 1935
    s 1(1) 138
Criminal Damages Act 1971 141
Criminal Jurisdiction Act 1975 137
Criminal Justice Act 1993
    ss 1–3 141
    s 3(2)(3) 135

Diplomatic Privileges Act 1708 73–75
Diplomatic Privileges Act 1964 .... 158, 159, 164, 171, 172
    s 2(1) 167
    s 3 .... 161, 167
    Sched 1 .... 161, 167

Environmental Protection Act 1990
    s 7(10) 248
Exchange Control Act 1947 138

Interpretation Act 1978 43

Marine Broadcasting (Offences) Act 1967 146
Merchant Shipping Act 1894
    s 686 136
    s 686(1) 140, 141
    s 687 136
Merchant Shipping Act 1995
    s 281 140

Protection of Trading Interests Act 1980 155

Shipping Contracts and Commercial Documents Act 1964 155
State Immunity Act 1978 .... 78, 157, 158, 172–74, 178
    s 1 168
    s 1(1) 168
    s 3 172
    s 3(3) 169
    s 4 170
    s 4(2) 168
    s 4(3) 170
    s 4(6) 168
    s 14 .... 174, 177
    s 14(1) 174
    s 14(2) 176
    s 14(2)(a) 175
    s 14(2)(b) 175
    s 16(1) 170

s 17(1) 169
s 22(1) 168

Territorial Sea Act 1987 140
Treason Act 1351 141

Foreign Legislation

Cuban Democracy Act 1992 (US)...154
D'Amato Act 1996 (US) 154, 155
Export Administration Act 1981 (US) 153
Export Administration Act 1982 (US) 153
Foreign Proceedings (Prohibition of Certain Evidence) Act 1976 (Aus)............155
Foreign Trade Anti-Trust Improvements Act 1982 (US)...............153
Helms-Burton Act 1996 (US) 154, 155
Limitation of Danish Shipowners' Freedom to Give
Information to Authorities of Foreign Countries (1967) 155
Proclamation No 5928 1988 140
Sherman Anti-Trust Act 1890 ....151, 152

TABLE OF CONVENTIONS

African Charter on Human and Peoples' Rights
Art 24..269

Basel Convention on the Control of Transboundary Movement
of Hazardous Wastes and Their Disposal 1989 ....232, 258, 266
Biodiversity Convention 1992
Art 14..270
Brussels Supplementary Convention on Third Party Liability
in the Field of Nuclear Energy 1963 250

Canberra Convention on Antarctic Marine Living Resources
(CCAMLR) 1980 258
Charter of the Organisation of African Unity 1963..297
Constantinople Convention 1888..40
Convention for the Pacific Settlement of International Disputes 1899..............298
Arts 10–36 300
Art 14...298
Convention on Civil Liability for Oil Pollution Damage 1992 250
Convention on Establishment of an International Fund for
Compensation for Oil Pollution Damage 1992 250
Convention on International Trade in Endangered Species (CITES) 1973
Art XI(7) 266
Convention on the Prevention and Punishment of Crimes Against
Internationally Protected Persons 1973..327
Convention on the Representation of States in their Relations with
International Organisations of a Universal Character 1975..........................297
Convention on the Settlement of Investment Disputes between States
and the Nationals of Other States 1965 ....11, 99

Espoo ECE Convention on Environmental Impact Assessment 1991
Art 2(6) 270
Art 3(8) 270
European Agreement for the Prevention of Broadcasting Transmitted
from Stations outside National Territories 1965..146
European Convention on Human Rights 1950...............................71, 272, 289, 290
Art 25...99
European Convention on State Immunity 1972..174
Art 27...174
European Convention on the Peaceful Settlement of Disputes 1957..................297

Final Act of the Congress of Vienna 1815..40

General Act for the Pacific Settlement of International Disputes 1928 ......297, 300
General Treaty for the Renunciation of War (Kellogg-Briand Pact) 1928........4, 53
Geneva Convention 1949 ....40, 99, 299

xvii

Art 6 122
Art 154 122
Geneva Convention for the Suppression of Counterfeiting
    Currency 1929 138
Geveva Conventions on the Law of the Sea 1958 197–99

Hague Convention 1899 ....4, 42, 119, 294, 297
Hague Convention 1907 ....4, 42, 119, 297

Inter-American Convention on Human Rights 1969
    Art 44 99
International Convention for the Elimination of all forms of
    Racial Discrimination 1965 99
International Convention for the Prevention of Marine
    Pollution 1973 260
International Covenant on Civil and Political Rights 1966 ....202, 273,
                                                                                                                                                            278–81, 284, 288
    Art 4 285
    Art 7 284
    Art 9 284
    Art 9(1) 203
    Art 10 284
    Art 40 ....279, 288
    Art 41 ....203, 279, 284, 288
International Covenant on Economic, Social and
    Cultural Rights 1966 ....273, 278

Law of the Sea Convention 1982 ....40, 179–201, 262, 264
    Art 3 ....140, 145, 191, 194
    Art 5 299
    Art 14 185
    Art 17 195
    Art 19 191
    Art 19(2) 191
    Art 27(1) 140
    Art 27(1)(b) 140
    Art 33(2) 191
    Arts 37–44 195
    Art 44 196
    Art 46 190
    Art 47 190
    Art 47(1) 188, 190
    Art 47(2) 188, 190
    Art 49 191
    Art 52 191
    Art 52(2) 191

Art 56	185, 192
Art 56(1)	200
Art 56(1)(b)	186
Art 57	192, 200
Art 58(1)	192
Art 61	196, 200
Art 61(1)	185
Art 61(2)	185
Art 62	200
Art 62(2)	196
Art 62(4)	200, 201
Art 62(4)(a)	200
Art 62(4)(a)–(e)	196
Art 62(4)(k)	200
Art 69	185
Art 70	185
Art 73(1)–(4)	200
Art 73(3)	203
Art 76(1)	192
Art 76(3)	192
Arts 76(4)–(7)	192
Art 76(8)	192
Art 76(9)	192
Art 77(1)	201
Art 77(3)	192
Art 77(4)	201
Art 91	202
Art 109	146, 147
Art 109(3)	146
Art 110	146
Art 110(1)(b)	147
Art 116(a)–(c)	201
Art 117	201
Art 121	190
Art 121(3)	188, 190
Art 194	248
Art 207(1)	257
Art 207(3)	258
Art 220	186
Arts 279–99	193
Arts 305–7	183
Art 308(1)	182, 199
Art 309	183

League of Nations Covenant

Art 1(2)	93
Art 10	318
Art 11(1)	318

Art 12...318
Art 13...318
Art 15(7)..318
Locarno Treaties 297
London Convention on the Prevention of Marine Pollution
  by Dumping of Wastes and Other Matter 1972.....................................232, 260

Madrid Protocol to the Antarctic Treaty on Environmental
  Protection 1991...265
Montevideo Convention on the Rights and Duties
  of States 1933...90, 325
Montreal Convention for the Suppression of Unlawful Acts
  against the Safety of Civil Aviation 1971...309, 310
  Art 5...310
  Art 7...310, 311
  Art 8...310
  Art 11..310
  Art 14(1)..306, 311
Montreal Protocol on Substances that Deplete the Ozone
  Layer 1987..232, 262, 265, 266
  Art 11(5)..266

Option Protocol to the International Covenant on Civil and
  Political Rights 1966..99
Oslo Convention on the Prevention of Dumping of Wastes in the
  Northeast Atlantic 1972..260

Pact of Paris 1928
  Art 1...319
  Art 2...319
Paris Convention for the Protection of Industrial Property 1883..........................42
Paris Convention for the Protection of the MarineEnvironment
  of the North Atlantic 1992..249
  Art 2(2)(a) 249
Paris Convention on Third Party Liability in the Field
  of Nuclear Energy 1960 250

Rio Convention on Biological Diversity 1992 232
Rio Declaration on Environment and Development 1992 ....232, 238–40, 246–51
                                                              263, 264, 269, 253, 257
Rio Framework Convention on Climate Change 1992..................232, 249, 265, 266
  Art 3(3) 249, 262

Statute of the International Court of Justice 1945
  Art 34(1) 97, 98
  Art 36(2) 301, 303, 304

Art 36(3)	304, 305
Art 36(6)	305, 306
Art 38	30, 39
Art 38(1)	15, 17, 18, 22, 27, 38, 232, 236
Art 38(1)(b)	23, 29
Art 38(1)(c)	24
Art 38(1)(d)	24, 34, 206
Art 59	24
Art 65–68	309
Art 65	309
Stockholm Declaration on the Human Environment 1972	229, 232, 238–41, 248, 253, 255–57, 263, 264, 269
Treaty Establishing the Organisation of Caribbean States 1981	297
Treaty of Frankfurt 1871	119
Treaty of Paris 1856	296
Treaty of Rome 1957	71
Treaty of Versailles 1919	
Art 304(b)	98
Treaty on Principles Governing the Activities of States in the Exploration and Use of Outer Space, Including the Moon and Other Celestial Bodies 1967	33
United Nations Charter 1945	40, 272, 291
Art 1	10, 319
Art 1(2)	117
Art 1(3)	273, 277
Art 2(1)	128
Art 2(3)	294, 331
Art 2(4)	4, 5, 54, 111, 117, 119, 148, 293, 316, 317, 319, 323, 324, 327, 328, 330, 331
Art 2(7)	272, 287, 308, 320, 322
Art 4	90, 93
Art 10	6, 31
Art 24	312
Art 25	310–12
Arts 30–51	315
Art 33	300
Art 39	312, 320, 332
Art 40	332
Art 41	332
Art 42	320, 321, 333, 334
Art 43	334
Art 46	334
Art 47	334

Art 51 .... 5, 119, 120, 148, 316, 321, 324, 325
327, 330, 331, 333, 334
Art 55 117
Art 55(c) 273, 277
Art 56 .... 273, 277
Art 97 321
Art 98 321
Art 103 311
Art 961 309
United Nations Convention against Torture and Other Cruel,
Inhuman or Degrading Treatment or Punishment 1984 .... 273, 278
United Nations Covenant on Economic and Social Rights 1966
Art 12 269
United States Constitution
Art IV 10
Art VI 70

Vienna Convention on Diplomatic Relations 1961 .... 22, 40, 158
159, 167
Art 1 .... 170, 171
Art 1(d) 168
Art 1(e) 168
Art 22 .... 159, 161, 163
Art 22(1) 159
Art 22(2) 162
Art 29 .... 167, 168, 172

Art 30 161
Art 39 171
Art 39(1) 171
Art 41 164
Art 41(3) 164
Vienna Convention on Substances that Deplete the
Ozone Layer 1985 262
Vienna Convention on the Law of Treaties 1969 .... 9, 34, 37, 38, 43, 44, 50, 53
.... 119, 187, 188
Art 2 53
Art 4 .... 34, 44, 57
Art 18 .... 25, 188, 189, 198–200
Art 18(a) 200
Art 18(b) 200
Art 30 .... 55, 199
Art 30(2) 55
Art 30(4) 55
Art 31 .... 45, 46
Art 31(1) 44
Art 31(2) 45

Table of Conventions

Art 31(3)	121, 316
Art 31(3)(a)	46
Art 31(3)(b)	46
Art 31(4)	46
Art 32	46
Art 34	55
Art 35	55
Art 36	55
Art 37(2)	56
Art 44	47
Art 46	53
Art 48	53
Art 49	53
Art 50	53
Art 51	53
Art 52	53, 54, 122
Art 53	47, 53
Art 54(b)	51
Art 56	50
Art 60	51
Art 60(2)(b)	51
Art 64	63

Vienna Convention on the Succession of States in
Respect of Treaties 1978 .... 56, 297
    Arts 8–10 56
    Art 11 56
    Art 12 56

Washington Convention on International Trade in Endangered
Species of Wild Flora and Fauna (CITES) 1973 .... 41, 42, 232
World Charter for Nature 1982 269

CHAPTER 1

THE NATURE OF PUBLIC INTERNATIONAL LAW

Introduction

Public international law is certainly, in one sense, unique among all law subjects in that it is the only area of law which has to justify itself as law. Who would doubt that the law of contract exists, or trusts or tort? Yet many have argued that rules created between States are, in truth, not rules of law at all, but merely serve as rules of morality.

This view gained a good deal of support, particularly in the last century, from the supporters of the Austinian positivist school of jurists. As a result of this, examiners frequently ask a question about the very nature of public international law. General issues which will need to be understood include:

- a definition of the meaning of public international law;
- the position and relevance of public international law today;
- the historical development of public international law, focusing particularly on the difference of approach adopted by the 'naturalists' and the 'positivists'; and
- whether public international law is really law at all.

It is rare to chance upon a problem question concerning this area of international law. Questions on this matter are, in almost all cases, posed as essay – rather than problem – questions.

Checklist

Students should be familiar with the following areas:

- the varying definitions that have been given of public international law;
- the modern development of the traditional view of public international law as simply being the law regulating the relationship between States;

- the need, historically, for the development of the legal relationship of certain rules of international behaviour;
- the different schools of thought: the development of natural law thought and the growth of positivism;
- the clash of the two schools over the genuine existence and status of public international law; and
- comment on recent innovations in public international law and on its general effectiveness.

Question 1

All of the important principles of public international law are modern innovations.

Discuss.

Answer plan

Upon reading such a question, the 2.2 standard student is likely simply to reproduce his or her checklist of historical 'high points'. The more astute student has to perform a careful balancing act. Whilst an historical survey is important, writers must address themselves to what might be deemed the truly important principles of public international law. Only in this way can the student give a satisfactory answer to the question.

The order of the treatment here will be:

- a brief definition of international law, stressing its historical development;
- to focus on some of the key principles of public international law, for example, the use of force;
- to comment that, whilst public international law has developed greatly in the last century, the background to the key historical principles have important historical roots; and
- new innovations in public international law.

Answer

Whilst public international law has developed hugely in the 20th century, any examination of what might be described as 'the principal rules' will be found to have an ancient pedigree. Certain key features will be highlighted below.

For the purposes of this essay, three key features of current public international law will be highlighted. The reader should come to understand that, in one sense, the statement in question is false: namely, that it is arguable that the important features of public international law do have an historical derivation. In another sense, the statement might contain a truth; that truth will depend first on what one means by 'modern' and, secondly, on whether one makes a distinction between principles developed in this century and those developed in previous centuries.

Traditionally, public international law concerned the legal relationship between State entities. Therefore, it has been argued that the true emergence of principles of public international law can only be dated from the period of the rise of the nation states. This process was spurred on by two key factors, the first being the breakdown of the spiritual authority of the Roman Catholic Church.

The Reformation made kings and princes throughout Europe dependent upon no external authority. As a consequence, they could conduct their relations with foreign monarchs in any way that they saw fit.

Secondly, in conjunction with the new freedom from external pontifical interference, European monarchies began to centralise their power within nation states. This enabled them to make personal pledges as to how each nation was to conduct its affairs with leaders of other nations, and for these pledges to be, in most cases, capable of being honoured.

With the breakdown of papal authority, it was feared that Europe – now made up of new sovereign States – would be plunged into anarchy. The appalling casualties and devastation resulting from the Thirty Years War compelled the new nation states in 1648 to recognise certain realities, namely, the sovereign equality of States and the principle of territorial independence. These factors became the bedrock of a new stability. This stability was based upon substantive rules of behaviour defining the rights and duties of States, including such rules as those governing the illegal use of force. These substantive rules were devised by such scholars as Grotius, Vittoria, Gentiles and others, who attempted to replace the papal with the new secular rules based upon Roman law, State practice, and (where the former where unclear), upon what became termed 'natural law principles'. Thus, the greatest of these scholars, Grotius, devotes the first two books of his treatise *De Jure Belli ac Pacis* to the question, 'What constitutes a just war?' – and in the last book discusses lawful methods of warfare. If the scholars could not exert authority to ban war, they could at least regulate its discharge. They outlined the few specific circumstances in which resort to war was justified, what might be termed the substantive law of war, and the rules with regard to how the conflict was to be conducted (now called 'humanitarian law'), which might be referred to as the 'procedural law of war'.

Regrettably, diplomats, until relatively recently, concentrated on the procedural aspects of the law (for example, the Hague Conventions of 1899 and 1907) rather than on the substantive aspects. This, in large part, was due to two factors: first, the belief (famously expressed by Von Clauswitz), that after a State had exhausted all peaceable means of obtaining satisfaction, it could legitimately exact redress for itself by force; and secondly, because international law was without any judicial administrative machinery to seek redress on behalf of States, thus leaving an aggrieved State, once diplomacy had failed, with little option but war.

However, following the two great conflicts of the 20th century, the substantive law of war was radically altered. First, the League of Nations Covenant accepted the obligation not to resort to war. By the Kellogg-Briand Pact of 1928, the high contracting parties 'condemned recourse to war' and, by Art 2(4) of the United Nations Charter 1945, all Member States agreed to refrain from the illegal use of force. Secondly, bodies were established to enable injured States to gain redress for an illegal injustice committed against them by a foreign State, namely, the Permanent Court of Arbitration in 1907, the Permanent Court of International Justice in 1920 and its successor, the International Court of Justice in 1946.

Today, the illegality of war sounds like a truism. To make it so was the great achievement of modern public international law. When Hall wrote his treatise on international law in 1880, he could write in all candour that:

> As international law is destitute of any judicial or administrative machinery, it leaves States, which think themselves aggrieved, and which have exhausted all peaceable methods of obtaining satisfaction, to exact redress for themselves by force. It thus recognises war as a permitted mode of giving effect to its decisions.[1]

No longer would such a view be legally tenable after Art 2(4) of the UN Charter. Whilst 'self-help' was to remain a part of the customary law on use of force, primary reliance was placed upon collective security as maintained by the world's great powers. It was these great powers which sat as permanent members on the UN Security Council. With regard to actions undertaken by individual States, Art 51 only permitted military action if it were used in self-defence.

Notes
1   Hall, WE, *A Treatise in International Law*, 8th edn, p 81.

Question 2

Is international law really law?

Answer plan

Hackneyed though this question is, time and again it reappears in one form or another. It is primarily a response to the extreme positivism which, in the field of legal philosophy, reigned supreme in the last century. Any answer will therefore require an understanding of the jurisprudential pedigree of public international law.

The following approach is suggested:
- a definition of public international law;

- the 19th century positivist (Austinian) view of international law;
- responses to Austin's view;
- admitted 'deficiencies' of international law compared to municipal law; and
- 20th century improvements in international law making

Answer

International law has been described as 'the sum of rules accepted by civilised States as determining their conduct towards each other, and towards each other's subjects'.[1] However, the application of these rules has often proved to be troublesome. Under the UN Charter, the General Assembly, the nearest thing to an international legislative forum, can only make recommendations and cannot, given the wording of the Charter (Art 10), make law. The UN Secretary General has no power to intervene in any conflict beyond that which is expressly permitted by the disputing parties or by the oft quarrelling Security Council. Despite the existence of the International Court of Justice, States cannot be compelled to answer for their actions before it if they choose not to. Supposedly binding treaty rules are often formulated in such vague terms as to be almost without meaning.[2] All too often, if a vague solution was not possible, all that could be agreed was to disagree and reveal the myth of a consensus among 'civilised' States.[3] The leading flagship of international law, the United Nations, stated boldly in the preamble to its founding Charter that it was 'determined to save succeeding generations from the scourge of war ...'. Since 1945, there has hardly ever been a time when a bloody conflict was not being fought between UN Member States.

It is little wonder that Austin, the great 19th century British jurist, wrote that international law, as law, did not exist. To constitute a legal system (so Austin learned from Hobbes), two elements were essential: commands from an individual sovereign; and the capacity for that sovereign to order sanctions should those commands be disobeyed. These were elements which existed in every 'civilised' legal system the world over. Noticeably, however, they did not apply to public international law. For amongst States there was no hierarchy of command: rather it was a brotherhood of equals. Some writers refer to this as a 'horizontal', as opposed to a 'vertical', system of authority. Moreover, any rules which may have been produced by this 'horizontal' system could not be described as laws because infraction of such rules could never be followed by sanctions. Call the rules 'international etiquette', 'rules of morality', 'rules of good neighbourliness' but never can you call them 'laws'. Whilst such a view prevailed, the development of public international law was severely hindered, particularly with regard to any extension of its rules to the municipal systems of law.

There are a number of responses to Austin's view. First, it can be argued that Austin's view of a successful legal system was too limited. He was describing one type of legal system, but there is no reason why others could not exist which had a different design, where, for example, laws were obeyed not through fear of sanction but for other reasons, equally compelling. It is hardly surprising that Austin took the view that he did of international law, given its primitive state at that time and the fact that one of the primary purposes of his work was to consider legitimising sovereignty and explaining obedience. Given the international law in evidence before him, joined with the objectives he was seeking, it was not surprising that he should adopt a jaundiced view of the subject. Few would dispute that public international law, when compared to municipal law, is, or can be, weak; given its structure, it is primitive. HLA Hart, another English positivist, states that to emerge from this primitive state and become a system of law, public international law must not just have a primary set of rules (which specify the standards of behaviour) but also a secondary set of rules which provide for a means for identifying and developing the primary rules. Without a central, sovereign, administrative body, this secondary set of rules cannot emerge. This has been faulted for exalting rules at the expense of principles and policies. In any case, to argue that a legal system is primitive (in the sense of basic) does not mean that it is not a legal system; it merely means that it is a legal system of a different type. Secondly, many rules are obeyed not because of compulsion, but for other reasons, comity being one of them.

When Austin was writing, the treaty structure was extremely primitive. Almost all of public international law was governed by custom. Making the distinction between non-binding usage and binding custom is a taxing task indeed, and it is little wonder that, given the obvious complexities involved, Austin viewed all such rules as based upon 'mere morality'. No doubt it might be argued that it was in the interest of States to perpetuate this resistance to the legally binding nature of rules of international behaviour.

Given an international system of States that were equals, that dealt with each other on an horizontal level, that recognised no sovereign body greater than their own, it can be appreciated that there might be resistance to any notion of being bound by the 'law of nations' rather than the law of the nation.

Yet curiously, as Sir Frederick Pollock made clear in his *Lectures on Jurisprudence* in 1873, there was still a desire within foreign ministries to justify foreign policy actions on the basis of legality rather than simply on morality. Secular States cannot rely upon religious justifications for their actions. If they, instead, appeal to some secular justification based upon the 'morality' of capitalism, communism, environmentalism or utilitarianism, they are unlikely to gain common agreement. Generally agreed international law, however, is a legal *lingua franca* that can legitimately clothe the exercise of State foreign policy. Thus there emerged a desire both to be bound and to bind others by such rules. Further that, when States do act in what might be deemed a controversial manner, it is rare to find a State that does not provide a legal justification for its actions. This might be to deflect international criticism and make penalties less likely. It might also be due to a recognition that if a State appears to violate international law without qualms, there might be citizens within its jurisdiction who feel that they can, on an equal basis, cast aside their obedience to municipal law. As such, an attack upon public international law is an attack upon one's own law.

It is certainly true that rules of international law are broken. However, because the rules of any legal system are broken does not mean that the legal system does not function. The laws on theft and speeding, for example, are broken many hundreds of times each day in the United Kingdom. That does not mean that the United Kingdom does not have a legal system or that there is little point in having laws governing theft and speeding. What is important is that most members of the community obey most laws most of the time. Their motivation for doing so can be mixed: socialisation, good neighbourliness, a calculation based upon Matthew ch 7, v 12: 'Therefore whatsoever ye would that men should do unto you, even so do ye to them.' Or, of course, their motivation could be the fear of being caught and subsequently punished. An interview with drivers stopping at traffic lights might prove to be revealing on this matter. What is of concern is that because the majority, for whatever reason, acknowledge the rules of the legal system, that legal system can be said to function. This can be just as readily said of the municipal systems as it can of public international law. It is true that the news reports might make it appear that public international law is ineffective. The frequent breaches of the rules on illegal use of force are pointed to as instances of this. Yet one might respond by pointing to the equally frequent and highly publicised breaches of the criminal law in the municipal sphere (for example, murder). The law on murder is (i) obeyed by the vast majority of citizens most of the time and, in any case, (ii) makes up only a tiny part of the legal system as a whole. The same is true with regard to the international law rules on the use of force. Little attention is drawn to the undramatic yet essential treaties on communications, airlines, waterways, postal regulations, etc, which work highly effectively and are products of public international law.

In modern public international law, the overarching sanction imposing sovereign body still does not exist. However, the production, application and enforcement of rules of international law have advanced dramatically since the time of Austin. Rather than matters being governed by customary law alone, there are now vast networks of treaties between States. These treaties are now governed by guidelines (for example, by the terms of the Vienna Convention on the Law of Treaties 1969) that might rival the 'secondary rules' of many a municipal State. Moreover, in the early years following the end of the Cold War, there was evidence that greater co-operation amongst the five permanent Members of the Security Council facilitated the efficient imposition of sanctions, both economic and military, in order to enforce collective security. (More recent events have cast some doubt on this.)

There is a recognition of the place of public international law not merely in the foreign ministries, but also within the constitutions and domestic judgments of states. The Constitution of the United States, for example, states that treaties are 'the supreme law of the land' (see Art IV, § 2). The domestic courts within the US also accord recognition to international law. Gray J, in *The Paquete Habana* (1900), stated in the US Supreme Court that:

> International law is part of our law, and must be ascertained and administered by the courts of justice of appropriate jurisdiction, as often as questions of right depending upon it are duly presented for their determination.

Similar expressions of recognition of the existence and importance of international law can be read in legal documentation of States the world over. Moreover, there is collective recognition of international law. The classic example of this is the UN Charter, which, in the very first Article, in para 1, states that the purpose of the organisation is to:

> ... maintain international peace and security, and to that end: to take effective collective measures for the protection and removal of threats to the peace ... and to bring about by peaceful means, and in conformity with the principles of justice and international law, adjustment or settlement of international disputes or situations which might lead to a breach of the peace.

Therefore, it can be seen that, despite the demands for State independence and equal sovereignty, there is still a persistent desire to have a set of rules guiding the international affairs of these same States, and that these rules shall have the force of law.

Notes

1 Near to that given by Lord Russell of Killowen in 1896 and which was judicially adopted in the *West Rand Central Gold Mining Co v Rex* (1905). This definition is admittedly somewhat old fashioned today. Now, international legal personality has been extended to international organisations. Moreover, in certain rare circumstances, individuals can be held guilty of a breach of international law, ie, piracy, war crime, crimes against humanity, etc.

2 See the Convention on the Settlement of Investment Disputes between States and the Nationals of Other States, 18 March 1965.
3 At the second Geneva Conference on the Law of the Sea, the 87 States that participated failed to agree to establish a general rule which would fix the width of the territorial sea. This repeated the lack of consensus which had existed at the earlier meeting: the Hague Conference of 1930.

Question 3

Account for the rise of positivism in public international law.

Answer plan

A clear kinship can be noted between this and the former question. Here, however, the key concern is the nature of positivism and the way in which the doctrine influenced the development and the effectiveness of public international law. Joined to this jurisprudential awareness must be an historical appreciation of the evolution of the law of nations.

The following approach is suggested:
- precursor to positivism: the natural law school of thought;
- the inherent problems of natural law philosophy;
- the growth of positivism and its influence on public international law;
- the emergent weaknesses of extreme positivism;
- the resurgence of natural law; and
- the present attempt at balance between the two schools of thought.

Answer

It can be argued that the positivist school had a greater influence upon the development of public international law than any other; that its influence, for good or ill, shaped the nature of the law of nations as we know it today. The essay will begin by briefly examining the development of the dominant theory prior to the emergence of positivism: namely, that of the natural law school. It will then be shown that the natural law school bore within it certain fundamental flaws, which led, particularly given the changing socio-political circumstances existing in Europe during the late medieval period, to a need for a new view of the legal relationship between States. This development led to the emergence of positivism, a doctrine which itself contained fundamental weaknesses. Finally, it will be shown that, following the Second World War, there has been a resurgence of natural law thought, a result of which has been that the two schools now appear to exist in equal favour.

The birthplace of public international law was Europe. Prior to the Reformation, Europe was dominated by one authority, that of the Pope. In theory at least, all monarchs within Europe acknowledged that, with regard to certain matters, the will of the papal authority was supreme. Moreover, infraction of the papal will could result in serious consequences for any recalcitrant monarch. King John of England suffered as a consequence of insubordination by being excommunicated. His Majesty was only able to obtain a withdrawal of the excommunication on conceding defeat and acknowledging papal authority. Moreover, kings such as John, as well as paying obeisance to the head of the Catholic Church, also viewed themselves as part of a brotherhood of Christian monarchs. As a consequence, should a dispute arise amongst them, a resolution could be reached upon shared Christian principles. This divine law was a product of God; God, by definition, would create nothing that was not founded upon reason. It was God who created all nature, including man, and in creating man in his image, He gave him reason. As a consequence, so wrote Aquinas, God's laws could be discerned in nature by the application of man's reason.

The fundamental place of reason had also predated Christianity. The law of nature, natural law, was a term greatly employed by Roman jurists. Rome boasted proudly of its own laws. Yet, as a large imperial State, it was compelled to deal with its neighbours. What became apparent was that there were some rules contained within Roman law that were found in every other legal system they encountered. These rules were labelled *jus gentium*, the 'law of peoples'. Why did they emerge? Why the coincidence of rules? It was argued that such rules had their foundation in reason. This was the basis of their fundamental validity. Given the Roman pedigree and existence of Christendom, natural law rules became means by which the principalities of Europe conducted their legal affairs. Yet that system was breaking down. The Reformation destroyed the temporal power of Rome, and Europe was fragmenting. With the end of the Thirty Years War in 1648, the Peace of Westphalia was said to mark the moment when the State system began. In a sense, the diminution of papal authority revitalised the dependency upon natural law theory. For now, with no overarching, pontifical authority, the desire that individual sovereigns should discern reason in nature became ever more vital if the peace and prosperity of Europe were to be maintained. Publicists such as Suarez urged rulers to employ natural reason to bring about agreement amongst them: if the old brotherhood was founded upon the recognition of papal authority and Christian society, the new brotherhood could be founded on the wisdom of monarchs in understanding God's will through reason.

Whilst this was laudable, it generated two fundamental problems. First, it has ever been possible for two reasonable and intelligent Christian men to come to very different conclusions upon the same issue. Secondly, the reason of God is open to endless speculation. The scripture is open to a multitude of interpretations on many matters. There therefore developed a new group of scholars who, though by no means abandoning natural law, began to supplement it. In particular, publicists such as Zouche and Grotius, rather than just looking at what States should do, supplemented these observations by looking at what States actually did. This is by no means an abandonment of natural law theory, for, as we have seen, a key element of that theory was the Roman rule of *jus gentium*. If a practice is generally followed, then it must be based upon reason. Thus State practice could be seen in treaties entered into and by practices followed. These rules were 'positive' in the sense that they were a product of the will of States. They had been 'put in place' as the name 'positivism' suggests (taken from the Latin *pono, ponere, positum* – to put, place). Here, examination of State practice is performing the role of anecdotal proof that a rule of natural law exists. It is an attempt to confirm the law, and not quite a full blooded assertion that State practice created the law. Two other elements were necessary for that to come about.

With the Enlightenment came the true diminution, at least to scholars, of the place of divine will. In its stead strode scientific discovery. At its extreme, this resulted in the belief that everything could be distinguished, determined, defined, not just by the application of the reasoning of mankind, but by the inventions of man. Just as the universe could be comprehended by the telescope and by mathematical calculation, the moral imperatives of mankind could be determined not by using reason to determine God's will[1], nor by examining collective State practice (for the generality of States could be mistaken), but by using an objective means of calculating what laws should be created. The most obvious example of this was the so called 'felicific calculation' devised by Jeremy Bentham. By this method, the greatest happiness to the greatest number could be mathematically deduced. Each State was capable of making such a calculation for itself. It was in the best position to evaluate what was in its own interest. Therefore the wisdom of following general State practice became less appealing.

Moreover, in the 19th century, science, in the misinterpretation of Darwinism, combined with another influential force. The second key element in the development of the modern positive law position on public international law was nationalism. The writings of Nietzsche were completely antipathetic to the medieval and pre-medieval notion of Christendom. Rather than there being a brotherhood of nations, there was a struggle of survival between States.

Furthermore, the communities that composed these States were quite distinct from one another: each State represented a different race. This had two consequences. First, States 'put in place' rules not for moral reasons, and certainly not for reasons of collective expediency; rather, State practice reflected each State's 'will to power'. This had an important influence upon the view of Western States, not only in their relationships with each other, but in their relationships with what became colonial territory.

Secondly, a law that was for the benefit of the German race and the British race need not have any bearing, so it was believed, on that of the French or the Spanish. A consequence of this was that a State could not be bound unless it had consented to be so bound.

It can be seen that one result of the 19th century view of positivism was State self-interest and self-advancement at all cost. One consequence of this was held to have been the disasters that befell the world between the 1914–18 and 1939–45 wars. With the resolution of these conflicts came a desire to reincorporate a natural law element into public international law. It was based on a desire to rebuild universal community and devalue national assertiveness. In terms of international law making, this marrying of the two elements can clearly be seen in Statute of the International Court of Justice, a reworking of the statute of the earlier Permanent Court of International Justice. Chapter 38(1) lists the sources the court will apply in order to decide upon disputes submitted to it:

(a) international conventions, whether general or particular, establishing rules expressly recognised by the contesting States;

(b) international custom, as evidence of a general practice accepted as law;

(c) the general principles of law recognised by civilised nations; and

(d) subject to the provisions of Art 59, judicial decisions and the teachings of the most highly qualified publicists of the various nations, as subsidiary means for the determination of rules of law.

Of this list, (a) can clearly be placed as a positive law element. A State can be bound by an agreement it has made. In (b), we still encounter an aspect of positive law; custom is based upon State practice – by what a State has actually 'put in place'. Yet here can also be noted natural law consequences, for there can be circumstances in which a State can become bound under customary international law even though it has never consented to such a rule. The two further divisions of para 1, namely (c) and (d), clearly reflect a need to attempt to incorporate natural law rules into public international law in order to avoid the worst excesses of positive law practice.

In conclusion, it can be seen that raw positivism was truly a product of its time. The two great human disasters of the 20th century led to the belief that State survival was best maintained not by each State pursuing its own self-interest, but by participating in the interests of the community of States as a whole.

Notes

1 Jeremy Bentham, populariser of utilitarianism, referred to natural law as 'nonsense upon stilts'.

Chapter 2

Sources of International Law

Introduction

Students usually find this topic, of all those taught on the public international law syllabus, by far the most difficult. In most of the textbooks the chapters are lengthy and weighty. Yet this is not essentially the problem; the same might be said of many topics in many areas of law. The problem lies in the fact that, particularly with regard to customary international law and general principles of law, the topic seems so amorphous. This can come as quite a shock to law students who are steeped in the black letter tradition. It is generally the case that students who have a natural bent towards legal philosophy tend to find this topic far easier.

Almost all answers on questions involving sources begin by discussing Art 38(1) of the Statute of the International Court of Justice. This is right and proper, but students should be aware that, strictly speaking, that article is only actually binding on the International Court of Justice (ICJ). It is, however, generally taken to be a highly authoritative statement of the sources as they exist in customary international law.

In answering a problem question, for example, the following issues should normally be considered:
- the nature of public international law (that is, the fact that there is no central law making body);
- the sources of international law with a concentration upon Art 38(1) of the Statute of the International Court of Justice;
- the possible hierarchy of those sources; and
- the implementation and enforcement of public international law.

Essay questions will often require you to discuss the creation of customary international law and the assessment of what 'general principles of law' are.

Checklist

Students should be familiar with the following areas:
- customary international law: what it is, the evidence for it, what amounts to *opinio juris*;
- international conventions: why they are obeyed;
- whether States can be bound without having given their consent; and
- the significance of the balance between positive law and natural law elements in the provisions of Art 38(1).

Question 4

In what way is custom a source of public international law?

Answer plan

Custom is the traditional method by which rules of international law are established. When the international community consisted of a small number of like minded States, this process worked reasonably efficiently. From the perspective of Anglo-Saxon lawyers, the rationale for the validity of such rules mirrored that of the common law. That is, such rules represented the distilled wisdom of wise and civilised counsel through the ages. However, with the expansion of the international community, the establishment of new customary rules became far more difficult. No longer were they established from the practices of a small club of nations. Rather, they represented, on any particular matter, the agglomeration of practices established by States with widely disparate interests. Moreover, as if to make matters worse, the categories of evidence of State practice were also expanding. The consequences of this are that establishing a new rule of customary international law can be a forbidding task.

Points to be considered are as follows:
- the nature of customary international law;
- the problem of determining rules of customary international law;

- the evidence of customary international law and where such evidence might be found; and
- the importance of *opinio juris* in establishing that State practice amounts to more than comity, but to a rule of international law.

Answer

Prior to the 20th century, international law effectively meant customary international law. This was formed out of usages that had developed between the relatively small community of civilised nation states. When a usage began, in time, to be thought of as obligatory, rather than being performed out of mere comity, it hardened into a custom and, as such, was legally binding on the international community as a whole.

A great number of these customary rules were created by the dominant States in certain fields; for example, many of the rules on shipping were dominated in the last century by British practice (see *The Paquete Habana* (1900)). Other customs, especially in the field of commercial law, found their basis in the practice of a small number of States, which, when followed, worked in the perceived collective interest.

On matters which worked to the benefit of all, there was little difficulty in the international community accepting the evolution of usage into binding custom. However, in other areas, the matter was less clear cut. Without an international court to establish a set of rules to define when a usage crystallised into a binding custom, the matter was left up to the foreign offices, which frequently disagreed. Thus, in many respects, customary law was uncertain. Not only was there contention over when usage became custom, there was also debate as to the weight to be attached to the State practice that was to be the proof of such an evolution.

When searching for evidence of State practice, clearly the diplomatic correspondence between States needs to be examined. Originally, this information was not easily accessible. Consequently, the matter was greatly influenced by the scholarly, interpretive role carried out by jurists to establish the rules of customary international law from what materials might be at their disposal. At first, the tendency of such writers as Grotius was to bridge inconsistencies in State practice by citing ideal objectives, discerned by natural reason. Later, however, the jurists restrained their speculations and confined themselves simply to reporting State practice.

Fortunately, the practice of States is now more easily learnt due to their official publications. For example, the US has produced a variety of digests, such as Moore's and Hackworth's, as have the UK, France and a number of other industrialised states. Moreover, due to the rise of information technology, more information on State practice is available than ever before, for example via the internet or on CD-Rom. This in itself has led to problems. First, customary law had long been resisted by many developing States because it was seen as a product of the developed nations. In a sense, this problem can only be exacerbated by the over-abundance of information about State practice in technologically advanced nations, as contrasted with the comparative paucity of material on the State practice of less advanced States. Secondly, information technology could well allow the expansion of the type of information that might contribute to State practice. Thus, a tribunal might be swamped with information regarding US State practice in a certain area and feel that they had to delve with equal care and depth into the archives of the other 190 nation States. This could have the effect of adding far greater difficulty to the judicial task as well as slowing down the already lengthy process of dispute resolution.

Whilst it is true that in some instances the tribunal will pay some attention to the State practice of the States that are more likely to have a real concern in the matter at hand (for example, with regard to a matter concerning maritime boundaries, the State practice of coastal States will be of greater weight than that of landlocked States), the fact remains that any judge who wishes to make a declaration based upon customary international law will need to employ enormous research in order to find convincingly that a practice generally exists, has existed for a long enough time to have been accepted as a general guideline, and that inconsistencies within the practice are rare and insignificant. Yet this is only the first hurdle.

To become a rule of customary international law, the usage must also have another quality, namely, that it be psychologically felt to be binding, or, as it is known, *opinio juris sive necessitatis*. For example, in the *North Sea Continental Shelf* cases (1969), the ICJ highlighted the fact that *opinio juris* involved a belief by States that they were conforming to what amounted to a legal obligation and that mere habitual action without more was not enough. Now, it would seem, not only is the court faced with establishing virtually uniform State practice amongst the majority of the 190-odd States in the international community, it must also establish that these States abided by that rule because they found themselves legally bound.

Thus, the rule must be believed to be legally binding prior to it becoming legally binding. The problem of proof should therefore be apparent. The consequence is that any State wishing to place reliance on what it claims to be a new rule of customary international law must meet a number of difficult hurdles to establish its case.

Question 5

Prompted by the slaughter of soldiers and civilians resulting from the Great Oil War of 1971–72, the General Assembly of the United Nations unanimously passed five resolutions between 1972 and 1997 by which it condemned acts of genocide. Such acts were stated to be violations of the 'basic and fundamental principles of humanity'. The resolutions insisted that States endeavour to bring to justice any person who commits such prescribed atrocities.

In 1997 Alobonia, Bolgova, Chinto, Dogrovia and Enspana, pursuant to these resolutions, concluded a treaty entitled the 'Genocide Punishment Convention' (GPC). This treaty was negotiated under the auspices of the United Nations. The GPC is currently in effect and Art XX of the treaty states that ratification is a condition for its binding operation. The purpose of the treaty is 'to increase the likelihood of the prosecution of individuals guilty of outrages against humanity'. The treaty, which is open to all States, provides that if any person guilty of such outrages is a national of a Contracting State and enters the territory of another Contracting State, the State whose territory the criminal enters

Q & A ON PUBLIC INTERNATIONAL LAW

must hand him over to the State of which he is a national for prosecution. Finbaria has signed the treaty but is yet to ratify it.

Manuel, 'The Butcher', is a national of both Chinto and Finbaria. He has been accused by the War Criminals Lobby Group, a non-governmental organisation based in State Chinto, of responsibility for acts of genocide during the Great Oil War. Last year he entered the territory of Alobonia as the Ambassador of Finbaria to that State. The Albonian Government, on reading the report produced by the War Criminals Lobby Group, handed him over to Chinto, where criminal proceedings have been instituted against him.

Finbaria claims that Albonia has thereby violated a rule of customary international law concerning the treatment of diplomatic representatives, citing as authority (i) a judgment of the International Court of Justice of 1987 confirming the existence of this rule of customary law and (ii) 'general international law'.

Discuss.

Note: When answering this question, do not make reference to the Vienna Convention on Diplomatic Relations; write as if it did not exist.

Answer plan

Problem questions on sources of international law are quite common and usually centre around the sources listed under Art 38(1) of the Statute of the International Court of Justice. They usually involve more than one of the sources. Indeed, one of the issues that may arise may be the question of the hierarchy of the sources listed. Time and space permitting, it would be advantageous to introduce such a point in answering this question.

Clearly, any useful discussion will require that the student is familiar with the details of the cases on sources which came before the International Court of Justice.

The examiner would expect to see the following matters discussed:

- the evidence of the existence of a rule of customary international law concerning diplomatic representatives;
- the legal significance of decisions by the International Court of Justice;
- the meaning of 'general international law; and
- the possibility of a new custom emerging from a General Assembly resolution.

Answer

In answering this question, there will first be an examination of the bases upon which Albania would be liable to Finbaria followed by an examination of Albania's response to such charges.

Upon what basis would Albania be liable to Finbaria? It might possibly be claimed that Albania has acted in violation of customary international law by treating the Finbarian diplomatic representative, Manuel, in the way that it has. To assess this claim, it is first necessary to establish whether an infracted rule of customary international law actually exists. Customary international law is formed out of actions of States. If a great many States – no precision has ever been given to the number – all respond to situation X in a certain, relatively uniform, manner for a certain period of time, and do so by a self-imposed compulsion,[1] then that response becomes law. It becomes binding on all States, unless they have clearly objected to the formulation of the rule whilst that rule was crystallising.[2] Evidence of State practice includes documents produced by States in their conduct of foreign relations, policy statements, press releases, opinions of official legal advisors, official manuals produced by governments, votes on international bodies (such as the UN General Assembly), etc. In order for Finbaria to claim that such a rule of customary international law exists, it would have to accumulate sufficient evidence of this kind to substantiate its claim.

Custom has been defined as a source of law for the International Court of Justice by Art 38(1)(b) of the Statute of the International Court of Justice. We are informed of an ICJ judgment of 1987 that confirms that such a rule exists with regard to the treatment of diplomatic representatives. Does this ICJ decision confirm Finbaria's claim? First, it should be noted that the decision of the court in 1987 only binds those parties who appeared before the court (see Art 59 of the Statute of the International Court of Justice). Thus, in this instance, the 1987 decision need not bind Albonia.[3] Despite this, Finbaria could contend that, although the 1987 decision was not directly binding upon Albonia, the decision itself gave a judicial imprimatur to the existence of a general rule of customary international law which should be binding on all States including Albonia. Article 38(1)(d) of the Statute of the International Court of Justice states that the court *shall* apply, subject to the provisions of Art 59, '... judicial decisions and the teachings of the most highly qualified publicists of the various nations, as *subsidiary* means for the determination of rules of law' (emphasis supplied). Thus, the 1987 decision might be viewed by international lawyers as being the expression of what the most authoritative international judicial body believes to be international law at a given point. Upon such a basis, Finbaria might argue that Albonia had violated international law.

Finbaria might further contend that Albonia had violated general international law. If, by this, is meant custom, then Finbaria would need to establish its case upon that footing (as discussed in the previous paragraph). Alternatively, Finbaria could be making reference to another source of international law, namely, 'general principles of law'. These are listed as a source of law for the ICJ under Art 38(1)(c) of the Statute. This was originally included as a source so as to allow the court (originally the Permanent Court of International Justice) avoiding a *non liquet*. Exactly what such 'general principles' consist of has never been clearly defined. Finbaria might argue that it consists of the general practice of States with regard to their municipal law. Thus, if a great majority of States had introduced municipal law giving diplomats immunity, then this rule might be viewed as a general principle of law. This might seem similar to custom, but unlike custom there would be no need to prove *opinio juris*. Such an approach to municipal law seems to have been adopted by the ICJ in the *Barcelona Traction* case (1970) with regard to limited liability companies.

Albonia might respond to the Finbarian claims in the following manner. First, it might place reliance upon the provisions of the

GPC. However, Finbaria could escape its obligations under the GPC upon the ground that it had not yet ratified that treaty. Article XX of the GPC stated that its provisions would not bind any State until it had ratified the treaty. However, Art 18 of the Vienna Convention on the Law of Treaties 1969 states that where a treaty is subject to ratification, signatory States, such as Finbaria in this instance, are under an obligation of good faith to refrain from acts calculated to defeat the purpose of the treaty until they have made their intention of not becoming parties apparent.

Secondly, Albania might argue that a new rule of customary law had emerged with regard to war criminals, which would prevail over any older rule with regard to the immunity of diplomats. The primary evidence for this would be the five unanimous General Assembly resolutions between 1972 and 1997. Sloan argues that: 'Resolutions that are adopted unanimously ... carry considerable weight as interpretations of the Charter, statements of law or quasi-judicial determinations.'[4] This approach was recently adopted by the ICJ in the *Nuclear Weapons* case, *Nicaragua v United States* (1997).[5] In para 70 of that judgment, it is stated that:

> The court notes that General Assembly resolutions, even if they are not binding, may sometimes have normative value. They can, in certain circumstances, provide evidence important for establishing the existence of a rule or the emergence of an *opinio juris*.
>
> In order to determine whether this new rule has in fact been created, it is necessary for the court to examine the particular resolutions in question, taking particular note of their content and conditions and as to whether an *opinio juris* exists as to its normative character.

As to the situation where there are a number of similar resolutions (as in the question), this may show the gradual evolution of the *opinio juris* required for the establishment of a new rule. Thus, it might be possible to state that a new rule of customary international law has been created by the General Assembly resolutions. As Finbaria must have voted in favour of the resolutions, there is added evidence that it wished to be bound by such an emerging custom. If the new custom could be said to exist, this would legitimise the action of Albania.

However, two factors might balk Albonia's case. First, Finbaria, in declining to ratify the GPC, might be indicating its active dissent to the development of a rule of customary international law. This might not only prevent the rule from so developing, it could be argued that, even if the rule had crystallised, Finbaria had been a persistent objector to such a rule. As such, it would not be bound by the new rule of customary international law. Furthermore, even if there were a new custom, that new custom would be to the effect that States should actively pursue a policy which would lead to the punishment of those guilty of genocide. Finbaria may believe that it is best to punish Manuel itself, even if they are bound by the new custom. Thus, the new custom, even if it existed, does not necessarily confirm Albonia's action.

In conclusion, the legitimacy of the actions of Finbaria and Albonia are seen in the light of applicable public international law. Sources of such law include treaty, custom, 'general principles of law' and judicial decisions. In order to determine the existence of such a rule in this instance, the relevant treaty and State practice must be scrutinised closely.

Notes

1 This sense of compulsion, the belief that a mode of behaviour should be followed as if it were law, is known as *opinio juris sive necessitatis*.
2 Known as a 'persistent objector'; this possibility was raised in the ICJ decision in the *Fisheries* case *(United Kingdom-Norway)* (1951).
3 As was stated in the *Nicaragua* case (1986), the court 'is bound to confine its decisions to those points of law which are essential to the settlement of the dispute before it'.
4 Sloan, 'General Assembly Resolutions Revisited' (1987) 58 BYIL 39.
5 Note that the far less cautious approach to GA Resolutions adopted by the ICJ in the *Nicaragua* case (1986) with regard to customary law on the use of force.
7 On this point see note 1, above.

Question 6

In 1976, a collision takes place between two aircraft – one Bolganian, one Slobenian – in which all the passengers are killed. The 'black box' is found and it clearly confirms that the crash was due to the negligence of the Bolganian captain.

Slobenia, through its diplomatic sources, makes clear to the Bolganian ambassador that it demands compensation for the death of its nationals. The Slobenian authorities point to a rule of customary international law which would suggest that it is generally recognised that, in the event of an air collision, the State in which the culpable aeroplane was registered should pay full compensation to any parties with valid claims.

The captain of the aeroplane, however, does not have Bolganian, but Dreamonian, nationality. Bolgania argues that a treaty between it and Slobenia establishes the rule that, in the event of an air collision involving negligence, compensation shall be paid by the State of which the negligent aeroplane captain was a national.

In 1970, a General Assembly resolution stated that, in the event of an air collision, even if it involved negligence, the State of which the killed or injured passengers were nationals should pay any compensation that is validly claimed.

Discuss.

Note: Confine your answer to the issue of sources of public international law.

Answer plan

This problem concerns the derivation, application and interaction of the different sources of public international law. Answers should concentrate upon two of the sources listed in Article 38(1) of the Statute of the International Court of Justice, namely custom and treaties. An examination will also be required of another potential source of international law, that is, Resolutions of the General Assembly.

The following approach is suggested:

- a discussion as to how the rules of customary international law are formulated;
- the nature of *opinio juris*;
- the importance of treaty provisions as a source;
- the General Assembly Resolutions as a source of International Law.

In conclusion, answers should address the question of which source might well prevail.

Answer

Rules of customary international law are based upon the accumulation of consistent State practice in support of such a rule, backed by *opinio juris*. In this instance, Slobenia will need to establish that the rule of compensation that it supports can be sustained by consistent general State practice which has the necessary *opinio juris*.

In order to establish such a rule, Slobenia would examine diplomats' correspondence, press releases, policy statements, official manuals produced by States, municipal laws and court decisions, bilateral treaties between two States and multilateral treaties between a number of States. This is the evidence of State practice which could help to support Slobenia's legal contention. It should be borne in mind that such State practice also has to measure up to further criteria which, with the possible exception of *opinio juris*, need to be traded off against each other. For example, there is greater possibility of the usage amounting to custom if such usage has been practised for a long period of time. Yet duration is not essential: in the *North Sea Continental Shelf* cases (1969) it was found by the ICJ that a usage could still amount to a rule of customary international law if it had evolved over a short period of time so long as the usage had been extensive and virtually uniform. Equally, inconsistencies, if relatively small and insignificant, would not destroy a usage long in practice from developing into a customary rule, but it could destroy the possibility of usage developing into custom over the short term. Then there is the perplexing question of generality. The question as to how many States need to abide by a usage in order to transform it into a rule of customary international law cannot be exercised other than to state that practice needs to be consistent and general and that, when a tribunal is assessing the matter of generality, it will give greater weight to the practice of those States that have a more direct concern with the matter at hand (for example, coastal States in the matter of rules regarding shipping).

Slobenia's legal representatives will find themselves highly taxed in performing such an enormous exercise in worldwide archive research, research they would find essential if they were successfully to establish that there was a rule of customary international law that supported their case. However, their real problem is not just to prove that States generally and consistently followed a particular usage: they must also establish, as Art 38(1)(b) of the Statute of the International Court of Justice demands, that they *'followed a general practice accepted as law'* (emphasis supplied). That is to say, those States behaved in the way they did not out of good neighbourliness, diplomatic tact or mere expediency, but because they felt that if they did not behave in such a way they would be transgressing a rule of international law. Thus, the Slobenian legal team needs to establish not only that consistent general usage exists but also that the generality of States had imposed upon themselves that rule as an anticipatory rule of public international law. As can be imagined, to prove such a rule is a task indeed.

Although Slobenia's task is difficult, it is by no means impossible, particularly if the rule of compensation is found to be a duty. That is, that States feel they must, in nearly every circumstance, abide by a rule. This can be distinguished from a rule which is found to be permissive (that is, which a State can, in circumstance X, use its discretion in applying). If the compensation rule falls into the former rather than the latter category, Slobenia will have a greater chance of succeeding in its action. Moreover, if the rule is found to be a duty, writers such as Chen suggest that, when delving into the documentary records of an individual State, that State is to be judged, not by its genuine beliefs and motives, but merely by its actions: 'By their works shall ye judge them.' Thus, if the generality of States did, by their actions, demonstrate that they believed that the State from which the aeroplane came that caused the airborne collision (through pilot error) should be liable to pay full compensation, that will be sufficient to determine a State's belief that such a general practice is being followed as law.

There is one further problem that the Slobenian legal team might encounter, namely, it might be the case that Slobenia had always indicated by its State practice that it was a persistent objector to the generalised usage. As such, it can, if it objected before the usage crystallised into custom, opt out of that nascent general State practice. An example of a State behaving in this way can be found in the *Anglo-Norwegian Fisheries* case (1951). This case concerned the drawing of maritime boundaries (amounting to 10 nautical miles) around the mouth of the coastal bays. As well as finding that, because of inconsistent usage, the rule had not hardened into a rule of customary international law, the court acknowledged that, even if it had done so, the rule could not apply to Norway's maritime boundary as it had always consistently protested at any attempt to apply such a rule to the Norwegian coast. If Bolgania had never opted out prior to the crystallisation of the usage into a custom (and would therefore be classed as a subsequent objector), or if it had simply acquiesced in the development of the usage into custom, Bolgania would potentially be bound by the alleged rule of customary international law.

Bolgania would be advised to place reliance on the treaty it has with Slobenia. Treaties – referred to in Art 38 of the Statute as 'conventions' – are regarded as a source of public international law. The existence of the treaty would certainly strongly militate against Slobenia's attempt to prove that State practice established the rule that the State in which the aeroplane was registered should pay compensation. For, as has been earlier stated, treaties, whether bilateral or unilateral, are State practice which forms evidence of rules of customary international law. Amongst academics, there is keen debate as to the hierarchy between the two main sources of public international law – debate which it would be fruitless to enter here. It might be said, however, that with the proven existence of a treaty (as in this instance), the balance is tipped against a contrary rule in customary international law being proven.

Lastly, there is the question of the effect of a General Assembly resolution. Could such a resolution have a legally enforceable effect? Could such a resolution amount to an instant creation of customary international law? This matter has also been hotly debated amongst scholars and a variety of views has emerged. At best, it could be argued that there are some General Assembly resolutions that might become legally binding, but that this would, in large part, depend upon the type of rule that was meant to be established and the degree of support it achieved. Evidence of the truth of this can be found in the reliance placed on the General Assembly Resolution on Use of Force and the intervention by the ICJ in the *Nicaragua* case (1984). It was implicit in the court's opinion that, at least for this area of international law, General Assembly resolutions are the primary register of all State practice.

Yet one should be cautious when arguing that this decision put General Assembly resolutions upon another legal footing. The UN Charter explicitly provides that the General Assembly's key purpose was not 'law making' but one of 'making recommendations' (Art 10) to other UN Member States, and to the Security Council in particular. There is a clear distinction to be made between recommending measures and directly creating rules which are the equivalent of international legislation.

Even if one discounted the ability of the General Assembly to legislate, this would not in itself mean that the resolution would have no influence upon this dispute. It may be noted that Bolgania makes a claim based upon customary international law. Anyone weighing up the legitimacy of this claim could not ignore the collective view of what the law is in the relevant area, as it had been expressed by the General Assembly. Arguably, therefore, the existence of the resolution could militate against the success of the Bolganian claim.

In conclusion, it would appear that Slobenia's claim based upon customary international law is unlikely to prevail. Indeed, the only rule of customary international law that might prove effective would be that favoured by the General Assembly resolution, and that would depend greatly on the view of the type of rule that was being created and the type of voting support it achieved. Even where such a rule of customary international law is said to exist, it might still fail to bind Slobenia and Bolgania, which might indicate that, whilst the relevant rule is crystallising into custom, in rejecting the nascent rule they (as persistent objectors) can never be bound by it. The bilateral treaty between the two States would be evidence of this. Indeed, it could be argued that, should a decision be reached upon the dispute, it would be upon the terms of this very bilateral treaty, and then be resolved in Bolgania's favour.

Question 7

What is the role of multilateral treaty making today?

Answer plan

Traditionally, international law was a product of State practice, State practice that, after a certain (indeterminate) length of time, developed into rules of customary international law. However, as the reader will have discovered, there are problems involving the determination of such customary rules: they take time to formulate, and their terms can often appear vague. How can we establish that customary rules are obeyed by States because those States regard such a custom as law?

Partly because of the inherent problems with the creation of customary rules, there has been a drive, since 1945, to create legal regimes founded upon multilateral treaties. In contrast to customary rules, mutlilateral treaties' terms can be clearly stated and, because such treaties, after 1945, permit certain types of reservation, they have proved to be popular. In answering this question, students will be required to demonstrate the importance that multilateral treaties have attained, and what matters the key treaties touch upon.

Students will be expected to discuss:
- the ways in which a multilateral treaty can shape international law;
- the formulation of the terms of a multilateral treaty;
- multilateral treaty making and 'soft law';
- the effects of 'soft law'.

Answer

One of the clearest ways in which international law is developing today is by the means of multinational treaties. At present, the United Nations is the depository for about 410 conventions, a great majority of which could be described as UN sponsored treaties. Furthermore, there are other multinational conventions for which other States act as depositories. For example, the Treaty on Principles Governing the Activities of States in the Exploration and Use of Outer Space, Including the Moon and Other Celestial Bodies 1967[1] is a treaty for which there are now three depositories: the Soviet Union, the United States and the United Kingdom. United Nations organisations have also been responsible for the formulation of such treaties. The International Labour Organisation (ILO) has produced over 160 conventions.[2] In total, there are around 1,500 multilateral treaties of which around half are products of the UN system. Furthermore, the rate of new multilateral treaties is increasing and has come to represent the way in which the international community formulates the guidelines for its future behaviour.

Clearly the importance of a multilateral treaty can be assessed in terms of the effectiveness of its application and in the number of States which wish to apply its provisions. Whilst this is true, it is a mistake only to look at such treaties as statements of hard law alone. Even prior to a treaty coming into effect, it can shape international law. This process begins when the experts set to work at codifying the relevant State practice into new norms that are to be regarded as law. This is carried out by a team of international law experts. The job of these experts is to determine the state of current international law on a particular issue. Once determined, whether it be from treaty law, customary law or from other less authoritative sources of law (known as 'soft law'), these same experts are responsible for coherently articulating international law in that particular area. This codification, the expert body of which is the UN's International Law Commission (ILC), demands that those who codify have a thorough understanding of the current law. One can see the reflection of such expertise in the reports submitted by such bodies. Indeed, because of the supposed expertise of such bodies, the statements made by them will be accepted as the legitimate statements of the law *ab initio*. As a consequence, while not constituting the law, they have been viewed as the equivalent of the teachings of the most highly qualified publicists, in the sense referred to by Art 38(1)(d) of the Statute of the International Court of Justice. As such, they can be regarded as subsidiary means for the determination of the rules of law.

This can also occur at the next step of the codification process when the reports formulated by the expert bodies are being formulated for the new treaty instrument. Whilst under expert consideration, most of these texts will be widely circulated amongst interested parties. The norms set out by such reports might well have an immediate impact on State practice. An example of this can be found in the reports that led to the Vienna Convention on the Law of Treaties 1969. While the reports of the ILC (and, from 1968–69, the UN Conference on the Law of Treaties) were being considered, their findings were clearly being regarded by States and international authorities as near authoritative. States wished to shape their policies to reflect the future state of international law with regard to treaties; the reports represented an authoritative presage of what those rules were to be. This proved to be of particular importance as, by Art 4 of the Convention, the agreement only applied to those treaties which were concluded after the 1969 treaty came into effect after it had been ratified by 35 States. That only came about in January 1980, and even then meant that the treaty was only to apply to the ratifying States. However, as States had, even prior to final formulation of the treaty document, moulded their own treaty practices around the wording of the expert reports as to what future treaty law would be, effectively the terms of the Vienna Convention were informally, universally in effect long before the treaty entered into force.

Secondly, what may be described as the laws' progressive development requires, above all else, experts who can comprehend the full nature of the problem that is yet to be tackled. It is the experts who then produce a statement of preliminary guidelines stating that the declared new rules have, at least in principle, gained a degree of international acceptance. This is effectively an ambitious statement of a desired norm. The hope is that, upon pronouncement, the wish will be fulfilled and that

State practice will be modified in such a way as to meet such a norm. In such a way, so called 'soft' international law is created.

Many such declarations are made under the aegis of the United Nations. After the General Assembly has determined that a solemn pronouncement of some importance should be made on a particular subject, which may be the first step in the formulation of a treaty, it will usually assign that formulation to one of its main committees. For example, in 1978, the General Assembly requested that the subcommission of the Human Rights Commission on Prevention of Discrimination and Protection of Minorities carry out a study with a view to determining guidelines for the protection of those detained on the grounds of mental ill health.[3] Thereupon the subcommission and a further *ad hoc* working group of the Commission formulated a number of Principles for the Protection of Persons with Mental Illness and for the Improvement of Mental Health Care. Subsequently, these guidelines were submitted to the General Assembly through the UN Economic and Social Council (ECOSOC) and were adopted by the General Assembly in 1990.[4]

After the adoption of such instruments, no signatures or other formal acceptance is required by States, though they are encouraged to adopt such resolutions as law. The hope is that they will, in some form, achieve the objectives of the resolution by transforming their own domestic law. The effectiveness of this soft law is measured by the degree to which this transformation into domestic law takes place. If this is done on a widespread basis, the non-binding norms can metamorphose from soft law into hard law. Any evidence which suggests that States behave in such a manner because they believe that such pronouncements constitute a valid statement of law lends weight to that principle having the necessary *opinio juris* needed to constitute customary international law. As such, they can become binding upon all States, except those States which have been persistent objectors to the formulation of a new rule of customary international law.

In conclusion, one can look at the formulation of multilateral treaty making in two ways. First, it can be noted that multilateral treaty making constitutes the most dynamic aspect of international law creation in the world today. Secondly, the process of multilateral treaty making produces byproducts which also contribute to the formulation of international law.

Notes

1. For a discussion of the terms of the treaty see: Darwin (1967) 42 BYIL 278; Cheng (1968) 95 JDI 532; Goedhuis (1968) 15 NILR 17.
2. The International Maritime Organisation (IMO) and the World Intellectual Property Organisation (WIPO) have also formulated many multinational treaties.
3. See UN Doc A/RES/33/53.
4. See UN Doc A/RES/46/119, Annex.

CHAPTER 3

THE LAW OF TREATIES

Introduction

Students will often be provided with copies of the Vienna Convention on the Law of Treaties 1969 in the examination. Consequently, a good many questions on this topic involve a detailed examination of that document. To be more proficient at answering questions in this area, students should make themselves very familiar with the layout of the Convention prior to the day of the examination.

In answering a problem question, the following issues should normally be considered:
- why treaties are generally adhered to;
- the status of the Vienna Convention on the Law of Treaties (for example, will it apply to the problem question before us?);
- whether the relevant treaty is in force yet;
- why some States will insist that the terms of the particular treaty should be fully applied while other States argue that the treaty is ineffective or, at least as far as they are concerned, avoidable; and
- whether there is any possibility of reservations being made to the treaty.

Checklist

Students should be familiar with the following areas:
- the methods by which treaties are made;
- the ways in which treaties are interpreted;
- the application and observance of treaties;
- the application of treaties to third States;
- modification and amendment of treaties;
- the validity of treaties;
- provisions on the invalidity, termination and suspension of treaties;

- termination, suspension and withdrawal of treaties; and
- the way in which treaties are registered.

Question 8

Assess the importance of the law of treaties in the latter half of the 20th century.

Answer plan

Treaty making is one of the most dynamic areas of modern international law. Students will be expected to have an understanding not just of the provisions of the Vienna Convention on the Law of Treaties 1969, but also of the development of the modern importance of treaties. This will require a knowledge of treaties in an historical context.

Issues which should be examined include:
- the nature of treaties as a source of international law;
- the modern importance of treaty making;
- the general nature of treaties prior to the Second World War;
- the expansion of international law making: ('universal legislation' by treaty?);
- by becoming part of customary law, the possibility exists that treaties might ultimately be capable (depending on the nature of the treaty) of binding States that were not party to the original treaty;
- the mechanisms within modern treaties which galvanise international law.

Answer

Treaties, though referred to as 'conventions', are listed as one of the sources of international law in Art 38(1) of the Statute of the International Court of Justice. Legally, this article only binds the International Court of Justice, but in practice it is taken as a truism of international law. It is to be noted that in the list of the four sources, treaties are listed first. Does this mean that hierarchically treaties are the primary source of international law and that custom, the general principles of international law, etc, have a subsidiary status? Theoretically, this is not so; for underpinning the very essence of convention making is the belief that terms contained within treaties will be abided by. This is a belief founded upon customary law; that is, *pacta sunt servanda* (agreements must be observed). More realistically, it is perhaps better to argue that the listing in Art 38 is based upon convenience rather than upon an hierarchical priority of the sources. Whereas the determination of customary law can take a great deal of time and study (and perhaps, even then, only be determined in an inconclusive fashion), black letter treaty law is determined easily.

Any cursory examination of texts on international law will reveal that the nature and expectation of treaty making have changed, in some cases dramatically, since the century's beginning. At the beginning of the 20th century, treaties were contractual in nature. They bound two parties and created mutual responsibilities and mutual duties. Conventions of this type are still formulated and are of importance to the nature of international relations. However, it might now be argued that the core of international law is no longer based upon the contractual model. Instead, they are based upon treaties which are 'law making'. These 'law making' treaties have been products of the desire to create 'black letter' rules that bind a community of States. They do not amount to international legislation but, in the absence of a Hobbesian world government, they are the nearest substitute. Multilateral agreements have taken the place of 'unicentric' laws. States feel themselves bound to compacts even though the essential element of a contract, the demand for reciprocity, is absent. For example, a multilateral treaty on human rights cannot be said to be contractual in nature (unless it is regarded as a 'social contract' in the sense that Locke, Rousseau or Rawls would recognise it).

At the beginning of this century, there were very few treaties that might be regarded as 'law making' rather than contractual.[1] The real blossoming of such treaties came with the establishment of the United Nations in 1945. This was partly a product of the unity and sense of idealism and community, if temporary, brought about through the war against fascism and colonialism, partly a rejection of the positivist perspective of international relations and partly the product of the many organisations that the UN established to formulate general rules of State behaviour. As a result, there are now around 1,600 such treaties, and the number is continuing to expand.[2] Some of these treaties are regional, some global; some set up and control military organisations; and some bring about peace. They differ in detail, but they have one similarity. Rather than just creating mutual obligations between two States, as treaties formerly did, these treaties create norms of behaviour. Leading examples of such treaties are: the United Nations Charter 1945, the Vienna Convention on Diplomatic Relations 1961, the Geneva Convention 1949 and the United Nations Convention on the Law of the Sea 1982. Each of these conventions binds many parties, creates a legal policy on an issue (the norm), and does so in black letter rules, sometimes of great complexity.

These modern law making treaties are increasingly beginning to resemble universal legislation rather than mere bilateral contracts. This is due primarily to their potential to bind non-party States and to their potential to bind parties to terms to which they had not originally agreed when first they signed and ratified the treaty.

The fact that treaties can bind non-parties is not a novelty in international law. The Final Act of the Congress of Vienna 1815 made Switzerland a neutral State and allowed for the free navigation of international waterways. The Constantinople Convention 1888 was, for many years, considered to accord rights of passage through the Suez Canal to States that were not parties to the original convention. However, these were rarities and, in a sense, almost accidental by products of contractual treaties. With the advent of multilateral treaties that created law and norms, there arose the possibility that the application to non-party States might become a key element. It should be stressed that this is not because non-parties to a treaty should be bound by that treaty; rather, it was because the possibility was raised that a norm creating multilateral treaty might, coupled with the necessary *opinio juris*, formulate a new rule of customary international law binding on all States. In para 71 of the ICJ's judgment in the *North Sea Continental Shelf* case (1969), it was stated that:

There is no doubt that this process is a perfectly possible one and does from time to time occur: it constitutes one of the recognised methods by which the new rules of customary international law may be formed. At the same time, this result is not lightly to be regarded as having been attained.

This possibility can be described as dramatic because it tentatively raises the possibility of law making treaties becoming more like universal legislation. Domestic legislation has been said to bind all citizens whether or not they have given their consent to a law. They have been born into, or have otherwise entered, a society and therefore have accepted the social contract which can legally require obedience. The possibility is raised that norm creating treaties might be capable of having the same effect upon States.

In addition to norm creating treaties forming customary law, such treaties are now very often formulated so that they can develop to meet new circumstances. Traditionally, conventions only determined obligations at the time of formulation. If a change of obligations was to be brought about, either a new treaty had to be introduced (involving another usually lengthy process of negotiation, signing and ratifying) or an amendment (often called a protocol) could be made to the original instrument. This process can be time consuming and, as such, might not keep pace with current circumstances. The modern, norm creating treaty is designed so that it is more easily adaptive to those changing circumstances. In an attempt to do so, they incorporate mechanisms for adding new norms that might not have been contemplated by the original drafters of the treaty. An example of such a treaty is the Convention on International Trade in Endangered Species of Wild Flora and Fauna 1973 (CITES). The purpose of the treaty is, as the name suggests, to protect certain species of flora and fauna being endangered by trade. In 1973, it was anticipated by those at the Washington Conference who produced the Convention that different species required different types of protection. In addition, with changing circumstances over time, new species might need protection, while others might no longer need protection. Under the treaty, a secretariat was established to co-ordinate activities. It also includes methods for eliminating any unforeseen textual loopholes which could be exploited by smugglers to circumvent the basic provisions of the

Convention. CITES also allows party States to adjust the protection given to a species by changing its position within three appendices that are included within the treaty. Biennial conferences are required by CITES to allow the 126 party States to discuss their new policies on endangered species. Party States can, if they wish, make reservations with regard to the classification of certain species.

It is true that, legally, this ability to adapt stems from provisions within the original treaty. Nonetheless, such adaptive provisions mark a major departure from the traditional notion that States are bound only by treaty obligations that they accepted at the time they entered into the original treaty. Arguably, this marks a move away from traditional contractual treaties and toward 'international legislation'.

In conclusion, the new breed of treaties that has emerged since 1945 is, perhaps, the most dynamic feature of international law. Increasingly, treaties are law making rather than merely contractual and, as such, come nearer to being 'international legislation'. This has been the major development in treaty law since the beginning of the 20th century.

Notes

1   See, for example, the 1883 Paris Convention for the Protection of Industrial Property. Also, the Hague Conventions of 1899 and 1907.
2   See Bowman and Harris, *Mulilateral Treaties: Index and Current Status*, 1984, and the supplements they have provided.

Question 9

Thalingia and Smallovia signed and ratified a treaty in 1995 entitled the Thalingian-Smallovian Cross-Border Pollution Treaty. The treaty came into effect in January 1996. Article 25 of the treaty, written in English, states that:

> If one of the parties to the treaty allows a noxious substance in any way to cross its border, then the party responsible for such a discharge shall pay compensation agreed by a committee established by this treaty.

The committee referred to in Art 25 was composed of five Thalingians, five Smallovians and was chaired by citizens of Spotsiland. Article 92 of the treaty states that the committee shall make its decisions based upon the principles of public international law and not upon the basis of a compromise.

In 1997, an explosion occurs in a military research laboratory in Thalingia, with the result that chemical substances are released into the atmosphere. One of these substances, called Raino 2000, was designed to promote heavy rainfall. The release of the Raino 2000 causes torrential downpours within Thalingia. Although there is no trace of Raino 2000 itself crossing the Thalingian/Smallovian border, nonetheless, given the usual direction of the winds, the clouds that rained heavily upon Thalingia moved to rain equally heavily on Smallovia. The rainfall in Smallovia caused considerable damage to crops there. Smallovia relies upon Art 25 of the 1995 treaty in order to gain compensation.

Article 26 of that same treaty addressed itself to the question of testing possible pollutants. It stated that an individual who had committed a criminal offence in one of the party States could be shipped to the other and used as a human guinea pig in experiments. These experiments will be used to ascertain what effect certain chemical substances used in factories have on the human body if released into the atmosphere. Three hundred individuals have been so shipped, of whom 50 had died in the experiments.

Discuss.

Answer plan

The similarity between the production of a deed, contract or legislative enactment and an international convention is clear. They all must be construed and there must, accordingly, be rules by which this construction is carried out. Whereas, within the municipal system, those rules are (with the exception of the Interpretation Act 1978) a product of the common law, in the international sphere, the rules of interpretation were traditionally part of customary international law. Since 1969, these customary rules have been incorporated into the Vienna Convention on the

Law of Treaties. Thus, any student attempting to answer the following question should have an understanding of the terms of this treaty.

The following considerations are suggested:
- the interpretation of Art 25 of the 1996 treaty;
- the methods established in the Vienna Convention on the Law of Treaties by which treaties should be interpreted;
- the use of *travaux preparatois*; and
- the validity of Art 26 of the 1996 treaty: is it a breach of a rule of *jus cogens*?

Answer

In this question, attention will be given to two matters. First, the interpretation of the meaning of Art 25 of the 1996 treaty, and secondly, the validity of Art 26 of that treaty.

The first point concerns the interpretation of Art 25 of the 1996 treaty. It might be argued by counsel for Thalingia that rain clouds could not be classed as a 'noxious substance' under that article. This matter would, in all likelihood, be governed by the Vienna Convention on the Law of Treaties 1969 (VCLT) which came into effect on 27 January 1980 (see Art 4). Even if Thalingia and Smallovia are not parties to this treaty, the treaty was a codification of pre-existing international law. As a consequence, unless the matter concerned is one of the few innovations brought about by the treaty, it is probable that the arbitrator or court would refer to its provisions as authoritative. The Vienna Convention rules on treaty interpretation are now used regularly as if they were part of customary international law (as seen recently in the *Maritime Delimitation and Territorial Questions* case (1995)). This is especially so, since we are informed that its proceedings are to be governed by principles of public international law and not be a compromise between the two parties.

Article 31(1) of the VCLT states that:

> A treaty shall be interpreted in good faith in accordance with the ordinary meaning to be given to the terms of the treaty in their context and in the light of its object and purpose.

The paragraph spells out the steps by which the arbitral committee will need to reach its conclusion. It will need to begin by focusing upon the ordinary or plain meanings of words within the article. This is also referred to as the 'textual approach'. In this instance, therefore, the committee would pay particular attention to the plain meaning of the word 'noxious'. In order to help the committee in this task, they can look at the treaty's object and purpose, if it is believed to be necessary. Thus, 'context, object and purpose' are not separate bases for interpreting the treaty, but auxiliary. This textual approach received approval by the International Law Commission's *Commentary* upon Art 31, in which is stated that:

> ... the jurisprudence of the International Court contains many pronouncements from which it is permissible to conclude that the textual approach to treaty interpretation is regarded by it as established law.[1]

The question for the committee would therefore be: 'Is the meaning of the word "noxious" clear and unambiguous?' If they believe it is, then they must apply it as it stands and not concern themselves with context, object, purpose or effectiveness. Arguably, however, the term 'noxious' does not admit of a clear meaning in this instance. Banks of artificially created rain clouds could possibly be viewed as noxious, but the matter is open to doubt.

In its ruling in *Competence of the General Assembly for the Admission of a State to the United Nations* (1950), the ICJ stated that:

> ... the first duty of a tribunal which is called upon to interpret and apply the provisions of a treaty is to endeavour to give effect to them in their natural and ordinary meaning in the context in which they occur.

As earlier mentioned, use of 'context' is also a supplementary method of determining the ordinary meaning. What can be used as context is set out in Art 31(2) of the VCLT. It allows, if the need to resolve the ambiguity of the meaning of a word arises, '... reference to be made to any agreement relating to the treaty which was made between all the parties in connection with the conclusion of the treaty', and/or, '... any instrument which was made by one or more parties in connection with the conclusion of the treaty and accepted by the other parties as an instrument related to the treaties'. Clearly, if such documents exist, they might readily prove of assistance in interpreting Art 25.

Further recourse can be had to subsequent agreements between the parties (Art 31(3)(a) of the VCLT), any subsequent practice between the parties relating to the treaty (Art 31(3)(b)), or any special meaning given to the term (Art 31(4)).

An example of a State attempting to rely on the special meaning of a term can be found in the *Eastern Greenland* case (1933) in which Norway tried to persuade the court that the word 'Greenland', as used by Denmark, did not mean the whole of the landmass but had a special meaning (that is, it only referred to the western area of Greenland that had been settled by the Danes). The court rejected this argument. In the case before us, it might also be argued by Thalingia that the word 'noxious' had a special meaning in the sense that it meant a non-natural cause of environmental damage.

When attempting to comprehend the appropriate meaning of the ambiguous word in terms of the 'objects and purpose' of the treaty, recourse might be had to the *travaux preparatois* of the 1996 treaty. These are materials that preceded the final draft of the convention (such as earlier drafts, minutes of meetings, discussion papers and the like) which might give a clearer indication than is available in the final document itself of what the object of the treaty was. Art 32 of the VCLT establishes that *travaux preparatois* can only be used as 'supplementary' aids to interpretation. They are only to be used to '... confirm the meaning resulting from the application of Art 31'. Such documents might also be used to help resolve the committee's problem of construction.

In addition, ambiguous terms are to be construed so as to lead to the effective application of terms of the treaty which can be inferred from the wording of Art 31. This is expressed in the maxim *ut res magis valeat quam pereat* (that the thing may rather have effect than perish). This means that the committee, when deciding between two or more meanings of the ambiguous word in question, would opt for that meaning which did not distort the treaty in question. In the words of the ILC *Commentary*:

> When a treaty is open to two interpretations, one of which does and the other does not enable the treaty to have appropriate

effects, good faith and the objects and purposes of the treaty demand that the former interpretation should be adopted.[2]

The rationale for such a principle is the desire to give effect to the provisions of the treaty in question in accordance with the will of the parties (see *Corfu Channel* case (1949); *Ambatielos* case (1948)).

The second matter for consideration concerns Art 26 of the 1996 treaty. It might be argued that such an article, as it involves human experimentation, is in violation of a rule of *jus cogens* and, as a consequence, is invalid. Article 53 of the VCLT states that: 'A treaty is void if, at any time of its conclusion, it conflicts with a peremptory norm of international law.' That peremptory norm, a norm that admits of no derogation in any circumstance, is the rule of *jus cogens*. Thus, if Art 26 of the 1996 treaty breaches such a peremptory norm when the treaty is concluded, it is immediately invalid. However, this raises two problems. First, can the obnoxious Art 26 be severed from the rest of the Treaty. Article 53 begins: 'A *treaty* is void ...' (emphasis supplied) suggesting that it can only apply to the *whole* treaty and not to a part of it. This is especially the case where the provisions of the treaty are believed to be non-separable. Judging by the terms of Art 44 of the VCLT and from an ICJ decision,[3] it might be suggested that the committee would be wary of allowing such separability and, as a consequence, the 1996 treaty might stand or fall as a whole.

The second problem is whether the terms of Art 26 of the 1996 treaty violate a rule of *jus cogens*. There is a good deal of dispute as to exactly what such norms are. Genocide is frequently mentioned, as is the illegal use of force, but beyond that, there is doubt. The ILC *Commentary* on Art 53 deliberately did not include any examples of rules of *jus cogens* because the mention of some cases '... might, even with the most careful drafting, lead to misunderstanding as to the position concerning other cases'.[4] Therefore it is difficult in the present instance to state with any degree of confidence whether either the provision in the treaty or the treaty as a whole is invalid for being in breach of a rule of *jus cogens*.

In conclusion, it can be seen by what methods the committee would set about construing the contentious Art 25. In addition, it could be suggested that Art 26, or the treaty as a whole, could be invalid as being in breach of a peremptory norm of international law.

Notes
1 (1966) YBILC II, p 220.
2 (1966) YBIL II, p 219. Application of the principle of effectiveness can be observed in the United States diplomatic and consular staff in *Tehran* case (1980). Here, the ICJ ruled that the fact that a dispute was still being dealt with by the Security Council did not prevent the court exercising jurisdiction. For Art 36(3) of the Charter stated that the Security Council should recognise that the primary organ for remedying disputes was the ICJ (see para 40 of the ICJ judgment).
3 See the decision of Judge Lauterpacht in the *Norwegian Loans* case (1957).
4 (1966) YBILC II, p 248

Question 10

In 1981, 32 States signed the Preservation of Sea Snails Convention (PSSC). Twenty nine states eventually ratify the Convention and it comes into force on 5 January 1989. Four of the parties, which are neighbouring States (Arcadia, Binrovia, Canbeera and Dreemovia), once had thriving sea snail fishing communities. Moreover, in each of these countries, the sea snail is a food of cultural importance. All the States which signed and ratified PSSC did so because they feared that the species was being overfished and would soon become extinct. By 1995, the governments in Arcadia, Binrovia and Conrovia come under great pressure from their fishing unions to resume the exploitation of the sea snail.

Arcadia decides to ignore the treaty's provisions and passes a law to permit its fishermen to renew their exploitation of the sea snail. The Binrovian Minister of Agriculture announces that his country, too, will resume fishing the sea snail, because they believe that circumstances surrounding fishing have changed so radically since they originally ratified PSSC that the treaty should be terminated. In particular, studies carried out by civil servants from

Binrovia have suggested that stocks of the sea snail are now large enough to allow fishing to restart.

Canbeera and Dreemovia wish to have the PSSC amended either generally or between themselves.

Ginolaria, a party to the PSSC, has a very powerful 'green lobby' and a population which refuses to eat the sea snail. The Foreign Minister of Ginolaria insists that the original provisions of the PSSC should not be altered. She disputes the recent statistics presented by the Binrovian research into the sea snail and, moreover, argues that renewed fishing will seriously impair attempts to enforce the PSSC.

Escoria and Frizonia, both parties to the PSSC, enter into a state of conflict. The fishermen of both States wish to know if they can now fish for the sea snail.

Answer plan

As with the previous question, this answer requires the student to have a firm grounding in the key rules contained within the Vienna Convention. In addition, the examination candidates will need to know a number of cases decided by international tribunals to support their contentions. Although there is no rule of *stare decisis* in international law, such decisions, nonetheless, can prove highly influential in shaping the law in a particular area.

In answering the problem question, the student should address attention to the following issues:
- the consequences of Arcadia's termination of the Preservation of the Sea Snail Convention;
- the question of whether a change in circumstances will permit Binrovia to terminate its treaty obligations;
- the possibility of Canbeera and Dreemovia either amending the treaty generally or modifying the treaty between themselves;
- the position of a State that objects to any alteration of the original treaty; and
- the effects of war upon a multilateral treaty.

Answer

This question demands discussion of the following matters. First, the consequences of Arcadia's termination of the Preservation of the Sea Snail Convention (PSSC); secondly, the question of whether a change in circumstances will permit Binrovia to terminate its treaty obligations; thirdly, the possibility of Canbeera and Dreemovia either amending the PSSC generally or modifying the treaty between themselves; fourthly, the position of a State that objects to any alteration of the original treaty; and finally, the effects of war upon a multilateral treaty.

The Vienna Convention on the Law of Treaties 1969 (VCLT) attempted to codify customary international law on treaties. It is highly probable that all of the parties concerned in this question are parties to the VCLT, but even if they were not, the VCLT would still be authoritative when used to interpret customary international law on any matter relating to treaties. For the purposes of this essay, it will be assumed that the relevant States are parties to the VCLT. It can be noted that the PSSC came into effect after the VCLT, and therefore its provisions will be interpreted in the manner prescribed by the latter treaty.

Arcadia, under pressure from its fishermen, simply wishes to withdraw from the PSSC. Most multilateral treaties tend to contain a special clause specifically allowing for withdrawal. Usually, such clauses incorporate a procedure whereby the other party States may be informed of the withdrawal. In addition, they also usually have an express provision which states that withdrawal can only take place following a set time period following notification of withdrawal. If such clauses do not exist, then it is to be suggested that reference should be made to Art 56 of the VCLT. Paragraph 1 of this article states that denunciation or withdrawal cannot take place unless (a) it is established that the parties intended the possibility of denunciation or withdrawal, or (b) a right of denunciation or withdrawal may be implied by the nature of the treaty. Paragraph 2 of this article additionally specifies that if the treaty makes no express provision for withdrawal '... a party shall not give less than 12 months' notice of its intention to denounce or withdraw from a treaty under para 1'. If neither condition (a) or (b) is met, then denunciation or withdrawal can only take place after 12 months. Thus, it could be suggested that the legitimacy of Arcadia's instant withdrawal could well be doubtful.

When a treaty is breached, the State in breach is to be held responsible for its actions. The Permanent Court of International Justice stated in the *Chorzow Factory* case (1928) that '... any breach of an engagement involves an obligation to make reparations'. The purpose of reparations would be, as far as possible, to repair any damage done in such a way that the *status quo anti culpa* is restored. In the case of the fished sea snails, this is not a simple matter. A retraction of the withdrawal, payment of monetary compensation to foreign fishermen, and perhaps a contribution toward a fund to carry out more research into the stocks of sea snails might be considered as suggested penalties. A key demand would be for a repeal of the legislation which permitted the fishermen to restart their fishing.

In addition, one or more of the other parties might invoke Art 60(2)(b) of the VCLT. The parties could either collectively suspend or withdraw from the treaty in the relations between themselves and the defaulting State or between all the parties; such a decision would require an unanimous agreement. A party specially affected by the breach of the treaty (as all the other parties could argue), could invoke the breach as a ground for suspending the operation of the treaty in whole or in part between itself and the defaulting State. Furthermore, any party (other than the defaulting State), whether specially affected or not, can 'invoke the breach as a ground for suspending the operation of the treaty in whole or in part'. Paragraph 1 of this article states that:

> A material breach of a bilateral treaty by one of the parties entitles the other to invoke the breach as a ground for terminating the treaty or suspending its operation in whole or in part.

One alternative which Arcadia might have pursued would have been to let the other party States allow it to withdraw from the PSSC. Here, one might consult VCLT Arts 54(b) and 60. Under the former article, a party may withdraw from a treaty 'at any time by consent of all the parties after consultation with the contracting states'.

Question 11

Arcadia, Binrovia, Canbeera, Dreemovia and Escoria ratify a multilateral treaty on border demarcation in 1979. They each border the Toby Desert and now wish, by this treaty, to establish firmly their border relations with one another with regard to this desert territory. The treaty is known as the 'Toby Desert Pact' ('the pact').

Arcadia is a small State that gains very little from the pact. It later alleges that the other party States had threatened sanctions against it unless it signed and ratified the multilateral treaty.

In 1994, a new treaty is signed governing the same territory. With the exception of Arcadia and Binrovia, all of the States which had signed and ratified the former treaty sign and ratify the new treaty (named the Toby Desert Convention (TDC)) By this new treaty, the Toby Desert is divided into sectors. One sector is granted to Frizonia, despite the fact that Frizonia is not a party to the treaty. The TDC contains a denunciation clause which states that any party State may withdraw after a period of six months following its notice of withdrawal to the other party States. The original pact has not been suspended or terminated.

Dreemonia, following a revolution, divides and becomes two new States, Dreemovic and Monaria.

Assess the legal position of each of the parties.

Answer plan

One of the areas referred to in the following answer concerns the question of whether a third, non-party State can be bound by the provisions of a treaty. Clearly, the answer to this question is particularly important to those who wish for multilateral treaties to be viewed, in certain instances, as universal legislation rather than limited consensual, contractual agreements. This matter has important repercussions for the influence of public international law, and students should anticipate a question concerning this matter.

The problem question will demand an examination and discussion of the following:

- the importance of the treaty's nomenclature;
- whether the pressure placed upon Arcadia means that this State can avoid its obligations under the treaty;
- the rules governing the succession of treaties;
- whether treaty provisions bind a third State; and
- the rules governing the succession of States.

Answer

Both treaties in this question came into effect after the entry into force of the Vienna Convention on the Law of Treaties 1969 (VCLT).[1] The latter treaty attempted to codify customary international law on treaties. As a consequence, its provisions are looked to even in circumstances in which one of the parties has not ratified the VCLT or in which the treaty concerned was signed prior to the entry into force of the VCLT.

It will be noted that the first document brought to the reader's attention is referred to as a 'pact'. Despite this nomenclature, it can still be regarded as a type of treaty. For a definition of what is considered a treaty, it is necessary to refer to Art 2 of the VCLT, which defined a 'treaty' as 'an international agreement concluded between States in written form and governed by international law ... whatever its particular designation'. It became common after the Versailles Settlement to use the word 'pact' as shorthand for a treaty; for example, the Kellogg-Briand Pact is more formally known as the General Treaty for the Renunciation of War 1928.

The first issue of note in this question concerns the position of Arcadia, which alleges that it did not sign the pact of its own free will but because of pressure placed upon it by foreign powers. The VCLT outlines four main grounds for impugning the validity of a treaty:

(a) the incapacity and corruption of the party who gave consent on behalf of the State (Arts 46 and 50);
(b) error or fraud involved in the signing of the treaty (Arts 48 and 49);
(c) coercion related to the treaty, be it of the representative or of the State itself (Arts 51 and 52); and
(d) those treaties made in violation of a rule of *jus cogens* (Arts 53 and 64).

In this instance, Arcadia might claim that the third ground for impugning the invalidity of the treaty arose, namely, that involving coercion of a State prior to signing and ratifying a treaty. Article 52 states that '... a treaty is void if its conclusion has been procured by the threat or use of force in violation of the principles of the United Nations'. Such a hard line was taken by the drafting body of the VCLT – the International Law Commission – because they wished the law on treaties to reflect the general prohibition on illegal use of force contained in Art 2(4) of the UN Charter.

Two points need to be made with regard to a breach of Art 52. First, the aggression concerned must be of the kind proscribed by Art 2(4) of the UN Charter. However, it is arguable whether the imposition of sanctions constitutes a breach of the article. Certainly the drafting history of the UN Charter, in particular Art 2(4), could indicate that economic pressure should not be included. Whilst the General Assembly Resolution 2625(XXV) 1970 does, in its section entitled 'Declaration on the Principles of Non-Intervention' prohibit economic coercion, in *Nicaragua (Merits)* (1986), the ICJ noted that US sanctions did not breach the principle of non-intervention. Secondly, Art 52 refers to the use of force used to gain actual acceptance of the treaty; it does not relate to those events involving force that might have historically led up to the signing of the treaty. Thus, the wars that preceded the Egyptian-Israeli Treaty of Peace 1979 would not become void under Art 52.

Given the above, it is arguable, on the first point raised, that Arcadia would be incapable of holding its acceptance to be void *ab initio* under Art 52. Secondly, in any case, it would be necessary for Arcadia that the pressure was exerted not in the ordinary way of international relations, but was a deliberate exertion of pressure to attain one end and one end only, namely, Arcadia's signature and ratification of the pact.

The next issue involves the succession of treaties. It can be noted that both Arcadia and Binrovia declined to become parties to the Toby Desert Convention (TDC). In their dealings with States party to the latter treaty, what rules are to govern their relationship? – the earlier treaty or the latter? If it is found that Arcadia did sign and ratify in breach of the VCLT Art 52, then the terms of the treaty, being void with regard to them, will not apply. In their stead will be the rules of customary international law. Failing this claim being made out, Arcadia, like Binrovia, would be bound by the terms of the pact.

The relevant rules as to the relationship between succeeding treaties on the same issue can be found in Art 30 of the VCLT. If either the pact or the TDC contained a clause giving priority to the other treaty, that provision should be followed (VCLT Art 30(2)). Should this not prove to be the case, then Art 30(4) should apply. This states:

> When the parties to the later treaty do not include all the parties to the earlier one [as here] ... the treaty to which both States are still parties [in this case, the pact] governs their mutual rights and obligations.

Thus, if, for example, a dispute took place concerning the Toby Desert border demarcation between Binrovia and Canbeera, the terms of the 1987 pact would be followed rather than that of the 1994 convention.

The next question concerns the rights conferred upon Frizonia by the TDC. The general position adopted in customary international law is that expressed in the maxim *pacta tertiis nec nocent nec prosunt* (a treaty does not create either obligations or rights for a third State without its consent), and this is expressed in VCLT Art 34. However, the VCLT makes a distinction between *obligations imposed* upon a third party and *rights conferred* upon a third party. In the former case, Art 35 demands that two tests are met:

(a) that the party States intended to confer obligations upon the third party; and

(b) that the third States accepted that obligation in writing.

In the case of rights (which would apply to the benefits Frizonia would gain under the TDC), arguably, Art 36 would apply. Again, two tests need to be met:

(a) as with Art 35, the parties intention to confer rights on a third party has to be established; and, critically

(b) the third party's 'assent shall be presumed so long as the contrary is not indicated, unless the treaty otherwise provides'.[2]

Moreover, Art 37(2) provides that '... such a third party right was intended not to be revocable or subject to modification without the consent of the third State'.

Thus, unless Frizonia makes it clear through its diplomatic channels and/or its municipal law that it refuses the rights conferred upon it by the TDC, then such rights will be granted to it, and any subsequent modification of those rights can only be made upon the terms of VCLT Art 37(2). There remains another possibility, and that is that the terms of the multilateral TDC become part of customary international law (because of factors such as the duration of the application of the treaty; its wide, if not universal, adoption; their possible norm creating character; and *opinio juris*). This would mean that the rules established under the TDC could become applicable to all States whether they had ratified the treaty or not.[3] Such a possibility was suggested in the *North Sea Continental Shelf* case (1969). However, it could be suggested that this would apply to only very few treaties indeed, and that it would be most unlikely to apply, because of the relevant circumstances, to the TDC.

Following the revolution in Dreemonia, the former State became two States. What are the legal obligations of the successor States with regard to the treaties? This is a matter to be determined not by an examination of the VCLT, but by the Vienna Convention on Succession of States in respect of Treaties 1978, which attempted to codify customary law on this issue. Whilst this treaty is still not yet in force, it does clarify existing customary international law, and thus would still be referred to as an authoritative guide to the law in this area. By Arts 8–10 of this convention, when succession occurs, the successor States are no longer bound by treaty commitments entered into by the former State; this is the so called 'clean slate doctrine'. However, an exception to this rule should be noted in Arts 11 and 12 of the 1978 treaty. In particular, Art 11 states:

> A succession of States does not as such affect:
>
> (a)   a boundary established by a treaty; or
>
> (b)   obligations and rights established by a treaty and relating to the regime of the boundary.

Thus, it could be argued that the two newly created States would inherit the rights and obligations contained in both the pact and the TDC.

In conclusion, it could be argued, first, that Arcadia, because military force had not been exerted against it, could not hold that its commitment to the pact is void. Secondly, that Arcadia and Binrovia, when conducting negotiations with States which signed the TDC, will follow the rules established in the pact. Thirdly, that Frizonia, unless it clearly indicates otherwise, can accept rights conferred on it by the TDC even though Frizonia is not party to that treaty. Lastly, Dreemonia and Monaria are still bound by the treaty commitments agreed to by the State they succeeded.

Notes

1 The VCLT came into effect on 27 January 1980 (see Art 4 of the Convention).
2 See also the remarks directed on this point made in the *Case of the Free Zones of Upper Savoy and Gex* (1932).
3 Unless it were shown that they were persistent objectors to the formulation of the rules established by the treaty. See *Anglo-Norwegian Fisheries* case (1951).

CHAPTER 4

THE RELATIONSHIP BETWEEN INTERNATIONAL AND MUNICIPAL LAW

Introduction

Rarely is a term time essay or an examination essay on this subject awarded anything above a 2.2 mark. The reason for this is straightforward: the topic has a tendency to provoke students to reproduce their notes, rather than trying to approach the question with any subtlety. For the examiner, the difficulty lies in formulating the question so that it will (a) be different from the one he set last year, and (b) allow good candidates the ability to demonstrate that they can do more than merely memorise their notes and demonstrate in writing that they have thought about the area and can apply this thought to answering the question.

A student who wants to see what the classic 2.2 answer looks like is advised to inspect that produced by J Collier in his excellent article in volume 38 *International and Comparative Law Quarterly* 924 entitled: 'Is International Law Really Part of the Law of England?' There can be no better piece to read for gaining an understanding of this subject.

In answering a problem question, the following issues should normally be considered, in the order given:
- a comparison between municipal law and international law;
- whether customary international law has to be transformed into English law by an Act of the legislature, or whether it is, like the common law, automatically part of our law (that is, 'incorporated') and capable of being applied by the courts as such; and
- the position of treaties and executive agreements and in what way their provisions become part of the law of the United Kingdom.

Checklist

Students should be familiar with the following areas:
- the meaning of international law;
- the way in which municipal law is enforced;
- the doctrine of legislative obedience;
- the cases involving the incorporation of customary international law into English law and of what genuine importance these cases are;
- the position post-*Trendtex* regarding the incorporation of proven rules of customary international law into English law;
- the distinction between self-executing and non-self-executing treaties; and
- the ways in which customary international law and treaty law become part of UK law.

Question 12

The position of English jurists and judges with regard to the application of the principles of customary international law within the municipal jurisdiction has been both inconsistent and irrational.

Discuss.

Answer plan

In response to a question such as this, the 2.2 student will simply produce a list of the key cases and what he or she believes to be their outcome. There will be no constructive critique to accompany the reporting. However, the student who wishes to gain a 2.1 and above will regard the lack of clarity that might be said to exist in the law on this subject as an opportunity to analyse the different positions, and in so doing, will be able to provide a more sophisticated and accurate, answer to the question asked.

The following order of treatment is suggested:
- the theoretical positions that have been adopted with regard to this question. Here, there will be a brief discussion of the Monist, Dualist and Harmonist positions;

- the above raises the obvious question of which position the English courts have adopted. Here there could be said to be four in number:
  (a) exponents of the statutory transformation doctrine;
  (b) exponents of the broad incorporation doctrine;
  (c) exponents of the incorporation following judicial adoption doctrine;
  (d) exponents of the *Trendtex* incorporationist exception to *stare decisis;*
- despite such an inconsistent approach, is it possible to predict how an English court would view the matter today.

Answer

With rare exception, the international community cannot enforce public international law directly. There is no single, all powerful body governing international law just as there is no police force to assert compliance with these rules. The legal rules can only have any effectiveness if they are applied as part of the municipal law of each legal system. This inspires two key questions. First, are the rules of customary international law automatically part of domestic law, and should they be enforced as such? Secondly, if the answer to the first question is 'yes', which rule is to prevail in the case of a conflict between the rules of the two legal systems? As will be shown in this essay, English courts and jurists have not always adopted a consistent approach to answering these questions.

It might be said that, in responding to these questions, English judges and jurists have associated themselves with four different schools of thought.

First, there are those who have been termed 'Dualists'; that is, they believe that municipal and international law are distinctly separate; they deal with different issues and operate in different jurisdictions. The municipal law has primacy over international law in municipal decisions, and that of international law has primacy over municipal law in international decisions. With regard to the role of English judges, four factors should be borne in mind in this regard. The first is the doctrine of judicial obedience. The historical position has been that, since the Glorious

Revolution of 1688, all English judges have recognised the supremacy of Parliament. In accordance with this rule, they will, in the event of any conflict with other rules, always give priority to and apply accordingly the latest Act of Parliament.[1] Moreover, judges will also feel themselves bound by precedent from courts of equal or higher status. Traditionally, they would give priority to such a precedent rather than to a current rule of customary international law.

Secondly, many judges and jurists, particularly in the last century, were heavily influenced by the writings of jurists such as Austin. To Austin, international law was not truly law but rather an accumulation of moral guidelines. This was so because such rules were not made by one sovereign body that issued commands, and any such vague rules that *did* exist could not be supported by a system of sanctions. Municipal law, on the other hand, was not simply a collection of moral guidelines, but imperative commands. As such, the law implementing bodies were bound to apply it, whereas rules of international law only bound their conscience. The only way to alter this position would be for Parliament to transform 'the rules' of international law, be it treaty law or customary law, into commanding municipal law. This puts the rules of customary international law on a similar footing to that of a treaty in the way in which they are viewed by English courts.

Thirdly, it should not be forgotten how difficult it is to establish rules of customary international law. The test usually adopted in order to ascertain whether usage has developed into obligatory custom is that it must be approved by the common consent of nations.[2] However, what if that consent is inconsistent? Not only might there be doubt as to whether the rule applies and doubt as to whether the rule is a compulsory one, rather than a voluntary one (even if it is established that it exists), but there might also be doubt when the rule is applied, because it is applied in a variety of ways. These factors proved to be of importance in the case of *R v Keyn* (1876), in which Cockburn LCJ demonstrated the lack of consensus over the supposed three mile maritime limit of jurisdiction.

Fourthly, it should be noted that, in *R v Keyn* (1876) the issue related to a penal matter. If the claim for UK jurisdiction had been made out, Captain Keyn might well have been jailed for manslaughter. If the court had been interpreting an ambiguous piece of UK statute law, it would have been obliged, by a rule of statutory interpretation, to have construed any obscurity or ambiguity contained within a section of an Act of Parliament to the advantage of the accused. How much more so would they have been willing to do this where the bench is applying inconsistent rules of public international law.

For the above reasons, both in theory and as illustrated in case law, the Dualist view received particular support. This was especially the case in the age of positivism and nationalism – the 19th century.

So, the strict transformationist approach denied the judges a mandate to introduce rules of customary international law into English Law unless that rule had been transformed by legislation into English law (in the same way that treaties entered into by the UK have to be).[3] However, there were those judges and jurists who went so far as to presume for the judges just such a mandate. Blackstone held that the great virtue of the common law was that it had been determined by the commonwealth and had stood the test of time. Such virtues could also apply to rules of customary international law. As such, once established, and as long as they did not run counter to a statutory provision, they could be adopted. Thus, on this view, the English courts could apply proven rules of customary international law in an English court in exactly the same way as they would apply English common law in that court. This might be viewed as the broad adoption doctrine of customary international law. It was a view that seems to have received judicial acknowledgment (though little more than that) in such famous cases as *Barbuit* (1737) and *Triquet v Bath* (1764).

In more recent times, the courts have favoured a narrower approach based upon the adoption doctrine, by which the judge still presumes a mandate from the sovereign to apply rules of customary international law, but only in a narrow set of circumstance. First, unlike common law, the rule of customary international law must be 'invited in' to English law by being given judicial endorsement. Until such endorsement has been given, the parties to an action could not appeal to the rule as of right. Such an endorsement would not be given if the rules of customary international law were inconsistent with pre-existing statutory rules.[4] No endorsement would be given until the rule was satisfactorily proven to exist. Unlike rules of foreign law, the rule does not need to be proven by evidence in court. Yet the judge needs to be satisfied that the rule is genuine and more than just the opinion of text writers.[5] This, as mentioned before, is not easily established. Even if the rule does exist, the court closely examines its content and will endeavour never to let a rule of customary international law extend beyond its original scope.[6] Lastly, as Lord Atkin made clear in *Chung Chi Cheung v R* (1939), no endorsement would take place if the proven rule was inconsistent with a previous common law decision 'as finally declared by their tribunals'.

The above approach might be thought to be a matter of judicial transformation. Just as the vast majority of treaties are transformed with English law by statute, so, it might be thought, customary English law, if it conformed to the adoption requirements, might be transformed by judicial endorsement into English law. Once this has been done, it would readily be acknowledged as part of the common law and would be capable of binding courts in later cases. This terminology might legitimately be used if it were not for an important legal fiction. By common law decisions, as distinct from statute, judicial decisions as to what the law *is* does have a retrospective effect on our law. Thus, when a judge in 1938 decides that rule X, a rule of customary international law, can be applied, it does not just mean that rule X becomes part of the common law in 1938. It means that from 1938 rule X should always have been viewed as part of the common law. Although the judge is actually transforming the rule in English law, the legal fiction exists that, once the judge has endorsed rule of customary international law X, it has *always existed* as a common law rule; in effect, that the rule had always been incorporated into English law. It can be argued that it is the existence of this legal fiction which is at the basis of all the confusion that exists over the judicial relationship between the common law and rules of customary international law.

If the court behaves in this way, rule X, as stated, will be binding in the normal way in subsequent cases. Yet the rules of customary international law could change; if the courts strictly applied the rule of *stare decisis,* the idea of the court having the capacity to adopt the contemporary rule of customary international law could be defeated. Adoption of a rule of customary international law could happen once; then the rule would become part of the common law, and bind subsequent courts.[7] Could it therefore be possible for the rule of *stare decisis* to be circumscribed so as to permit the introduction of new rules of customary international law? Lord Denning, in *Trendtex v Central Bank of Nigeria* (1977), seemed to give the answer in the affirmative. This could be done where the rule of customary international law could be proven (as far as one can prove a rule of customary international law). Further, the issue at hand must turn solely on the matter of *customary* law. Why could rules of contemporary customary international law bypass the rule of *stare decisis*? It was because customary international law recognised no rule of *stare decisis.*

In conclusion, it can be seen that any inconsistency of approach adopted by the courts might, in the main, be attributed to one key factor, that is, the very nature of the English legal system. Being a non-codified system, there is no clear statement about the status of international law nor, indeed, of the power of judges to interpret it.

Notes

1 Although historically this has certainly been the case, the situation might change in the 1990s. First, because *obiter dicta* comments in *Macarthys v Smith* (1979), and *Factortame* (1990) seem to indicate that the courts might be willing to 'dis-apply' a part of UK legislation if it should contradict European law. The only possible exception to this would be where the English statute expressly announced its intention to contradict European law. In those circumstances the courts would, most likely, uphold the English law. Otherwise, it might be argued that the rule of implied repeal, whilst applying to UK statutes, no longer applies to European law. In addition, when the European Convention on Human Rights becomes law within the UK, English judges might find that they can question the legitimacy of certain pieces of legislation produced by Her Majesty in Parliament.

2   On how an individual State indicates its consent, see Chapter 2 on Sources of International Law.
3   This is not entirely true, for there are some rare treaties known as 'self-executing'. For this type of treaty, legislation is not required, although it is common practice to pass such legislation in any case.
4   See the opinion of Lord Atkin in *Chung Chi Cheung v R* (1939).
5   See the judgment of Lord Alverstone in *West Rand Central Gold Mining Co v R* (1905); also Cockburn LCJ in *R v Keyn*.
6   See the judgment of Lord Oliver in *Maclaine Watson v Department of Trade and Industry* (1989).
7   Obviously, much would depend upon the hierarchy of the court structure. The House of Lords, since 1966, might well wish to introduce a new rule of customary international law. The key point here is the way in which lower courts are bound by *stare decisis*, just as Lord Denning should have been bound in *Trendtex* (1977).

Question 13

In 1932, the United Kingdom signs and ratifies the Freedom of Shipping Convention, a treaty by which it agrees to place no restrictions upon the type of vessel that can use its port facilities.

Following a number of disastrous oil spillages off the British coast caused by old, overly capacious and badly maintained oil tankers, Parliament passes the Sea Safety Act 1995. This prohibits vessels that are 'unseaworthy' from using any port in the United Kingdom. In 1996, the House of Lords, in *Boondoggle v Trollope Shipping*, decided that the word 'unseaworthy' in the statute included oil tankers over 60,000 tons. In 1997, the Foreign Secretary signs an agreement with the State of Tinko allowing oil tankers of any capacity to enter British ports.

Flexxon Shipping is a British oil import company. They wish to use the services of the 80,000 ton Tinkoese registered oil tanker *The Fang U*. Tinko is also a party to the convention of 1932. *The Fang U* would be required to dock at the British port of Hilford Mavern to unload its imports.

Flexxon Shipping seeks your legal advice before the company signs the contract. Advise them.

In what way would your answer have been different if the matter had been governed by US law?

Answer plan

Most students will be expected, and expect, to answer an essay type question on this topic. However, they should always be prepared for a problem question. As with all other questions, students should be advised to ask themselves, at the end of each paragraph: 'Am I actually answering the question asked of me?' If you ask that question *at the very end of the essay*, it is too late; the damage will have been done.

In order to answer the above question, the following approach is suggested:

- an examination of the relationship between domestic legislation and international law (that is, between the Freedom of Shipping Convention obligations and the Sea Safety Act of 1995);
- an examination of the position the English courts must adopt when faced with a conflict between the terms of statute and international obligations;
- an examination of the legal status of the executive agreement made between the Foreign Secretary and the State of Tinko; and
- a discussion on how such issues would be viewed in US law.

Answer

In order to answer this question, it is necessary first to examine the relationship between domestic legislation and international law; that is, between the Freedom of Shipping Convention obligations and the Sea Safety Act of 1995. Secondly, the position the English courts must adopt when faced with a conflict between the terms of statute and international obligations will be examined. Thirdly, there will be an examination of legal status of the executive agreement made between the Foreign Secretary and the State of

Tinko. Fourthly, each of these issues will be examined from the perspective of US law.

A distinction must be drawn between the application of customary international law within the United Kingdom and that law created by treaty. The proposition has been accepted by the courts that customary international law is, unless it runs contrary to statutory provisions or decisions of higher judicial authority, part of the law of United Kingdom. Moreover, it is law agreed to by the community of States; it is the collective and refined wisdom of States; it is the 'common law' of States. Treaty law, on the other hand, is different in two senses. First, rather than being the product of a collective, a treaty obligation could, and often is, a bilateral act between two States. Secondly, it is the product not of the concurrent conduct of the vast majority of States, but of the British executive using its prerogative powers. Whilst the courts cannot impugn the power of the Crown to make treaties, the terms of those treaties cannot be operative within the United Kingdom unless Parliament has passed an enabling statute. With the exception of the conduct of war and the cession of territories, Parliamentary sanction, in the form of an Act of Parliament, is essential if any treaty obligations entered into by the Crown are to effect private rights within the UK (see *Walker v Baird* (1892)).[1] As stated by Lord Oliver in *Maclaine Watson v Department of Trade and Industry* (1989): 'Quite simply, treaty is not a part of English law unless and until it has been incorporated into the law by legislation.'[2] As a consequence, unless Her Majesty's Government passes legislation incorporating the Freedom of Shipping Convention into English law, it is not part of English law.

However, there is a judicial presumption that legislation, in this case the Sea Safety Act 1995, is to be construed so as to avoid a conflict with international law. As Lord Diplock noted in *Saloman v Commissioners of Customs and Excise* (1967): 'Parliament does not intend to act in breach of international law, including therein specific treaty obligations.' The Lords of Appeal in Ordinary would acknowledge this presumption when construing the Sea Safety Act in *Boondoggle v Trollope Shipping*. However, where the words of a later statute are clear, unobscure and unambiguous, their Lordships would have no choice but to apply the terms of the statute even though it means that the Crown will violate its treaty obligations (see *Ellerman Lines v Murray* (1931)). Despite

Lord Simonds in *IRC v Collco Dealings Ltd* (1962) stating that an exception might be made to this rule where 'broad considerations of justice or expediency' are involved, it would be unlikely in the extreme that an English court would disapply part of British statute in favour of the term of a treaty obligation.[3] In advising Flexxon Shipping, one should state that, unless the decision in *Boondoggle* can be distinguished, the interpretation of the word 'seaworthy' is binding upon all courts. The position can only be altered by a subsequent Act of Parliament or by the House of Lords overruling its previous decision.

The failure to give legal effect to the UK's treaty obligations under the 1932 convention will place the UK in violation of international law. Lord Atkin, in *Attorney General for Canada v Attorney General for Ontario* (1937), stated that, whilst a treaty might bind the contracting parties, the UK Parliament could still refuse to enshrine those obligations in English law (and by so doing, bind English courts) and thus bring the State into default. The only remedy for that default would be for an action on the international level between one of the contracting parties and the UK. Given this, one might advise Flexxon Shipping to try to persuade the Tinkoese government (for Tinko is a party to the Freedom of Shipping Convention), to put diplomatic and/or legal pressure on the UK to alter the terms of the 1995 Act and abide by its treaty obligations.

Flexxon Shipping should be advised that it is rarely probable that a court of law will enforce the terms of the executive agreement between the British Foreign Secretary and Tinko. Some executive measures are capable of being self-enacting. However, those that affect the private rights of British subjects, or which involve any modification of the common law or statute, require enabling legislation. As the terms of the executive agreement run counter to both the terms of the 1996 statute as construed in the *Boondoggle* case, an enabling statute would have to be passed in this instance.[4] Authority for this proposition can be found in *Laker Airways Ltd v Department of Trade* (1977).

Any differences on the US position in these matters would be due to the position of treaties within US constitutional law. In the UK, the Crown is solely responsible for the negotiation, the signature and the ratification of treaties. However, it does so under the proviso that the passing of such provisions as it has agreed to is a matter to be left to Parliament. In the US, the President may only ratify a treaty on one condition: that the Senate has approved that treaty by a two-thirds majority. Following that ratification, those treaty provisions can, directly and immediately, be part of the law of the land. As Art VI, para 2 of the US Constitution states:

> ... all Treaties made under the Authority of the United States, shall be the supreme Law of the Land; and the Judges in every State shall be bound thereby, anything in the Constitution or Laws of any State to the contrary notwithstanding.

Would this mean that Flexxon Shipping should be advised that the Freedom of Shipping Convention would apply in this instance? Two points need to be made here. First, it is stated above that such treaty provisions can' directly and automatically be incorporated as part of US law. Whether they will be depends upon whether they are deemed by the courts to be self-executing' or non-self-executing'. To be self-executing (that is, able to come immediately into force without requiring enabling legislation), the 1932 convention will need to have terms which, in the view of a US court, can be directly applicable in US municipal law. This can be gauged by the nature or by the express terms of the convention.[5] Secondly, under the US Constitution, if the treaty is self-executing it becomes an equal to federal legislation. Thus it can effectively, by implied repeal, supplant earlier laws which differ from it.[6] Equally, as the case of *Edye v Robinson* (*The Head Money*) (1884) demonstrates, if later federal legislation is passed which has different terms from those contained within the treaty, the court will apply the later piece of federal legislation. Thus, whilst a US court, when construing their equivalent to the Sea Safety Act 1995, would still presume that its legislature had no wish to depart from international law (see *Cook v United States* (1933)), if the terms of the new federal law were clear, the US courts would apply them in preference to the provision of the 1932 convention.

As to the executive agreement made by the British Foreign Secretary, the following could be suggested. The President of the United States can make such agreements without the two-thirds approval of the Senate. This can be achieved following a joint resolution of both Houses of Congress or because the agreement was made pursuant to the President's power to conduct foreign relations. These agreements have been enforced by US courts (see *United States v Belmont* (1937)). However, the ability to make such executive agreements has not been extended to the US Secretary of State (the US equivalent of the Foreign Secretary).

In conclusion, Flexxon Shipping should be advised, for the reasons mentioned above, that they would be unlikely to legalise the docking of *the Fang U* in either a British or a US port.

Notes

1 The rationale behind the lack of need for Parliamentary sanction is due, presumably, to the fact that the alteration of the rights and duties concerned does not in any sense attenuate the power of Parliament. Certain administrative measures, as long as they do not alter private rights, can equally be self-executing.
2 See also *Attorney General for Canada v Attorney General for Ontario* (1937), *per* Lord Atkin.
3 Two caveats should be added here. First, following the case of *Factortame Ltd v Secretary of State for Transport* (1990), this rule may no longer be true with regard to UK obligations under the Treaty of Rome 1957. Secondly, the position of the UK courts on the matter of the European Convention on Human Rights is to be altered. One has yet to see how that will affect English law.
4 See also the first instance decision of Phillimore J in the Court of Admiralty, Divorce and Probate in *The Parlement Belge* (1874–80). Although this decision was subsequently reversed in the Court of Appeal, it is now regarded as good law.
5 Clearly, if the convention is non-self-executing, legislation will be required before its terms can become operative. See *Sei Fujii v The State of California* (1952). It should also be noted that if the convention is believed to deal with a matter over which Congress has exclusive legislative powers, the convention will be considered as *prima facie* non-self-executing. This will be the case irrespective of the express terms of the convention.
6 Unless, of course, the provisions in the treaty are deemed to violate the Constitution.

Question 14

Has there ever been any validity to the incorporationist doctrine? Is there now?

Answer plan

Yet again the student attempting this answer should avoid falling into the trap of producing the Collier model student answer if he or she wishes to gain a 2.1 or above. What is required is more than a knowledge of names of the cases; the student is also called upon the recognise the significance of these authorities.

A suggested answer plan would be as follows:
- the incorporationist view and its rival position;
- an historical analysis of how the view of incorporation came about;
- why the incorporationist view became ousted by transformationism;
- *Trendtex* and the incorporationist revival;
- whether *Trendtex* amounts to a new exception to the rule of *stare decisis*; and
- what has been the long term result of the *Trendtex* decision

The student should not forget that much of what Lord Denning and Lord Shaw stated, in relation to this topic, in *Trendtex* was *obiter dicta*. To find out whether it would alter the law, one needs to see whether such views have been followed in later judicial decisions.

Answer

For many decades, English texts on international law have engaged in the debate concerning the relationship of the rules of customary international law to English law.[1] Are such rules, once proved, to be treated as being on a par with common law authorities or do they have a different status? Do they have to be transformed into English law by a legislative Act? Any examination of this problem requires an examination of the case law.

Traditionally, such an examination begins with *Barbuit's* case (1737) and *Triquet v Bath* (1764). These are both hailed as cases which demonstrate the so called 'incorporationist doctrine', that is:

> ... the view that customary rules are to be considered part of the law of the land and enforced as such, with the qualification that they are incorporated only so far as is not inconsistent with Acts of Parliament or prior judicial decisions of final authority.[2]

Under the opposing transformationist doctrine, such rules could enter into English law 'only so far as the rules have been clearly adopted and made part of the law of England by legislation, judicial decision, or established usage'. Both cases involved the construction of the Diplomatic Privileges Act 1708. The circumstances whereby this Act was introduced were somewhat unusual. Prior to 1708, any valid foreign ambassadors were not immune from civil suit in English courts. This was contrary to practice in the majority of major states. In 1708, the ambassador of Peter the Great, Andrew Mattueof, was arrested and taken out of his coach for debts which he had contracted. Blackstone relates:

> This the Czar resented very highly, and demanded (we are told) that the officers who made the arrest should be punished with death. But the Queen (to the amazement of that despotic court) directed her ministers to inform him [the Czar] that the law of England had not yet protected embassadors [sic] from the payment of their lawful debts; that therefore the arrest was no offence by the laws; and that she could inflict no punishment upon any ... of her subjects, unless warranted by the law of the land'.[3]

In order to appease the wrath of the Czar and other ambassadors the Diplomatic Privileges Act was introduced. It referred to the arrest that had been made and states that such an arrest was:

> ... in contempt of the protection granted by her Majesty, *contrary to the Law of Nations*, and in prejudice to the rights and privileges which ambassadors ... have at all times been thereby possessed of, and ought to be kept sacred and inviolable [emphasis supplied].

By the 'Law of Nations', the statute referred essentially to what we would now refer to as customary international law. This privilege applied to ambassadors or other public ministers but not to their servants.

In *Barbuit's* case (1737) and *Triquet v Bath* (1764), the issue arose as to who could count as members of the diplomatic staff of an embassy and therefore be immune from suit. In the former case, Talbot LC, noted that the 1708 Act was only declaratory of the 'antient [sic] *jus gentiu*,' as the statute had made clear. He then proceeded to make a distinction between ambassadors and public ministers, who would come under the protection of the statute, and consuls, who would not. As Barbuit served as a consul, he would not, therefore, be immune from civil suit. When a similar dispute arose in *Triquet v Bath* (1764), Lord Mansfield reflected upon this earlier case and remembered the Lord Chancellor stating:

> That 'the law of nations was to be collected from the practice of different nations, and the authority of writers'. Accordingly ... the Lord Chancellor turned to the writings of Barbeyac, Wincquefort, &c, there being no English writer of eminence, upon the subject.

What do these cases actually establish? They might be claimed to establish that, in circumstances in which a statute sets out to be declaratory of customary international law, where a question arises regarding construction of that statute, the rules of customary international law can be an authoritative guide. Further, to establish those rules, one can turn to the works of learned authors. This seems to have been a perfectly reasonable approach in both the above cases. The statue had made its purpose clear: to bring English law on diplomatic privilege in line with that of other States. There were no English authorities on the matter, not even authoritative works of English authors. Moreover, it should not be forgotten that the doctrine of the sovereignty of parliament was, at this stage, not adhered to as firmly as in the century that followed; the same could be said of the rule of *stare decisis*. Indeed, it might be argued that because there were far fewer authorities to follow in the 18th century, it was natural, in cases of doubt, that the Bench should turn to the common law of nations in order to procure an answer.

The position adopted in the above cases should be contrasted with those decided over a century later, when Parliament had enormously increased the number and size of legislative enactments. The industrial revolution and the improvement in the court structure in the 19th century together led to an enormous increase in the number of legal authorities. Judges were adhering far more strictly to the will of Parliament and to the rule of *stare decisis*. Perhaps, above all, the prevailing legal philosophies were heavily influenced by positivism and, to a degree, nationalism. This can be observed by contrasting the decision in *Barbuit's* case and *Triquet* with *Engelke v Musmann* (1928) – a 20th century case on privilege. In the 18th century cases, the interpretation of the Act of 1707 depended on an interpretation of customary international law, an interpretation based upon the works of a small selection of learned non-English authors. Whilst, in the 18th century cases, 'customary international law to its full extent was part of the law of England', in *Engelke* Lord Phillimore stated that such rules are part of the 'common law of England'.[4] This does not mean that the incorporationist view is incorrect. What it does mean is that, by the 20th century, customary international law seemed to be reduced to a position of very little relevance to English law. It could only be employed (a) if the rule had been clearly proven – and when assessing the works of learned authors, a distinction should be made between statements *lex lata* and *de lege ferenda* (see obiter comments of Lord Alverstone in *West Rand Central Gold Mining Co Ltd v The King* (1905)); (b) if it were not inconsistent with the clear provisions of a statute (which would equally apply to a common law authority) (see *Mortensen v Peters* (1906)); (c) if such a rule was not inconsistent with the rules enacted by statutes or declared by their tribunals (*per* Lord Aitkin in *Chung Chi Cheung v The King* (1939); and (d), even if the rule has been established and does not run counter to a statutory term of a binding rule of common law, the rule must be proscriptive or prescriptive but not permissive (see *R v Keyn (The Franconia)* (1876). The existence of these high hurdles led to the belief that the UK had in effect adopted the transformationist position.[5]

However, *Trendtex Trading Corporation v Central Bank of Nigeria* (1975) seemed to defy three of the above criteria and resurrect the incorporationist doctrine. The issue involved in the case was that of State immunity. There was not, as yet, any statute law on the matter.[6] Binding common law authority clearly supported the absolute view of immunity.[7] At first instance, Donaldson J based his decision upon these authorities. Despite the stance taken by the UK, foreign State practice demonstrated that the restrictive approach had been adopted by many States. Lord Denning examined the view of one writer and the practice of the European Community States (and others). Denning and Shaw LJ stated *obiter dicta* that, as rules of customary international law are not governed by the rule of *stare decisis*, they could not only be immediately incorporated into English law but could do so in such a way as to overrule previous common law authority. In the words of Lord Denning:

> I now believe that the doctrine of incorporation is correct. Otherwise I do not see that our courts could ever recognise a change in the rules of international law. If this court today is satisfied that the rule of international law on a subject which has changed from what it was 50 or 60 years ago, it can give effect to that change – and apply the change in our English law – without waiting for the House of Lords to do it.

Further, his Lordship stated:

> I see no reason why we should wait for the House of Lords to make the change. After all, we are not considering here the rules of English law on which the House has the final say. We are considering the rules of international law. We can and should state our view as to those rules and apply them as we think best, leaving it to the House to reverse us if we are wrong.

In the opinion of Stephenson LJ, if such incorporation were to take place in such a way as to overrule previous binding authority, it should be performed by the House of Lords.

It should be noted that the rule of customary international law on immunity, should it have existed, was permissive; that is, States could chose to adopt it or otherwise.

The key questions following *Trendtex* were twofold. First, did the courts indicate that the restrictive (international customary law) approach had been accepted? Secondly, was any judicial support given to the view that a new exception had been introduced to the rule of *stare decisis*? In *Uganda (Holdings) Ltd v The Government of Uganda* (1978), Donaldson J refused to follow *Trendtex*, believing that it had been decided *per incurium*. Lord Denning reasserted the validity of the decision of the Court of Appeal in *Hispano Americana Mercantil SA v Central Bank of Nigeria* (1979).[8] The decision in *Trendtex* was later applied by the House of

Lords in *I Congreso Del Partido* (1981). In this latter case, Lord Wilberforce said of the landmark decision in *Trendtex* that:

> The case was not appealed to this House, and since there may be appeals in analogous cases it is perhaps right to avoid commitment to more of the admired judgment of Lord Denning than in necessary. Its value in the present case lies in the reasoning that if the act in question is of a commercial nature, the fact that it was done for governmental or political reasons does not attract sovereign immunity.

In conclusion, *Trendtex* would seem to demonstrate that there is still life in the incorporationist doctrine. Rules of customary international law can be incorporated directly into English law as long as they are proven and do not run counter to a clear statutory term. Whether they can provide an exception to the rule of *stare decisis* has yet to be established.

Notes

1 For example: Westlake, J, 'Is International Law a Part of the Law of England?' (1906) LXXXV LQR 14; Brierly, JL, 'International Law in England' CCI LQR 24; Lauterpacht Grotius, H, 'Is International Law a Part of English Law?' (1939) Society 51; Collier, JG, 'Is International Law Really Part of the Law of England?' (1989) ICLQ 924.
2 Brownlie, I, *Principles of Public International Law*, 4th edn, 1990, Oxford: OUP, p 43.
3 *Blackstone's Commentaries on the Laws of England*, Vol 1, p 247. See also Lord Phillimore in *Engelke v Musmann* (1928).
4 Hence, rules of customary international law could not be viewed as a 'source' of English law in the same way that case law is a source and statute is a source. If asked which authority or statute on a point of law you would apply to a given situation you would respond 'that latest one governing that particular matter'. If you fail to admit rules of customary international law as a separate source of English the same claim cannot be made for it. Lord Denning dealt with this problem in *Trendtex* and his response seems to imply that rules of customary international law should be viewed as a source.

On this point see the article by Brierly referred to in note 1 (above), p 31.
5 See the decision of the Court of Appeal in *R v Secretary of State for the Home office ex p Thrakar* (1974). Note Lord Denning's later reflections on his judgment and its implications for the relationship between customary international law and English law, in this case. In his complete *volte face* a year later in *Trendtex*, the Master of the Rolls conceded that his decision in *Thrakar* was inconsistent with the incorporationist doctrine.
6 That situation was altered by the passing of the State Immunity Act 1978.
7 *Baccus SRL v Servico Nacional del Trigo* (1956); *Rahimtoola v Nizam of Hyderabad* (1957); *Thai-Europe Tapioca Service Ltd v Government of Pakistan* (1975); *Philippine Admiral (Owners) v Wallem Shipping (Hong Kong) Ltd* (1976).
8 He states: 'It was suggested that the decision in *Trendtex* was per incurium ... All I would say about that is that *Trendtex* was not decided *per incurium*.'

CHAPTER 5

PERSONALITY AND RECOGNITION

Introduction

Recognition of statehood is crucial in public international law, for without such recognition, an entity lacks sufficient *locus standi* to participate in the legal relationship between States. It should be pointed out that this area of law is liable to make the black letter lawyer more than a little uncomfortable. Even the smallest investigation of the matter will reveal that recognition of statehood is more accurately to be described as being based upon political rather than legal considerations. It is perhaps for this reason that older textbooks on international law, far more influenced by Austin than the positivists, and totally uninfluenced by sociology and international relations scholarship, paid almost no attention to the topic. Despite this, the fact remains that few modern syllabuses decline to consider the matter, and so we need to consider it here.

For the black letter lawyers, some relief is provided by the discussion of recognition of governments. Modern judicial developments have indicated that in recent cases the courts have been put in a position whereby they, rather than following government diktat as to whether they could recognise that a particular government could bring or defend a suit in an English court, have been forced, where the expression of Foreign Office fiat is obscure, to adopt a more creative or interpretive role.

To answer questions on this topic, it is necessary to have a good grasp of the nature of statehood. Why should recognition be of any real importance at all? Students should examine the criteria that have been used to establish whether a State does exist. To critique these supposed attributes is, perhaps, to reveal the political substructure that underlies them.

A knowledge of the historical development of the position of the British Foreign Office on recognition of governments is required. Why is governmental recognition of any importance? Why should governments have any form of difficulty at all in according recognition to any established regime? What has been the relationship between the courts and the Foreign Office in recent years with regard to governmental recognition?

In answering a problem question, for example, the following issues should normally be considered:
- the attributes that contribute to statehood;
- whether these attributes are legal or political in nature;
- whether or not foreign intervention can have a major impact upon the accord of recognition of statehood;
- in what sense the British position on recognition of statehood differs, after 1980, from its position on the recognition of a foreign government; and
- to what extent recognition of a government can have a retrospective effect upon a legal claim before an English court.

Checklist

Students should be familiar with the following areas:
- recognition of statehood;
- bodies other than States which have international legal personality;
- the criterion for establishing the recognition of governments;
- the consequences in international law of the non-recognition of a *de facto* government;
- governmental recognition and municipal law.

Question 15

The real problem regarding recognition of foreign governments is that governments want to leave it for the courts to decide, and courts believe that it is the responsibility of their government to decide. Until this problem is clearly resolved, the matter of governmental recognition will be far from satisfactory.

Discuss.

Answer plan

The student will need to understand the importance of the recognition of governments in public international law. This will include not just a comprehension of the contemporary legal position in the United Kingdom, but also an historical grasp of the different views that have prevailed. The issues to be considered are:

- what is meant by recognition of governments;
- why recognition of governments is important;
- what the traditional approach of the UK has been;
- the position that has now been adopted by the UK government; and
- whether this position is satisfactory.

Answer

At the outset, a distinction should be made between recognition of the existence of a State (thereby according a State international legal personality) and recognition of a government. The former involves a procedure under which regular membership of the international community is formally acknowledged. This acknowledgment is made by an existing member or members of the international community. Its effect is to grant that a territorial entity, hitherto not holding membership of the community, is now entitled to it, and, as an incident of membership, to all the rights and privileges of other members of the community. When recognition is formally accorded by an individual member of this community, it can obviously confer no more than the individual State has to give; that is, it makes the newcomer a member only in so far as the State giving recognition is concerned. Other States are free to postpone their recognition for an indefinite period, or, possibly, to refuse it altogether. This, then, is recognition of a State.

Recognition of a government likewise depends upon the actions of individual States. There may be no question as to the personality of the State that the government claims to represent, yet each member of the international community is placed in the position of deciding whether that particular government can legitimately represent it.

Problems over the recognition of a governments are most likely to arise when that government comes to power by means which are unconstitutional, bloody or by foreign intervention (or, indeed, a combination of all three). This is especially troublesome when the overthrown government has been accorded recognition by other members of the international community. This places foreign States in something of a dilemma: if they accord the new regime recognition, they appear to endorse it. Such an endorsement might appear to legitimise methods of attaining power that could be viewed by some States as illicit, and it might bring forth regimes that apply policies which they find repugnant. Recognition might thus threaten the basis of their own regime as well as running counter to the maintenance of their State *Weltanshauung*. On the other hand, non-recognition can prove equally problematic. What might become, say, of defence contracts made between a private company in State X and a deposed regime in country Y in a situation where State X refuses to recognise the new State Y government? How would State X gain compensation for its nationals when they had been maltreated while in State Y by agents of that State?

In such instances, the answer for State Y might be to design the form of its recognition in such a way as to acknowledge the existence of the new, unpalatable government without in any way allowing that acknowledgment to be construed as any form of endorsement or seal of legitimacy. This, certainly, is the view now adopted by the United Kingdom and the United States, yet, as will be indicated, it has not always been so.

Why, then, is the recognition of a government a matter of any legal importance? It is because English courts have refused to give any effect whatever to the acts of unrecognised governments. As plaintiff, the unrecognised government has no *locus standi* in an English court (*The City of Berne v Bank of England* (1804); as defendant, the unrecognised government cannot claim immunity in an English court (*The Annette; The Dora* (1919)). There is also the matter of the courts' cognisance of the legal acts of an unrecognised government. By English law, the validity of legislative acts of unrecognised governments will not be acknowledged. This will include, for example, contracts entered into by unrecognised foreign governments (*Taylor v Barclay* (1828)) and a change of nationality entered into pre-recognition (*Murray v Parkes* (1842)); and legislation winding up companies, or in any other way altering their legal status, will not be given cognisance (*The Eastern Carrying Insurance Co v The National Benefits Life and Property Insurance Co Ltd* (1919)) – an obvious example of which is that of nationalisation (*Luther v Sagor* (1921)). The legal position of unrecognised governments before the courts of the United States is based on the same lines.[1]

The traditional approach adopted by the United Kingdom and the United States in these areas has at times differed. To be simplistic, one might state that there are two possible positions that a government might adopt. One focuses solely upon objective factors. Here, the determining factors are not, or should not be, coloured by any political considerations. One simply asks: Does government X truly have control over the territory and population of State Y? If the answer is 'yes', then recognition is accorded; if 'no', recognition will not be forthcoming. Alternatively, the subjective approach is one centred around political considerations. One not only asks whether government X truly controls the territory and population of State Y, but also a number of other essential questions. Do we, as a foreign State, approve of the means by which this new government came to power? Although this new government may control the population, is it merely by fear, or do the people – no matter how distasteful the new regime may appear from abroad – give their genuine allegiance?

Traditionally, the British government has adopted four different official positions:

(a) one of non-recognition (based very possibly on the subjective test), that is, the Foreign Office had issued no certificate of recognition;
(b) where the Foreign Office had certified *de facto* recognition;
(c) where the Foreign Office had certified *de jure* recognition; and
(d) where the Foreign Office will merely certify whether or not dealings existed between itself and the regime.

Here, (b), (c) and (d) could be said to be based upon the objective approach.

Non-recognition, as mentioned above, leads to the consequence that English courts will refuse to give effect to any laws produced by an unrecognised government. Although, in 1951 Herbert Morrison, the then British Foreign Secretary, by implication stated that there would be no question of the United Kingdom government refusing to recognise a new government, the reality was to prove otherwise. Thus far, the issue of non-governmental recognition has only appeared before English courts in circumstances where the government concerned is believed to be simply the creature of another foreign government, and for that reason has been denied recognition. The question that has arisen is simply this: if a legal dispute arose involving the government of this State, what position would the courts be expected to adopt? The issue arose in the case of *Carl Zeiss Stiftung v Rayner and Keeler Ltd (No 2)* (1967), in which the plaintiff was the Karl Zeiss foundation, established under the law of the German Democratic Republic (GDR), a State to which the UK had not accorded recognition. Could this non-recognition prevent the plaintiff from bringing a claim in the first place? The House of Lords looked at the special circumstances surrounding the State in question and demonstrated a determination not to allow considerations of *Weltpolitic* to prevent a private party maintaining private rights bringing suit in an English court.

When the court examined the Foreign Office certificate, it found that the position of the UK government was that the *de jure* government of the GDR was still the Soviet Union. At an earlier date, the Court of Appeal had interpreted this to mean that any action taken under the authority of the GDR was discrete and unrecognisable. The House of Lords took the view that, rather than being separate, the government of the GDR was a subsidiary body of the *de jure* Soviet regime. The actions carried out by the GDR were to be regarded as having been done with the consent of the Soviet Union. The Soviet Union had been accorded *de jure* recognition by the United Kingdom. As a consequence, an English court could give cognisance to those acts carried out by the subsidiary body. Both Lords Reid and Wilberforce stressed the importance of the unfortunate consequences to private rights (for example, the status of East German marriages and divorces) if the doctrine of non-recognition were pressed too far. Thus, in this instance, it was with the legal fiction of subsidiarity that the House of Lords upheld that the interests of 'justice and common sense' should prevail over doctrines of international relations.[2] Here, the existence of a State is heavily intertwined with that of the existence of a government. The new policy of governmental recognition adopted by the UK in 1980 (see below) would not therefore mean that a foreign office certificate of status would be deprived of meaning or effect. Indeed, should a case such as *Carl Zeiss* arise before the court today, there is no reason to believe that the effect of the Foreign Office certificate would be any the less telling.

The distinction between *de facto* and *de jure* regimes was primarily one of convenience. Imagine that a new regime comes into power. The British Foreign Office is not certain whether this new government will last long. The revolution may be short lived; the rebel forces may be defeated. To ignore the existence of the new government would create a legal vacuum, much abhorred by international law, which could have serious consequences for the security of UK nationals abroad in the territory effectively occupied by the rebels, and could affect the private law created within that territory. The solution to the problem is to accord the rebels a token or *de facto* recognition. The prevailing tendency, though ignored in some instances such as the non-recognition of East Germany (above) and Lithuania, Latvia and Estonia, has been for the Foreign Office to categorise recognition into one of these two groupings. However, the significance of the separation has been of little importance. For example, in the case of *The Arantzazu Mendi* (1939), a dispute arose over the ownership of the eponymous vessel, then docked in British waters. The owners of the vessel had accepted the decree of the rebel nationalist government in claim of ownership. One claimant was the *de jure* Republican regime, the other was its opponent, the Nationalist government of General Franco which the UK had accorded *de facto* recognition. The latter government relied upon the *de facto* status to enable it to be immune from suit in an English court. It should be emphasised here that, although the vessel had docked in an English port (that is, outside Spanish territory), the question concerned the status of the Spanish nationalist decree. The House of Lords held that the Nationalist *de facto* government was indeed immune from suit. Thus, there were few distinctions of any importance between being granted *de facto* or *de jure* status. Only two distinctions were of any real significance: first, where the court is not concerned with the validity of acts in relation to persons or property in a foreign State, but with private rights (such as contractual relationships, for example, or title to a debt recoverable in England), then the *de jure/de facto* distinction could be conclusive (*Haile Selassie v Cable and Wireless Ltd (No 2)* (1939)); secondly, full diplomatic relations, involving the exchange of diplomatic agents, would only exist between the UK government and the *de jure* regime.

In the early 1980s, this *de jure/de facto* distinction become increasingly embarrassing for the Foreign Office. Whilst the certification of the recognition of States was a matter of little controversy and could be maintained, the position of Her Majesty's Government with regard to the recognition of governments, such as Pol Pot's regime in Cambodia, was becoming untenable. Other States, such as Belgium and France, had adopted a position whereby they would decline to give official governmental approval to a foreign government. In 1980, the British Government decided to adopt this policy.[3] The then Foreign Secretary, Lord Carrington, stated that the question as to whether a foreign government will be recognised will still depend upon the court examining a foreign office certificate. However, from this point forth, rather than stating overtly that it gave the regime *de jure* or *de facto* recognition, it would issue a certificate allowing the court to infer whether the United Kingdom had any dealings with the regime in question, particularly those dealings on a government to government basis. The inference to be drawn from the certificate was to be conclusive. In effect, although this still means that the government is certifying recognition, it simply means that they are being more circumspect and discreet in doing so. The courts are still expected to follow the will of the Foreign Office and 'speak as one voice' upon such matters. Although such a policy is not difficult to follow where the certificate is clear,[4] it leaves the courts in a difficult position when the Foreign Office line is obscure and where the original 'one voice' obfuscates.

Such a situation arose in the case of *Republic of Somalia v Woodhouse; Drake v Carey Suisse) SA* (1993) concerning the recognition of the government of Somalia. In this instance, two factors played a key part in the decision. First, the Foreign Office did not give a clear view in the certificate as to the course of its dealings; secondly, the position of the Foreign Office was not surprising given the near anarchy that prevailed in that country. As a consequence, Hobhouse J was left to determine what the 'one voice' that the British Government should employ should be. To do so, he had to look to factors other than the words contained in the certificate, important evidence though they were. The court examined the following factors:

(a) whether the alleged government is the constitutional government of the State;
(b) whether the UK government has any dealings with it, and if it does, the nature of those dealings; and
(c) in limited cases, the level of international recognition that had been accorded to the government.

This, it could be argued, was the only reasonable position the court could have adopted on what may be viewed as rare circumstances. One can only speculate on the position of a court of higher judicial authority if such an instance were to arise again.

Thus, it can be seen that the British government has always been theoretically eager to adopt an objective approach to the recognition of foreign governments. However, for two different reasons, the courts have been put in the situation in which they had to make what was essentially a political decision: first, where the Foreign Office had not certified any form of recognition of the government in question (a clearly unsatisfactory situation that puts the judiciary in an invidious position); and secondly, when the policy that the British government adopted in 1980 proved of little assistance to the court. By this policy, it has changed the language contained within the conclusive certificates which are given as instructions to the court. This, no doubt, was instituted so as to save embarrassment for Her Majesty's Foreign Office in our dealings with some of our more distasteful neighbouring governments. However, the consequence of such sibylline certificates, if only to judge by one (possibly unique) case, might be to force the courts to apply their own criteria in order to resolve such a matter. This can be little welcomed by the Bench and seems to be an unworthy chicane on the part of the Foreign Office.

Notes

1. *Bank of China v Wells Fargo Bank & Union Trust Co* (1952) (regarding whether the controlling authority of the Bank of China was that of the new unrecognised *de facto* regime – the Peoples Republic of China – or whether it be the recognised *de jure* regime – the Nationalist Government of China – which had recently fled to Formosa/Taiwan).
2. Note the support given to this practical approach by Lord Denning in *Hesperides Hotels v Aegean Holidays Ltd* (1978).
3. Hansard, HL, Vol 408, cols 1121–22, 28 April 1980.
4. See *Gur Corporation v Trust Bank of Africa Ltd* (1987). Note that although this recognition primarily concerned recognition of a state, the existence of the Ciskie government was also reflected within the wording of the Foreign Office certificate.

Question 16

The State of Arcadia was created in 1974 after being granted independence by the former colonial power. In 1976, it was admitted as a Member State of the United Nations. When the States of this region were created by the colonisers, they had drawn boundaries to suit their needs and not in order to match the tribal patterns which already existed in the locality. Moreover, the former colonial powers which governed the neighbouring State of Binrovia had failed to agree on the border demarcation for a small area known as Simbartoo, a sparsely populated area of desert populated by a nomadic tribe called the Oinkers. The Oinkers have strong cultural ties with the Arcadians and have indicated through plebiscites that they wish Simbartoo to be part of Arcadia.

Simbartoo constitutes 80% of Arcadia's border with Binrovia. The moment Arcadia is granted independence, a civil war breaks out.

Discuss.

Answer plan

Whereas Answer 15 concerned the recognition of governments, this question concerns the recognition of States. Examination of this area does have a tendency to make the black letter purist feel somewhat uncomfortable. The reason for this being that much of the debate on this matter is not essentially legal at all, but rather one of international relations. Recognition is thus a high political act, not motivated by essentially legal factors. However, it is important that the student has an understanding of the area because, whilst the motivation of recognition may well be political, such recognition produces legal consequences.

The following matters require discussion:
- what the notion of recognition means and whether Arcadia might qualify for that recognition: (the Montevideo Criteria);
- the way in which recognition takes place;
- the possible attitudes of foreign States to the conflict in Arcadia; and
- the question of the status of nomads and their position with regard to recognition.

Answer

Public international law primarily governs the legal relationship between States. A State must have personality; that is, those essential qualities that distinguish an independent State from, say, a *terra nullius* or a territory still dominated by a foreign power. This international recognition is important, for without it, Arcadia cannot play a role in international affairs, and its citizens and their property can be afforded no protection on the international level. In this essay, the following matters will be discussed: first, a discussion of what the notion of recognition means and whether Arcadia might qualify for that recognition; and secondly, the status of nomads and their position with regard to recognition.

Although the Montevideo Convention only binds 15 American States, its provisions as to the qualities that are necessary before a State will be deemed to have personality in international law are commonly taken to be useful, if not authoritative, guidelines. The first two criteria, a permanent population and a defined territory, are not generally difficult to meet. The need for a permanent population was arguably the product of the ingrained beliefs of developed States. If a State is a credible international entity, then it must have a coherent structure of administration, an administration co-ordinated from a focal point (a city or a town). If this were not to exist, the rules of international law could not – so it was believed – be appropriately applied within the territorial entity.

The second factor listed in the Montevideo Convention was that of defined territory. We are informed that 80% of Arcadia's border has not yet been clearly defined and is still, perhaps, disputed. Might this threaten the existence of Arcadia's statehood? This is unlikely, given that the requirement has never been viewed very strictly (observe the cases of present day Israel or that of Albania in 1913). The essential element, to quote from the decision of the arbitral tribunal in *Deutsche Continental Gas-Gesellschaft v Polish State* (1929), is a 'sufficient consistency'.

The next two criteria of the Montevideo Convention provide far greater difficulty in being met, partly because most decisions based upon these factors are not essentially legal acts but high political acts (and hence highly subjective in nature). It is also because such decisions are *sui generis* and leave little room for the interpreters to formulate general principles. These criteria are (a) that the State should have a government and (b) that it should have the capacity to enter into relations with other States.

It will be noted that Arcadia was admitted as a Member State of the United Nations. This, in itself, will not compel other UN Member States to recognise Arcadia. The UN (unlike the League of Nations)[1] does not recognise a notion of collective recognition. The admission of new Member States is based upon a 'recommendation' by the Security Council, which is then to be followed by a 'decision' of the General Assembly[2] (that is, an affirmation vote of seven, including the permanent members of the Security Council, followed by an affirmative vote by two-thirds of the General Assembly). The only criterion for membership established by Art 4 of the UN Charter is that the State be 'peace loving' and willing to carry out its international obligations. In 1950, the then UN Secretary General, Mr Tygve Lie, stated that: 'To establish the rule of collective recognition by the United Nations would require either an amendment to the Charter or a treaty to which all members would adhere.' Although the European Union, in its 1991 'Guidelines on Recognition of New States in Eastern Europe and in the Soviet Union', has made an attempt to establish a more objective criterion of recognition (to include respect for international law, guarantees for racial minorities, etc), this approach has yet to be extended to the UN. The most one might state is that membership of the UN might, in doubtful cases, be further evidence to support an entity being accorded recognition as a State.

As can be seen, this choice of recognition is, on the whole, not made collectively but by each individual State based upon its own criteria. To quote Senior Ruda, a former member of the International Court of Justice (ICJ), recognition of a new State is a 'unilateral act, whereby one or more States admit, whether expressly or tacitly, that they regard the ... political entity as a State'. Historically, individual States have been influenced by a number of factors in this regard, including whether the new State has been accepted as a major international organisation (such as the UN); the importance of recognition in order to enforce law (for example, the UK's recognition of the Barbary Coast was an attempt to contain the breaches of international law by the pirates of that region); the prejudice against admitting 'uncivilised' people peoples to the family of advanced western States; reasons of *Weltpolitic* (that is, when should it be acknowledged that a State has become truly independent from its occupation by another power? Note, for example, the long lasting non-recognition of the GDR by the UK because of the dominance of Soviet forces in that territory); and humanitarian considerations (for example, the non-recognition of Rhodesia because of its institutionalised racist policy). Factors such as these decide whether a State chooses to admit that another has a government and the capacity to enter into foreign relations with other States.

The political and historical circumstances surrounding Arcadia's position augur well to its being recognised as a State post-1945.[3] It has had a settled and governed population; it seems to be 'peace loving' it has been admitted to membership of the UN; many Member States must have looked favourably upon its existence as a State; and, perhaps above all else, it accords with the collective wish of the UN for decolonisation. Therefore, despite the existence of the civil war in Arcadia, which would leave it bereft of both government and the capacity to enter into foreign relations with other States (who would be the foreign minister? Who would the ambassadors be?), many individual States would still be likely to grant it recognition.

A comparable case might be that of the Belgian Congo in 1960. Upon the departure of its former colonial rulers, the State erupted into a civil war. Yet recognition was still granted by many individual States. It could be further argued that, even if one ignores the factors favouring recognition of post-colonial regimes, there is evidence of State practice which would indicate that, once a State has been established, a subsequent civil war shall not deprive it of its right to recognition by foreign States. For example, the Lebanon, which in recent times endured both a civil war and foreign occupation, continued to be recognised as a State. Thus, it can be argued that Arcadia, due to both its physical and political circumstances, could well be accorded recognition by a great many foreign States.

It can be noted that along Arcadia's border live a nomadic tribe, the Oinkers. If it is the case that this nomadic tribe makes up a small proportion of the population of Arcadia (and, indeed, of Binrovia), then there would be little question of their existence bringing the legal personality of these two States into doubt.

There remains the possibility, especially given the plebiscite, of Simbartoo becoming associated with Arcadia. Whether this took place in actuality would depend largely upon political considerations in the region. Legal considerations would only be addressed if either Arcadia and Binrovia submitted the case to the ICJ (under Chapter III of the Statute of the International Court of Justice), or if the ICJ were requested to make an Advisory Opinion by the General Assembly or any other UN organ, One might make two remarks about the considerations that the ICJ might take into account when adjudicating or making an Advisory Opinion. First, there is the relevance of the rule of *uti possidetis*. This is a Roman law doctrine meaning 'as you possess you should continue to possess' and has proved to have been of great importance in maintaining stability after the departure of former colonial rulers, especially in Latin America and Africa. In 1986, a special chamber of the ICJ stated that the principle was of 'exceptional importance' in resolving a dispute between Bukino-Faso and Mali. Indeed, the

Organisation of African Unity has agreed that colonial boundaries within Africa are to be viewed as permanent, despite the fact that they have the effect of dividing the same tribal, ethnic or linguistic groups between different States. Further support was given to non-colonial use of the *uti possidetis* principle by the 1991 Conference on Yugoslavia Arbitration Commission with regard to the drawing up of the boundaries of the secessionist States. Given the continuing importance of this doctrine, one would predict that it would be unlikely that the 20% of Arcadia's border that was strictly defined by the former colonial powers would be redrawn today.

The second point to note concerns the status of the Oinkers. As has been stated earlier, the fact that Simbartoo has a small nomadic population would not in any sense deprive it of the right of being deemed a State by the other members of the international community. What could be of of significance is that, whilst the Oinkers may frequently cross over the State borders, there is, at least, a proportion of the Oinker population that is ever present in Arcadian territory. In the *Western Sahara* case (1975), the issue arose as to whether a territory with a nomadic population constituted a *terra nullius*. The ICJ found that, at the critical date (1884), '... the State practice of the relevant period indicates that territories were not regarded as *terra nullius*'. Such territories came under colonial control, not through 'mere occupation' by colonial troops, but through agreement by cession with local tribal rulers. Further, in the *Western Sahara* case, the court stressed the great value to be placed on the matter of self-determination in modern international law. Thus, when deciding the fate of the Oinkers, rather than stressing the cultural or historical links between themselves and neighbouring States, a premium was put on the population of the territory determining its own fate. If the matter came before the ICJ as a border dispute between Arcadia and Binrovia, the plebiscite favouring union with Arcadia might prove to be a great influence upon judicial decision making.

Thus, it can be seen that given the circumstances, Arcadia arguably has a strong chance of being accorded recognition as a State by individual States in the international community. Equally, given the plebiscite vote of the Oinkers, one would expect an international arbiter or the ICJ to grant their desire, should Arcadia wish it, of being united with that State.

Notes
1 Article 1(2) of the League of Nations Covenant.
2 Article 4 of the UN Charter.
3 Note the contrast between the attitude of the international community to the Belgian Congo in 1961 (where the standards of 'government' and 'capacity to enter into relations with foreign States' were set very low), to that of the *Åland Island* case (1920). In the latter instance, the Commission of Jurists seem to have set far higher standards to be met in order to allow a State (in that case Finland) to qualify for recognition.

Question 17

Rumpi-Pola is one of the leading multinational companies in the world. It is incorporated in the United States of Tarnacia, the most powerful capitalist State in the international community. A subsidiary of Rumpi-Pola operates in Escorlia, a small backward State. Escorlia is the perfect location for the Rumpi-Pola Corporation because it allows them to exploit the cheap labour force in that country – the child labour – and take advantage of the very lax laws on worker safety and welfare. By a process of transfer pricing, the subsidiary of Rumpi-Pola is selling its product to the parent company for less than the market price, so depriving the Escorlian State of badly needed foreign revenue.

Escorlia is part of the continent of Apricot. Each State on this continent is a member of the League of Apricot States and is bound by the founding charter of that organisation. Under Art 21 of the charter, a Court of Justice (the Apricot Court of Justice) was founded. Article 21(5) states that:

> If a national of any State party to the Charter suffers loss, whether economic or personal, as the result of actions by a party State, that aggrieved individual may bring a claim before this court.

Pedro is an Escorlian citizen who is holidaying in the neighbouring State of Comodia. Whilst there, he is roughly treated by Comodian police officers. During the struggle Pedro, loses his left eye. On his return to Escorlia, Pedro is determined to seek redress against Comodia, a member of the League of Apricot States, though the Leagues' Court.

The Escorlian Prime Minister enquires of you, the Attorney General, as to whether it is possible to bring a suit against Rumpi-Pola under international law. Pedro also desires to know whether he can bring his action against Comodia.

Answer plan

This question requires an understanding of two key issues: first, the status of multinational companies in international law; and secondly, the question of whether an individual can have sufficient personality in order to bring an action against a State. In other words, are there circumstances in which an object of international law can bring an action against a subject of international law?

The following approach is suggested:
- an introduction which outlines the classical view of personality;
- an outline of the importance in international relations, if not in international law, of the powerful transnational corporation;
- a brief discussion of the guidelines and rules which are said to govern the activities of these leviathans;
- why they do not, as yet, have the status of international persons; and
- a discussion of the status of the individual in international law.

Answer

In this essay, two concerns will be discussed: first, the possibility of Escorlia bringing an action against Rumpi-Pola; and secondly, the possibility of Pedro bringing his own action against Comodia in the Apricot Court of Justice.

To be actionable under public international law, a party must have 'personality'. In contradistinction to the municipal system of law, where all citizens of a certain age usually attain full rights and responsibilities under that system, international law only allows certain bodies to have that status. In classical international law, the only bodies which were said to have this personality were entities recognised as States. They alone could qualify as international legal persons and be deemed the *subjects* of public international law. All lesser entities, individuals, organisations, etc, were the *objects* of international law. They might have a political importance and they might be capable of bringing actions in private international law, yet before an international tribunal, they would lack any form of *locus standi*.

However, since 1945, there has arguably been an extension of those entities which are said to have the necessary personality. For example, following the landmark opinion of the ICJ in the *Reparation for Injuries suffered in the Service of the United Nations* case (1949), in an Advisory Opinion, the ICJ found that the UN had full international personality. In the question, the Attorney General will need to address whether such personality had been extended to multinational corporations.

A good number of the world's leading companies have budgets greater than those of many States. Whilst being incorporated in one State, they may have many subsidiary organs operating abroad. Due to this cross border impact, they are frequently referred to as 'transnational companies' or 'multinational enterprises' (MNEs). These subsidiaries can often have a huge impact upon the State in which they operate, and this brings with it great social and political problems. For example, if the MNE's contribution to a State's economy is significant, it might lead to the internal policy of that State being dictated by a foreign board of directors. Whilst the host State might wish to see the MNE not only employing its cheap workforce but introducing new technology, this might be resisted by the parent company. The MNE might find a market for stock in the host State that was prohibited from sale domestically[1] (for example, medical products) or abide by safety and design standards in the host State that would be illegal domestically. Moreover, they might, as in the question, employ the policy of transfer pricing. Here, the affiliate sells its product to the parent company at less than the market price. This gives the parent company an immediate profit and prevents the host State from receiving badly needed foreign currency.

Given their economic and social power, it has been argued that MNEs should be given rights and responsibilities under international law. Since the mid 1970s, there have been attempts by the international community to set guidelines for these organisations. For example, in 1976, the Organisation for Economic Co-operation and Development (OECD) set down its Guidelines for Multinational Enterprises; the International Labour Organisation (ILO) devised its Tripartite Declaration of Principles concerning Multinational Enterprises and Social Policy. In 1990, a UN commission produced a revised draft Code of Conduct on Transnational Corporations, and two years later, the World Bank produced its Guidelines on the Treatment of Foreign Direct Investment. However, the guidelines and codes have created more dispute than problem resolution, particularly (and predictably) between industrialised and non-industrialised States. If such regulations became regarded, either through treaty or customary international law, as imposable by a host State against an MNE, and equally, by an MNE against a host State, then it might be possible to claim that MNEs had achieved personality. That day, however, has not come yet. The Third Restatement of US Foreign Relations Law states that, whilst MNEs are a major feature of international relations, they have '... not yet achieved independent status in international law'. It should be further noted that Art 34(1) of the Statute of the International Court of Justice proclaims that: 'Only States may be parties in cases before the Court.' Until this article is widened (as the Institute of International Law suggested it should be in 1954), the extension of personality to MNEs will not be completely fulfilled.

Traditionally, Pedro could only have sought redress by hoping that his government, to which he owed allegiance and which, in return, owed him protection, would bring the action on his behalf. This was so because an individual was an object rather than a subject of international law. If Pedro's government had refused to bring an action on his behalf, then, sadly, he would be without means of redress.[2] This places the individual in a position similar to a child who relies on the protection of another agency, whether it be a parent or guardian or the social services. It could produce unfairness and injustice, in particular when either the citizen fails to persuade his or her government to bring the action; where the government did bring the action, succeeded, and refused to pass on the compensation to its citizen (see *Rustomjee v The Queen* (1876); or where the citizen had no nationality.

In this century, certainly after 1945, the classical position with regard to individual claims has altered. The primary inducement to this change has been the development, through international treaties, of agreement on human rights. However, even before this development, it was established that individuals had been accorded personality under treaties. This was first brought about under a 1907 treaty between five Latin American States which set up the Central American Court of Justice. This approach was further adopted under Art 304(b) of the Treaty of Versailles 1919. This provision allowed nationals of the allied powers to bring a case directly against Germany before the Mixed Arbitral Tribunal. The first major case in which this assertion of individual rights was established was in the PCIJ decision in *Jurisdiction of the Courts of Danzig (Danzig Railway Officials)* case (1928). This case concerned a treaty between the Free City of Danzig and the Polish State. A key part of the treaty concerned the conditions of employment of Danzigers working on the Polish railways. Poland attempted to rebut the action by claiming that the courts of Danzig could not hear a dispute between objects of international law (the railway workers) and a subject of international law (the State of Poland). The agreement had been between two internationally recognised persons and could not confer on individuals rights which a municipal court could enforce. In their decision, the PCIJ demonstrated its refusal to accept this Polish contention. For the treaty had been designed so as deliberately to create definite rules creating individual rights and obligations and to be 'enforceable in national courts'. Thus, from this point forth, there could be certain, rare situations in which individuals could be accorded personality under a treaty. Certainly, since the Danzig decision, there have been an increasing number of treaties which allow individuals to bring action against a State directly.[3] The key point here is the actual wording of the treaty. As mentioned above, Art 34(1) of the Statute of the ICJ would prevent an individual bringing a claim before that tribunal. Yet in the question before us, we read that both Escorlia and Comodia are parties to a treaty which permits individuals to bring claims before the Apricot Court of Justice. One cannot tell whether there is a system of compulsory jurisdiction, or whether, once Pedro has filed his memorial and the action is not viewed by the court as vexatious, Comodia can be compelled to attend the proceedings. All that can be said is that, theoretically, Pedro should be legally entitled to bring his action. Effectively, all the parties to the charter have agreed, in certain circumstances of abuse, to accord personality to a national and, by so doing, make him a subject rather than an object of international law.

In conclusion, the Attorney General of Escorlia would regretfully inform the Prime Minister of Escorlia that the most he might be able to do would be to put diplomatic pressure upon the United States of Tarnacia. The hope would be that this pressure would lead to internal demands within Tarnacia that their MNEs abide by a Code of Guarantees to which their government has agreed. As MNEs do not have any international personality, it would not be possible to bring an action in international law directly against Rumpi-Pola. Secondly, Pedro, given that he has been given legal personality under a treaty, might well be able to bring his suit before the Apricot Court of Justice.

Notes

1 See, for example, the worst industrial accident ever, the Bhopal disaster on 10 December 1984.
2 Note the classical expression of this view by the Permanent Court of International Justice in *Panevezys v Saldutiskis* (1939); *Mavrommatis Palestine n Concessions (Jurisdiction)* (1924). For the situation where an absence of protest by the state of nationality leads the lack of means of redress see *US v Noriega* (1990).
3 The Fourth Geneva Convention of 1949 grants civilians who are captured by the enemy during conflict a wide range of individual and collective rights which they are entitled to enforce directly. Article 25 of the European Convention on Human Rights 1950 allows for such an assertion of direct individual personality as does Art 44 of the Inter-American Convention on Human Rights 1969. One can also find a similar provision in the Optional Protocol to the International Covenant on Civil and Political Rights 1966, the International Convention for the Elimination of all forms of Racial Discrimination 1965 and the Convention on the Settlement of Investment Disputes 1965.

Question 18

A civil war breaks out in Myopia and, following a bloody street battle, the elected government is deposed on 25 May 1995. The revolutionaries who take power are claiming to represent the people. They are, in fact, the Myopian Pretorian Guard (MPG) who took power when not given the pay rise that they had asked for from the then government. The deposed government, the Myopian Republican Party (MRP), claims diplomatic asylum in the United Kingdom, and this is granted.

The exiled MRP is badly in need of financial support. Fortunately, a company, the Emu Oil Company, owes the government of Myopia £5 m sterling. Their contract stipulated that any legal dispute between them should be resolved by an English court.

On 9 June, the MRP sends faxes from its office in London to all Myopian government employees. These faxes state that if the civil servants immediately leave their jobs they will receive what they would have earned had they been in work, directly from the MRP. As a direct result of this offer, 3,000 of the 4,000 Myopian government employees resign from their jobs.

Solicitors for the MRP request that the Foreign and Commonwealth Office define the status of Her Majesty Government's relations with the MRP and with the MPG. The Foreign and Commonwealth Office respond in the following manner:

> Her Majesty's Government has had dealings with the MRP after 25 May 1995 in relation to a variety of government contracts. It has dealt with the MPG between 10 July and the present with relation to matters of immigration and policing.

Ten States have accorded recognition to the new MRP government.

Discuss.

Answer plan

This is another question on recognition of governments and the consequences of such recognition within domestic courts. It is worthy of such emphasis as, generally, such questions, whether they be problem questions or essay questions, are far more common than questions on, say, the personality of international organisations. However, that is not to suggest that this latter topic should be neglected.

Students should consider the following points:
- identify the key questions to be resolved in this answer;
- whether the exiled government can lay a legal claim in an English court to any of the money that it claims was owed to it as the former regime;
- whether this question is outdated, given the new policy adopted by Her Majesty's Government in 1980;
- why, because of the nature of the Foreign and Commonwealth Office certificate, the court is faced with a problem of inference; and
- whether the public service employees who placed reliance upon the contract with the former regime can force the MRG to honour its commitments in an English court.

Answer

This question centres upon two matters: first, whether the exiled MRG can claim the money that is arguably owed to it; and secondly, whether the exiled government will be obliged to honour its contractual commitment to the 3,000 Myopian civil servants who left the employ of the MPG regime.

It can be noted that the Emu Oil Company (EOC) owes the government of Myopia £5 m sterling. Should this money be owed to the MRP government in exile or to the new regime in power in that country, namely that of the MPG? In order to answer this question, it is necessary to compare the legal situation regarding recognition of governments that has been adopted by the UK government. Prior to 1980, Her Majesty's Government made a distinction between so called *de jure* and *de facto* regimes. This distinction was, for the most part, of little real significance. The primary purpose of the distinction was to allow the UK, using *de facto* recognition, to recognise political realities without necessarily conferring any type of legitimacy or approval. However, there did remain two potential distinctions between regimes the UK recognised to be *de jure* and those it deemed to be *de facto*. The first distinction would be that there would only be an exchange of diplomats, that is to say, official diplomatic relations, with a government recognised as being *de jure*. Secondly, there would be a distinction where the legal dispute concerned persons or property outside that of the State concerned.

An illustration of this second attribute belonging solely to regimes recognised *de jure* can be found in the case of *Haile Selassie v Cable and Wireless Ltd (No 2)* (1939). In this case, the recently exiled Emperor of Ethiopia, Haile Selassie, was bringing an action against a British company for money contractually owed to his government. When the action was first brought, the Foreign Office adopted the following position: they recognised the deposed Emperor as the *de jure* leader and the invading Italian authority as the *de facto* ruler. At first instance, the court found that, as the debt was recoverable in England (that is, it was not a domestic Ethiopian matter concerning the validity of its domestic acts), then the *de jure* ruler had valid title to the debt. However, prior to the hearing of the defendant's appeal, the Foreign Office changed its position. It accorded the Italian regime *de jure* recognition. The real significance of this is that such recognition is retrospective in effect. The purpose of this would seem to be the unwillingness of the UK government to interfere in the internal affairs of a foreign State. It would hardly be in the interests of comity for there to be a period when legislation, wills, marriages, divorces, etc, made within State X between *de facto* and *de jure* recognition should be invalidated in perpetuity. Thus, from the moment of the Foreign Office certification of *de jure* recognition, the Court of Appeal backdated such recognition to the time when the Foreign Office had originally given the Italian regime recognition *de facto*. The Foreign Office had given such *de facto* recognition to the Italian regime before the case had been heard. As a consequence, the former Emperor of Ethiopia was informed that he had now lost any right to sue for recovery of the money that had been owed to him.

Given the above facts, can the question of the money owed to MRP by the Emu Oil Company simply be resolved by asking of the Foreign Office whether it is recognised (still) as the *de jure* regime? The answer is 'no', given that the Foreign and Commonwealth Office changed its policy on according recognition to governments in 1980.[1] No longer would they make a distinction between *de jure* and *de facto* recognition. From this point forth, they would do nothing more than certify that they did or did not have dealings with the regime in question. This response would conclude the matter. One consequence of such conclusiveness should have been to end the type of problem that emerged in *Haile Selassie* involving the co-existence of *de jure* and *de facto* governments. However, in our question it could be argued that what the Foreign and Commonwealth Office is certifying is somewhat ambiguous. Are they having dealings with both governments at the same time? Or, following the dealings of 10 July with the MRP, can the court infer that the UK government would now only deal exclusively with the new, revolutionary government? It should be noted that it is the responsibility of the court to infer from the certificate what the position of the Foreign and Commonwealth Office is. Moreover, as Sir John Donaldson stated in *Gur Corporation v Trust Bank of Africa* (1987), the court should pay heed to 'the undesirability ... of the national courts appearing to speak in terms which are not consistent with the nation's foreign policy and diplomatic stance ...'.

A similar such ambiguity appeared before the court in the case of *Republic of Somalia v Woodhouse Drake and Carey (Suisse) SA* (1993), involving the question of the legitimate government of Somalia. Hobhouse J was faced with an inconclusive Foreign Office certificate and therefore had recourse to the following criteria. He asked, first, whether the regime was the constitutional government of the State. In the case before us, we know that the MPG can lay claim to that title in distinction to the MRP. Secondly, he questioned the comprehensiveness of control exercised by the regime in question. It could be argued that, whilst the MPG have donned the mantel of executive control, the vast majority of the government's servants, who controlled the apparatus of government, have demonstrated that they owe their allegiance to the deposed regime. Thirdly, Hobhouse J examined the nature and type of dealings that the UK has with the regime. Following 10 July, we notice that the dealings between the UK government and the new MPG government concerned 'immigration and policing'. Arguably, these could be described as 'high governmental functions'. The court could draw an inference from this. Finally, Hobhouse J suggested that, in marginal cases, the court take cognisance of the view taken by the international community. We are informed that 10 States have accorded recognition to the MPG regime. However, in an international community numbering some 190 States, this is far from conclusive. Clearly, on all four of these bases, the court will have to make its own determination as to whom the UK government truly has dealings with. If it determines that those dealings are with the MPG, then the former regime loses any claim to the £5 m that had been owed to it.

There is also the matter of the contract made between the MRP in exile and the former government employees. Could such a contract be enforced by an English court? A similar problem arose in the case of *Gdynia Ameryka Linie v Boguslawski* (1953). Throughout the Second World War, the exiled Polish government, based in London, had been recognised by the British Foreign Office as the *de jure* government of Poland. It exercised authority over Polish seamen such as Boguslawski and the Polish shipping line (the appellant) which had remained out of German control for the duration of the war. Following the Soviet occupation of Poland in 1945, a communist regime was established on 28 June. On that date, the communist regime was accorded *de facto* recognition by the British Foreign Office. On 3 July, a minister of the *de jure* Polish government offered a number of Polish seamen compensation if they wished to leave their current employment rather than serve under the *de facto* communist government. Such an offer was made under powers under existing Polish law that had not as yet been revoked by the *de facto* regime. The compensation was to be payed by the employers of the sailors (in this case the appellant). At midnight on 5–6 July 1945, the British Foreign Office withdrew its *de jure* recognition of the government in exile and declared its *de jure* recognition of the new communist regime.

The two respondents in this case had accepted the offer of the exiled regime. When the shipping line refused to abide by the terms of the agreement, they sought to recover compensation in the English courts. The former appellants refused to honour on the ground that the UK recognition of the communist government on 5–6 July had a retroactive effect. It was retroactive to 28 July, and, as such, would make any agreement by the exiled Polish regime after that date nugatory. Lord Reid, with a unanimous House of Lords, rejected the appeal. Retroactivity did not have a 'blanket' effect: 'I do not accept the argument for the appellants that this necessarily or logically involves antedating for all purposes the withdrawal of the recognition for the old government.' If the matter was beyond the control of the new government and in the control of the old government (as in the case of the shipping line in this instance) then the old regime should honour its commitments.

One might ask, therefore, whether the MRP, though in exile, was still in control of the Myopian public employees in the same way that the exiled Polish government could control the shipping line by implementing current Polish law? The *Gdynia* case turned on Polish law. In this instance, we cannot tell whether the MRP were using powers still existent under their State's law. If they were not, the matter ends there. If they were, the question becomes one of their exclusive control over the Myopian public employees. It is certain that they could influence them, for this they did. Could they, however, legally command them independently of the *de facto* regime? If the answer is 'yes', then the MRP, based on the precedent of the *Gdynia* case, will have to honour their contractual obligations. If not, then such obligations can be avoided.

In conclusion, it can be seen that, due to the vagueness of the Foreign Office certificate, the court in this instance will be placed in the unsatisfactory position of having to infer from dealings and other matters what body is the legitimate ruler of Myopia. Secondly, the MRP's obligations to the 3,000 civil servants will turn upon the nature of then existing Myopian law and the level of independent control they exercised over the Myopian civil service.

Notes
1   Hansard, HL, Vol 409, cols 1097–98, 23 May 1980.

CHAPTER 6

THE ACQUISITION OF TERRITORY

Introduction

To answer questions on this topic, it is necessary to have a good grasp of the key modes of acquisition. This not only includes the traditional modes, much beloved by the older textbooks, but also those factors which have received approval in ICJ decisions on territorial claims.

When preparing a plan in order to answer a problem question, students should always address themselves to the following preliminary questions:

- what type of geographical entity the claimed area comprises (for example, an island or a stretch of desert, etc);
- whether the territory is habitable and if there is any form of population;
- whether all of the contending parties actually laid claim to the territory before the issue arises in the question; and
- Before what body the case might be brought for determinations.

Each of these four points can make a crucial difference to the outcome of the case and can help the student avoid needless errors.

Essay questions will frequently require candidates to understand the flaws that existed with the traditional modes of acquisition. Students should have a knowledge of the ICJ cases in which new factors (such as self-determination, economics, culture, etc) were better able to help resolve complex problems of relative title.

Checklist

Students should be familiar with the following areas:
- the traditional modes of acquisition;
- the doctrine of intertemporal law;
- the arbitral decisions and cases that have emerged on the issue of acquisition; and
- the factors which are said to have superseded the traditional modes of acquisition. In particular, students should know and be able to discuss the importance of self-determination in resolving such disputes.

Question 19

The old means of acquisition of territory are no longer of any relevance in the modern world.

Discuss.

Answer plan

In answer to such a question, it is all too easy to produce a shopping list of half-remembered revision notes. What the examiner is looking for is an approach which exhibits the fact that the student has thought about the issues involved. Thus, to gain a 2.1 or above, the list must be disguised as much as possible, and to the forefront must come a critical analysis of the transformation that has taken place in the international community with regard to legitimate title over territory.

The following approach is suggested:
- a short introduction outlining the traditional modes by which territory was believed to have been legally acquired;
- the meaning of the term *terra nullius*;
- the need to renew title – the doctrine of intertemporal law;
- problems with the traditional modes of acquisition;
- the possible displacement of the traditional modes of acquisition; and
- new factors which are now taken into account which are more consonant with contemporary circumstances and values.

Answer

The purpose of this essay will be to set out the traditional modes by which territory has, in the past, been peacefully acquired. It will then proceed to criticise the application of these modes and demonstrate that, whilst they are by no means redundant in the modern world, they have, to a degree, been superseded by other considerations.

The traditional modes of acquisition are occupation, prescription, cession, accretion, conquest, papal grants and, possibly, novation. The history of the application of these modes is essentially the story of colonialism and the expansion of trade empires by the European powers.[1] If a State representative discovered a *terra nullius*, that is, 'a land belonging to no one', then it was believed that it could be claimed by that representative for his sovereign. Indeed, until the mid 18th century, a single proclamation of symbolic title might have been adequate in the eyes of international law. The expression 'a land belonging to no one' would suggest that the territory was uninhabited. In such an instance, there would be no question of the territory being considered a *terra nullius*. However, it became clear that what *terra nullius* in practice meant was that the entity either had no population or had a population that was not organised in such a way that Europeans could understand or with which they could negotiate. For example, the tribes in the northern island of New Zealand had a hierarchical structure. As a consequence, the acquisition of this territory by the Crown was not by occupation of a *terra nullius*, but rather by way of a treaty of cession between the British Crown and a representative of those tribes. However, the peoples of the southern island of New Zealand were not organised in a fashion that the British could recognise. Consequently, the acquisition of that territory was by occupation of a *terra nullius*. A similar situation arose in the colony of New South Wales. A question arose in *Cooper v Stuart* (1889) as to whether English land law could apply in this colony. The Privy Council found that it could, holding the native aboriginal population to be insignificant and, as a corollary, their rights of no significance.

Acquisition of territory by occupation of a *terra nullius* was of less significance in colonial expansion than is often thought. Most acquisitions, it appears, were made either by conquest or by way of treaties of cession with local rulers. Moreover, when the competition for colonial possession became more intense, greater rivalry emerged amongst the European powers over the fewer and fewer spoils. Quite early in the period of colonial expansion, it become clear that, at least where an entity had a permanent population, a one time proclamation of sovereignty would be insufficient to maintain good title. This title could only be maintained by active administration. The claim to title had to be continuous more than merely symbolic.

Good title might therefore be acquired by a State which had not been the first to proclaim symbolic title but which had appeared at a later date and had actively administered that territory. This process is known as gaining title 'by prescription'. There are two basic types of prescription: immemorial prescription and adverse possession. Under the first type, State X occupies a territory, and the original claimant is unknown or unremembered. Adverse possession has far more significance. Here, the original claimant is known, but, because they have failed to renew their title by administration, because they have failed to exclude other powers from administering the entity in question, their title becomes extinguished. Questions which this type of acquisition inspire include the following: did the original claimant protest at the activities of the other State? If not, acquiescence seems apparent, and that State could be estopped from rejecting the claim of the second claimant (*The Temple of Preah Vihear* case (1962)). However, if they *did* protest, then the title by way of adverse possession could be invalidated (*The Chamizal Arbitration* (1911)).

Treaties of cession have already been mentioned. A treaty of cession transfers the title to territory from one State to another. Two key questions arise with regard to such treaties. First, did the transferor actually have good title in the first place? If the transferor did not, then the treaty of cession will be valueless: *nemo dat quod non habet* ('no one can give what he does not possess'). Secondly, was the treaty directly obtained by unlawful military force? If so, then its validity, given current international law, can be doubted.

Accretion occurs where new territory is added as a result of geological change, for example, the change of a river bank along a border between two States, or the creation of a new island as a result of an underwater volcano.

Conquest was, for most of colonial history, regarded as one of the key means of acquisition. Conquest might have forced a treaty of cession from a defeated foe. In other circumstances, the former foe might have been annihilated so as to render any treaty of cession unnecessary. However, conquest is no longer a legitimate means of acquiring territory. Article 2(4) of the United Nations Charter makes illegal, with some notable exceptions, military conflict. Articles 42 and 43 of the Hague Regulations establish that belligerent occupation achieves but a substitution of the occupier's rule for that of the legitimate sovereign. This has been borne out by General Assembly resolutions (such as GAR 2625(XXV) of 1970) and by Security Council resolutions (such as SCR 242 of 1967 concerning Israel's possession of the occupied territories).

For many years, papal grants legitimised foreign conquest and occupation, but are now relics from another age. Novation might be classified as a type of prescription. It concerned the situation in which one sovereign, Y, with full title, granted another sovereign, X, limited rights in a territory. After the passing of many years, sovereign X can acquire full rights to that territory.

Problems with the traditional modes of acquisition should be apparent. Acquisition of a *terra nullius* is no longer likely to occur. Those States which gained their original title by this means will need to renew it by, say, administration. The doctrine of intertemporal law as expounded by Max Huber in the *Island of Palmas Arbitration* (1928) requires that title should be renewed by the application of modes which are consonant with current international law. Thus, the solitary proclamation of title is unlikely to be enough; there must also be administration. Prescription, particularly adverse possession, can still be of some value but can lose validity in the face of protest. Accretion is rare and almost insignificant. Cession can be invalidated by questionable original possession and tainted by the question of undue military influence. Acquisition by conquest is now illegal in public international law.

These problems with the traditional modes should hardly surprise us. They were borrowed from Roman land law in order to clothe with legitimacy an imperialism which is now abhorrent to international law.[2] Further, as disputes are a matter of relative title, one is unlikely to encounter a dispute in which one mode is in conflict with another. A far more subtle approach is required, and one that is consonant with the current demands of the international community.

Although by no means entirely redundant, the majority of traditional modes are too simplistic to help resolve modern disputes. Now, tribunals, particularly the ICJ, are more likely to take other factors into account. Historical factors are important, especially when applying the rule of *uti possidetis* (see the ICJ Chamber decision in *Burkina Faso v Mali* (1986)). Geographical factors can also be of importance, as was demonstrated in the *Anglo-Norwegian Fisheries* (1969) case. Economic considerations played a key part in the *Fisheries Jurisdiction* case *(Merits)* (1974), in which the ICJ, in a dispute over maritime territory between the UK and Iceland, declared that they were prepared to recognise the latter country's 'preferential rights'. This was due to that State's economic dependence upon the fishing industry. Lastly, and perhaps most importantly, there is now far more willingness to let the people of the territory determine their own fate. Considerations of self-determination featured prominently in the *Western Sahara* case (1975) and have been supported by other acts of international law.[3]

In conclusion, whilst the traditional modes of acquisition are not without relevance they have now largely been superseded by new modes which allow for greater complexity in the face of relative title and of equity in terms of the populations concerned.

Notes

1   Towards end of the 19th century the United States also became an imperial power.
2   Note, for example, Art 7 of the General Assembly Resolution on the Definition of Aggression 3314(XXIX) of 1974.
3   See the Charter of the United Nations (especially Arts 1(2) and 55); in General Assembly Resolutions 334 (1949); 545 and 567 (1952); 2200 (1966); 2625 (1971).

Question 20

In 1673, a merchantman named Van Clapp in the employ of the Fudgian East India Company discovers an uninhabited island in the centre of an international seaway. He lowers a boat and heads for this island and, by raising the Fudgian flag and saying a solemn prayer, claims the island on behalf of his sovereign. He then departs 'Van Clapp Island' with his vessel, never to return.

In 1760, a religious group settles the island, the Seekers, who are fleeing from persecution in their native land, Funlovia. They map the island and build a lighthouse at the far end of it.

In 1850, Fudgia suffers defeat in a major conflict with its neighbour Contona. In the peace treaty that Fudgia signs, it is stated: 'We hereby declare all territories formally under the rule of Fudgian Crown, Contonian. Fudgia disclaims any right to these territories in the future.'

In 1966, Contona controlled many islands in the region. Contona, following pressure in the United Nations to decolonise, had decided to allow referenda to take place on each of these islands so as to allow the native people to decide their own future. However, they chose to make an exception in the case of Van Clapp Island. This may be because the island is in a strategic position and recent research has shown that it may be surrounded by deposits of crude oil.

Following Contona's refusal to allow the referendum, there are claims by Funlovia and Fudgia that the island should rightfully belong to them.

You are employed as Fudgia's Attorney General. Assess the basis of your nation's claim to Van Clapp Island vis à vis the other claimants.

Answer plan

There is more than one way to answer a problem question on acquisition of territory. The two most obvious and logical ways are as follows. First, you can consider the arguments that might be put forward by each of the parties. Where the question states 'advise the parties', it is suggested that this approach should be adopted.

Secondly, the candidate might choose to answer the question chronologically. By whatever method the candidate chooses, she should be carrying out essentially the same task, that of putting forward the relative claims of each of the parties concerned. It should be remembered, however, that students should do more than cite the traditional modes of acquisition in their arguments; they must also represent those modes that have been looked upon with favour in ICJ decisions.

What matters above all else is that the candidate adopts a logical approach to answering such a question. This makes planning on the examination paper a prerequisite for any 2.1 answer. The key issues to be considered are as follows:
- the Fudgian claim would be based upon occupation of a *terra nullius*;
- whether there is, therefore, a direct parallel with the *Clipperton Island* case (1931);
- the *Island of Palmas Arbitration* (1928) – the doctrine of intertemporal law;
- the relevance of the *Western Sahara* case (1975); and
- the relevance of the *Temple of Preah Vihear* case (1962).

Answer

In order to answer this question, the nature of the claim put forward by each of the parties will be examined. It is necessary to speculate upon which of the parties has the best relative claim.

The Fudgian claim would be based upon occupation of a *terra nullius*. That is to say, in 1673, when Van Clapp made his discovery, the island belonged to no one. As a consequence, it could legitimately be claimed by Fudgia. Such declarations of occupation where accepted as legitimate grounds to peaceful acquisition at this date. As the island was unoccupied, there would arise no question of title through conquest or treaty of cession with the natives. The classic example of good title to a remote island being brought about through occupation of a *terra nullius* is the *Clipperton Island Arbitration* of 1931.

Clipperton Island is small, remote, uninhabited and pretty uninhabitable. It lies in the Pacific Ocean some 670 miles south west of Mexico. Upon gaining independence from Spain, Mexico succeeded to all legitimate claims made by Spain in its conquest of the area. Spanish vessels had spied the guano-spotted coral island, as had English vessels at various times. Yet this, in itself, does not amount – so Victor Emmanuel found in his arbitration – to a symbolic taking of possession. As a consequence, until such an act took place, Clipperton Island remained a *terra nullius*. In 1858, a French vessel, following official instructions, sailed around the small island and proclaimed possession of it on behalf of France. This was followed by notice of the French claim in an Hawaiian newspaper. Moreover, the French consulate in Honolulu informed the Hawaiian government of the French claim. There were no other claims to sovereignty until 1897, when a dispute arose between France and Mexico as to which was to have jurisdiction over two US guano collectors. Victor Emmanuel had to decide which of the two States had the better claim at this time (the so called 'critical date'). He found that France's claim was the more substantive. If Clipperton had had a population, the mere assertion of sovereignty at one instant without more (such as administration) would have been insufficient to establish a claim by way of occupation of a *terra nullius*. However, given the special nature of the island, the one time display of sovereignty would suffice to establish good title.

When Van Clapp claimed the island for Fudgia, it was unpopulated. Is there, therefore, a direct parallel with Clipperton in this instance? Are there any weaknesses in the Fudgian claim? First, its occupation can only be valid if it is undertaken by a State agent. In the *Clipperton* case (1931), the French naval officer was carrying out instructions given to him by his government. In this instance, it is not clear as to whether Van Clapp is a State agent or not. It will be seen that in the *Island of Palmas* case (1928) (below), the activities of agents of the Dutch East India Company counted as State agents. Therefore, the activities of Van Clapp might amount to the activities of a State organ. Secondly, in *Clipperton* it was a matter of balancing two rival claims. Both claims were very weak and the victor could be said to be the State which had the 'least-worst claim'. Here, however, the rival claim of Contona is far more substantial than that of Mexico in *Clipperton*. As a consequence, the outcome of the dispute of Van Clapp Island might be different. Thirdly, in *Clipperton*, until the temporary settlement of the US guano farmers, the island had continuously been uninhabited. This is not the case with Van Clapp Island. It had been settled by religious emigrés from Funlovia.

If Fudgia wished to maintain its claim, it should have done so in 1760, at the time the Seekers settled there. By so doing, Fudgia would have renewed its title to Van Clapp island.

This can be demonstrated by examining the *Island of Palmas Arbitration* (1928). The original discovery of this island had been made by Spain in the mid 16th century. Palmas is situated in the Philippines, 60 miles south of Mindanao. Spain had symbolically taken possession of the island which, at that time, would have been enough to give Spain valid title to a *terra nullius*. Following the defeat of Spain by the United States in 1898, Spain signed the Treaty of Paris. This was not only a peace treaty but also a treaty of cession, under which all of Spain's Philippine territories were transferred to the United States.

The Dutch, however, also laid claim to the island. Since 1677, agents of the Dutch East India Company had been making contracts with local rulers in the area. These rulers had successively exercised suzerainty over the island. The dispute over sovereignty erupted in 1906 when the United States discovered that the Netherlands regarded the island as part of the Dutch East Indies.

The arbitrator in this instance was Max Huber. He had to decide which of the two States, the US or the Netherlands, had the best relative title. Clearly, the strength of the US title depended upon a claim that, once a *terra nullius* had been occupied and there had been a symbolic declaration of title, that title was good. Thus Spain had valid title, and that title transferred at the 'critical date', 1898. The Dutch claim emphasised their own administration and control, which never aroused any protest from Spain. This administration, they hoped, would supersede any solitary symbolic claim made by Spain. If Spain's title had indeed lapsed before 1898, it could not have transferred that title to the United States in the Treaty of Paris: *nemo dat quod non habet*.

Huber found for the Dutch on the basis that they had the best relative title. Whilst the proclamation of title might have been sufficient in the mid 15th century, as competition between the colonial powers become fiercer and territories fewer, mere proclamation without more was not enough. Title had to be renewed by a method which was consonant with those changing conditions. Those new conditions required administration and the capacity to apply international law within the disputed territory. This Huber referred to as the 'doctrine of intertemporal law'. He stated that 'occupation, to constitute a claim to territorial sovereignty, must be effective, that is, offer certain guarantees to other States and their nationals'. Of the two parties, it was the Dutch who had exercised effective authority of the island, and it was that assertion of authority that was vital to keeping their title alive and which evidenced the lapse of the Spanish title.

It might be argued, therefore, that Fudgia's title is fundamentally weakened because Fudgia had failed to renew that title and had not made an attempt to administer the Funlovian settlers after 1760. Equally, if Fudgian title had lapsed after 1760, that would have meant that they were prevented from transferring that title by a treaty of cession to Contona. Furthermore, it is arguable that, even if Fudgia had maintained good title, Contona had gained possession of the island by means that, though legitimate in 1850, are illegitimate today (see Art 2(4) of the UN Charter). Therefore, given the doctrine of intertemporal law, they would have to renew their title by a means that would now legitimise their claim. Given the priority given to self-determination in international law, probably the best way to achieve this result would be by permitting a free referendum on the island. This emphasis can be found in the *travaux preparatoires* to the UN Charter (especially Arts 1(2) and 55); in General Assembly Resolutions 334 (1949); 545 and 567 (1952); 2200 (1966); 2625 (1971); and in the Advisory Opinion of the ICJ in the *Western Sahara* case (1975).

Lack of any form of administrative activity by either the Fudgians or the Contonians with regard to the Funlovian settlers should be noted. The Funlovian's might argue that they had acquired good title by prescription. That since 1760 their citizens had populated and administered Van Clapp Island and had done so peacefully and without protest from any other power. Indeed, such time has now passed as to estop any foreign claimant from disputing the Funlovian claim. They might point to the ICJ decision in the *Temple of Preah Vihear* case (1962) in support of this proposition. However, it should be argued that the Funlovian claim could not succeed, for none of the activity that took place upon the island was State activity, and this is fundamental to any acquirement of good title.

In conclusion, it can be seen that none of the parties has a particularly strong title to the island. Which of them has the best relative title would depend both upon a rigorous examination of the detailed facts and upon the choice of critical date (probably to be fixed at 1966). It could be suggested that any legitimation of good title would depend upon an assertion of self-determination by the people of the island. This would be consonant with current trends in international law and hence would meet the requirement of Huber's doctrine of intertemporal law.

Question 21

In 1997, the small State of Illusia comes under a series of attacks. All of its neighbouring States impose sanctions against it. Each of those neighbours has mobilised its army, and these forces are, to the best belief of Illusian intelligence, poised to invade its territory.

In order to defend itself against a military attack, which Illusia believes to be certain, it attacks first. It not only destroys the forces of each of its neighbours, but also occupies substantial tracts of land belonging to those States.

After the conflict ceases, Illusia refuses to return those lands which it gained in the conflict.

Is there any way in which Illusia could justify its acquisition of the territory of its neighbours by military force?

Answer plan

Historically, conquest was one of the most important means of acquiring territory. Following the UN Charter, this mode has been defined as illegal. However, the matter is still of relevance to the modern world for two reasons. First, because the doctrine of intertemporal law demands that good title depends upon renewal of that title by means consonant with contemporary values. Thus, if title to territory was legitimately acquired by X by conquest in

1620, for that title to remain legitimate it must be renewed by a mode which is now lawful. How is this renewal to take place and by what means? Secondly, despite Art 2(4) of the UN Charter, States still continue to acquire territory through conflict. What is the legal status of such territory?

The following matters should be considered when answering the question posed above:
- the way in which a territory could traditionally be acquired by conquest;
- the position of modern international law on acquisition of territory by conquest;
- the importance of community rights;
- the breadth of Art 51 of the UN Charter;
- relevant General Assembly resolutions, the Hague Conventions and the Vienna Convention on the Law of Treaties.

Answer

One of the traditional modes of acquisition of territory was by conquest. Where a conflict was believed to have been 'just', particularly where it had received the endorsement of the papacy, then any territory absorbed by the 'just' aggressor was legitimately acquired. Such territory could be acquired in two ways. First, it could be acquired following implied abandonment. Here, the defeated power withdrew its forces from an area allowing unresisted admittance of the victor, for whom one of the spoils of war would include the acquirement of the abandoned territory. The word 'implied' is incorporated here because there has been no express statement by the defeated power that it has permanently abandoned the territory and that it accepts and acknowledges the rule over that territory of the victorious power. This acknowledgment can be expressly made by a treaty of cession. An example of this would be the Treaty of Frankfurt 1871, by which the French transferred dominion over Alsace-Lorraine to the newly created Germany.

The other type of acquisition through conquest was through subjugation or *debellatio*. Here, the invaded country would not merely concede territory, it would cease to exist as an independent State. The victor would entirely absorb the former State into its territory. As the vanquished State had been totally defeated, it had ceased to have recognisable personality; it therefore became a *terra nullius*. As a result, when writing of subjugation, it might be more correct to say that it was justified as being acquisition by occupation following the creation of a *terra nullius* through conflict.

Modern international law no longer permits conquest to be a legitimate mode by which territory may be acquired. This has been the result of a general rejection of the acceptance of State self-interest and the adoption of a more communitarian view amongst States. Since the end of the First World War, it has increasingly come to be believed that permitting aggressive conflict and the reward of aggressive conflict is an affront and danger to the international community and should be proscribed by law. This applies even when the State concerned, such as Illusia in our example, was arguably acting in self-defence.

There is a further reason why postwar international law restrains acquisition of territory by conquest. It is a product of the modern conception of not just State rights, but also community rights and individual rights. It might well be the case that the neighbouring States to Illusia did provoke an act of anticipatory self-defence by Illusia. Yet should that mean that their peoples in the subsequently occupied territories should suffer the consequence of this? Modern international law, as will be shown, responds in the negative.

Could Illusia justify its acquisition of territory upon the basis that it was legitimately using force in self-defence? Under Art 51 of the UN Charter, self-defence can be justified in international law. Clearly, the legitimacy of this justification turns upon the particular circumstances in question. In theory, the right of self-defence exists until the Security Council can act in accordance with the appropriate provisions of Chapter VII of the UN Charter and maintain peace and order. State practice would demonstrate that this position is unrealistic and that the aggrieved State will continue defending itself regardless of the way in which the Security Council acts.[1] Furthermore, it has been (controversially) argued that Art 51 maintains the right to self-defence that preexisted under customary international law. This is important, as permissible military action in customary self-defence was wider in scope than that permitted under the strict wording of Art 51. Indeed, some have argued that the pre-existing and preserved rule was wide enough to allow for anticipatory self-defence.

Even if one accepts the argument that anticipatory self-defence is legitimate under the UN Charter, this would not, in itself, legitimise the acquisition of territory captured in such a conflict. Article 31(3) of the Vienna Convention on the Law of Treaties 1969 states that the interpretation of a treaty may be affected by the subsequent practice of the parties to it. This being the case, it seems clear, when one interprets UN resolutions, that the acquisition of territory by military force is itself illegal, regardless of whether the conflict was originally legal in international law. In 1967, Israel launched attacks on its neighbours, attacks which it then claimed were by way of anticipatory self-defence. In so doing, Israel, like Illusia in the question, occupied the Sinai Peninsular, the Gaza strip, the West Bank and the Golan Heights. Security Council Resolution 242 of 22 November 1967 declared the 'inadmissibility of the acquisition of territory by war'.

One may further examine General Assembly resolutions upon the same matter. Resolution 2625(XXV) (General Assembly Declaration on Principles of International War) states that: 'No territorial acquisition resulting from the threat or use of force shall be recognised as legal.' This would be so, no matter what the original legal justification for the conflict may have been. Moreover, this point was further elaborated by General Assembly Resolution 3314(XXIX), the Resolution on the Definition of Aggression. Article 5(1) states that: 'No consideration of whatever nature, whether political, economic, military or otherwise, may serve as a justification for aggression.' This should be read in conjunction with Art 5(3), which states that: 'No territorial acquisition or special advantage resulting from aggression is or shall be recognised as lawful.' One may interpret this to mean that, no matter who originally inspired that conflict, none of the parties involved in that conflict should exploit any gains thereby made. Secondly, any legitimation of continued occupation of territory for strategic reasons (such as the creation of buffer zones, or the garrisoning of key strategic points for future self-defence) would be illegal. Thus, although the Golan Heights occupy a key strategic position that might prove invaluable to Israel's self-defence, this would still not legalise occupation. Illusia would equally be deprived of this argument by way of justification.

These authoritative interpretations of the Charter should be accepted by UN Member States. Consequently, they have a duty to refuse to recognise the acquisition of those territories by Illusia.[2]

Given that Illusia wishes to flout international law, what is the status of its illegal occupancy? Articles 42 and 43 of the 1907 Hague Regulations establish that, at best, all occupancy in such circumstances can be a temporary substitution of that of the original sovereign. Furthermore, Art 43 declares that a State such as Illusia, in these circumstances, would be prevented from altering the pre-existing laws in the territory. One of the key aspects of sovereignty is the ability to apply one's laws throughout one's territory. Thus, this article would, arguably, prevent Illusian annexation from ever being legalised. The imposition of its own laws in the territory would forever be invalid, and other States are under an obligation not to recognise their effectiveness. Article 45 would deny it the possibility of gaining the allegiance of the inhabitants. Article 46 would place it in the position of trustee, rather than the new owner, of the former sovereign's public property.

Furthermore, even after the conflict between Illusia and its neighbours had ended, their obligations to the conquered population would not cease. Under Art 6 of the Fourth Geneva Convention of 1949 for the Protection of Civilian Persons in Time of War, Illusia would remain bound to abide by the regulations of the convention even though the conflict had ended over a year previously. Article 154 of this convention specifically maintains those rules contained in the Hague Regulations. The terms of the Geneva Convention accord with the tendency in modern international law to place far greater emphasis on the importance of peoples and populations as opposed to the rights of States.

Finally, is it therefore impossible for Illusia to acquire title over its occupied territory in the circumstances mentioned? It is possible, but only by a treaty of cession or by prescription. In the current circumstances, both these modes could be problematic. Article 52 of the Vienna Convention on the Law of Treaties 1969 invalidates the terms of any treaty procured as a direct consequence of force. In the given circumstance, it would be difficult for Illusia to argue that any such treaty of cession had not been procured in such a fashion. Prescription means that a new ruler acquires possession following the lapse of the old ruler's title. This, however, can only occur over a period of time, and there must be evidence that the former ruler has acquiesced in the activities of the conquering State. Any form of diplomatic protest by the conquered State would signal that it had not acquiesced, and any chance of Illusia relying upon prescription would be dashed (see *Chamizal Tract Arbitration* (1911)). If one is to judge by State practice in the Middle East, it is most unlikely that the conquered States would fail to protest in these circumstances.

In conclusion, it can be seen that, although Illusia might continue to occupy the territories it gained during the defensive conflict, it would do so in defiance of international law.

Notes

1 Note, for example, the action of Kuwait during the Gulf War of 1990–91.
2 Indeed, Professor Ian Brownlie, in his book *International Law and the Use of Force by States* (1963), argues that failure to abide by this duty makes refractory States equally as culpable as the aggressor State.

Question 22

Shark Island is positioned at the southernmost tip of a series of small islands within an an archipelago. The nearest significant land mass is Palpania, 20 miles to the west. Palpania has, from time to time, been visited and occupied by a tribe of nomadic people, who have their own established social and political systems, and whose 'territory' extends to some of the neighbouring islands within the archipelago, including Shark.

The archipelago was discovered in 1482 by a Vanbasten privateer who mapped the entire archipelago, landed on the main island proclaiming Vanbasten title to the whole, and then left. Since 1800, Gropian sealers have used Shark island as a hunting base. In 1810, members of the navy of the State of Darthvadia settled on the main island of the archipelago, and, in 1820, Darthvadia proclaimed title over the whole. Shark island is, however, an inhospitable place, and no Darthvadian administration has ever been established there.

In 1840, Palpania declared war on Darthvadia and conquered the main island of the archipelago, proclaiming the annexation of the whole. Ten years later, Darthvadia drove Palpania out of the archipelago but considered that a proclamation of annexation would be an undesirable acknowledgment of Palpania's putative title and declined to issue one.

In 1935, the Gropian sealing fleet was nationalised and the Gropian Sealing Conglomerate (GSC), an organ of the State of Gropia, established an office on Shark from which it has uninterruptedly administered Gropian seal hunting ever since.

Advise all the parties as to their title to Shark Island.

Answer plan

Another archetypal problem question on the acquisition of territory. As suggested above, there are two ways of approaching such a question and once again, one might choose to adopt arguments of the parties' approach rather than the chronological method.

Note that the student does not have to produce a definite answer as to who would 'win' any battle over title. Candidates would need far more information before they could even begin to make a judicial decision upon that matter. What students are expected to do is to make the best case they can given the information that has been provided. At most, they might merely suggest that one of the parties might have the better relative claim because of a certain factor. In such an answer, dogmatism is not required; sensible and well informed discussion is all.

Candidates should deal with the following matters in their answer:

- the basis of Vanbasten's claim: for and against;
- the basis for Gropia's claim: for and against;
- the basis for Darthvadia's claim: for and against;
- the basis for Palpania's claim: for and against; and

- conclusion: the considerations that should be borne in mind when assessing the merits of the relative claims to title.

Answer

In order to answer this question, it is necessary to examine the merits and demerits of the cases that would be presented by each of the parties that might make a claim.

Vanbasten's claim would be based upon the acquisition by occupation of a *terra nullius*. As the island was 'inhospitable', little authority would be needed in order to establish good title; planting the flag and attempting to gain recognition by foreign States might be said to be enough. Examples of this can be found in the *Clipperton Island Arbitration* (1931) and the *Eastern Greenland* case. It could be argued that the ICJ case of *Minquiers and Ecrehos* (1953) was not relevant because Shark Island is not in an area of the world where the recognition of the permanent application of sovereignty is common. This was a key element in the decision making process in the latter case.

Against Vanbasten's claim, based on discovery of a *terra nullius*, it might first be argued that, as the discovery was carried out by a private individual, it would invalidate good title. The discovery and claim must be made by a State agent. For example, in *Clipperton Island* (1931), the French declaration of title was made by a naval officer following official instructions. Secondly, in the *Eastern Greenland* case (1933), it was essential that Denmark included Eastern Greenland in legislation and had attempted to gain international recognition of its claim. There is no evidence that Vanbasten can be said to have made these efforts with regard to Shark Island. Thirdly, there is the doctrine of intertemporal law to consider. In the *Island of Palmas Arbitration* (1928), Max Huber stated that inchoate title had to be developed in a manner consonant with the developing demands of international law. This would mean that Vanbasten would have needed to maintain its title by administration since the discovery in 1482. This is especially the case as we are informed that the island had been visited by the local nomads (that is, it was not permanently uninhabited as in *Clipperton* and possibly *Eastern Greenland*) and given that there were rival claims for the island. Fourthly, there were no attempts to rebut the claims of Darthvadia. This could bring about the possibility of Darthvadian title by prescription and estopp Vanbasten from denying its rivals' claims. See, as an example of this, the *Temple of Preah Vihear* case (1962). This non-rebuttal might also add to the evidence that Vanbasten's inchoate title had not been developed.

Gropia has two possible bases for title: discovery of a *terra nullius* and one based upon prescription. Their legal representative might claim that, when the sealers first visited the island in 1935, Shark Island was still a *terra nullius*. For Vanbasten could not base its claim solely upon discovery, given the doctrine of intertemporal law as mentioned above. Arguably, because that inchoate title had not been developed, it had lapsed. Darthvadia bases its claim to Shark Island upon its declaration of 1820. Did it have a right to claim all the islands of the archipelago without, in some way, exerting State activity throughout all of the islands? Evidence of its lack of will to exert sovereignty over Shark Island is seen by the fact that it failed, seemingly, to exercise authority over the Gropian sealers who were present on the island. Moreover, no attempt has been made by Darthvadia to include Shark Island in legislation and gain internationally recognised title. This was essential in the *Eastern Greenland* case. There was also no attempt to renew Darthvadia's title after the war of 1840.

As to Palpania, even if that State's original title to Shark Island by conquest was legitimate in 1840, intertemporal law demands that this title be renewed by legitimate means (see the *Island of Palmas Arbitration*). This, Palpania has failed to do. In addition, the *Island of Palmas Arbitration* demonstrated that contiguity is, by itself, not sufficient to give title.

Therefore it might be argued that, in 1935, the State agents of Gropia (for the company was nationalised) made an implicit claim, as a corollary of their administrative acts, to a *terra nullius*.

Secondly, it might be argued that Gropia had prescriptive title following from continuance of occupation. Even if Vanbasten, Darthvadia and Palpania once had good title, that inchoate or, perhaps, once good title had lapsed. Further, Gropia had shown by the action of its State agents that it effectively administered the area and could therefore apply international law on Shark Island, which none of the other claimants could do. See, in this instance, the *Island of Palmas Arbitration*. Vanbasten, Darthvadia and Palpania have had 60 years to rebut Gropia's claim and they have failed to do so. Therefore *Qui Tacet Consentire Videtur Si Loqui Debuisset ac Potuisset* (See the *Temple of Preah Vihear* case). The period of 60 years could be long enough to gain prescriptive title (50 years was deemed long enough in the *British Guinea v Venezuela Boundary Arbitration* (1899–1900). The argument that Vanbasten, Darthvadia and Palpania were unaware of Gropia's State activity will not be acceptable. See the judgment of Carneiro in the *Minquiers and Ecrehos* case (1953).

Against Gropia's claim based upon prescription, it could be argued that Gropia has never claimed Shark Island. Contrast with the *Clipperton Island* and *Eastern Greenland* cases. Moreover, is Gropia's activity on Shark Island really State activity? Given the modern notion of State immunity, can one not distinguish between the activity of a nationalised company governed by the private law of transactions (*jure gestionis*) from those activities which are essentially vested in the State as an expression of its governmental authority (*jure imperii*)? If so, even if one accepts that Gropia did make an implicit claim to Shark Island, it will be invalid, as any such claim has to be made by a State agent. (See *Brazil-British Guiana Boundary Dispute*.) It should be noted that the action of the French in *Minquiers and Ecrehos*, in buoying and lighting the islands, was not enough, by itself, to establish sovereignty.[1]

Darthvadia might base its title on both occupation of a *terra nullius* and prescription. As to occupation, Darthvadia might argue that, in 1810, Shark Island was a *terra nullius*. The inchoate title of Vanbasten had not been developed and in any case was invalid because a privateer was not a State agent. However, the Darthvadian navy proclaim Darthvadia's title just as the French title to Clipperton Island was made by a French naval officer. It is true that Darthvadia only occupies the main island of the archipelago, but in the *Ares Island* case, this contiguity was enough to give good title.

As to Darthvadian title by prescription, because of the nature of Shark Island, little effective authority is necessary (see *Clipperton Island* (1931)); hence, administrative inaction does not deprive it of sovereignty. In addition, there is, a presumption against reversion to the status of *terra nullius*, a presumption not easily rebutted because territories without a sovereign are not only rare but a standing challenge to the legal order. See *Clipperton Island* (where French inaction did not relieve it of sovereignty) and the *Eastern Greenland* case (where knowledge about Danish sovereignty over Eastern Greenland persisted because 'the tradition of the King's rights lived on'). Note also the Falkland Islands, where, despite the British absence of 58 years, because there was no rival claimant (or so the UK claims), the UK claim was still good. Furthermore, it could be argued that there was no need to renew title after the 1840 war vis à vis Palpania because the original title was valid. Palpania could not gain legitimate title by conquest.

As for Palpania, its title was originally based upon conquest, following which it forced Darthvadia to sign a treaty of cession. As mentioned above, conquest is no longer considered a valid means of acquiring territory (see Art 2(1) of the UN Charter, GAR 2625, etc). Further, the doctrine of intertemporal law (see the *Island of Palmas Arbitration*) would require Palpania to renew its title by means that are now considered legitimate and sufficient.

In Palpania's favour, one could mention that it is the only one of the claimants which has attempted to establish its sovereignty, in 1840, over the whole of the archipelago, including Shark Island. Also, attention could be drawn to the fact that there is a degree of contiguity between Shark Island and Palpania. Could it not be non-industrialised States that have suffered over the centuries from the intrusion of outside colonial powers? Might not Vanbasten, Gropia and Darthvadia be such powers? It is arguable that its resistance to colonial powers is 'legitimised' in modern international law and that contiguity might be the crux of its claim. Note the attitude of the international community to the Indian invasion of Goa. Moreover, we are informed that there is a cultural connection with the nomadic population. This, too, could prove to be an important element in Palpania's claim for title (see *Western Sahara* case (1975)).

Lastly, if Palpania had constantly protested at occupation by Darthvadia (as is suggested by Darthvadia's reluctance to reassert its title after 1840), then the legitimacy of Darthvadia's title based upon prescription might well be in question (see the *Chamizal Tract Arbitration* (1911)).

In conclusion, it might be stated that, when a court or arbitrator is considering the above factors, it will take into consideration three elements. First, the determination of the successful claimant will be based upon that State having the best relative title vis à vis the other claimants. This can only be determined after a detailed scrutiny of the facts. Secondly, the 'critical date' is a crucial determinant of which State will prevail. This should be the date upon which title began to be disputed. It is not always easy to guess what date a court or arbitrator will pick (for example, in the *Clipperton Island* case, it seemed obvious; in the *Minquiers and Ecrehos* case, it was not obvious). Thirdly, it is probable that, if the ICJ decides the matter, it is far more likely to take into consideration so called modern determinants of title (for example, self-determination, anti-colonialism, etc), than to place reliance upon those bases of title derived from Roman law (such as prescription, occupation, etc). This would obviously be of greatest importance to the State of Palpania.

Notes

1 A response to the above argument might be that the administrative active which tipped the balance in favour of the Dutch in the *Island of Palmas Arbitration* (1928) was that conducted by the Dutch East India Company. Might that not be an early version of a nationalised industry?

CHAPTER 7

JURISDICTION

Introduction

To answer questions in this area, examination candidates will need to have a good understanding of the principles upon which criminal jurisdiction is based as well as an understanding of the attempts that have been made to apply civil jurisdiction extraterritorially.

Three key words students should be aware of are prescription (the ability to make laws), enforcement (the ability to enforce the laws prescribed) and custody (without which no enforcement can take place). The distinction between these elements is crucial in order to understand this topic. For example, Australia has passed legislation (prescribed) to make it illegal for any of its nationals to engage in child sex tourism anywhere in the world. However, they would not be able to enforce such rules against a national unless that national returned to the Australian jurisdiction. Upon return, the Australian authorities would then have custody and would have the legal capacity to press charges.

Questions can arise as to how custody has been obtained. There are instances in which the courts have refused to try a case where the accused has been returned to the territorial jurisdiction in breach of due process. It is to be remembered that the preferred way of obtaining custody by the nation that wishes to press charges is by way of a treaty of extradition.

In answering questions, the following issues should normally be considered:
- whether the question poses issues of criminal or civil jurisdiction;
- if the question is one of criminal jurisdiction, what principles of extraterritorial criminal jurisdiction might be applied;

- the relative value of the different principles of criminal jurisdiction and whether they have all been accepted as equally valid by the international community; and
- if it is a matter of the extension of civil jurisdiction, how municipal courts have reacted to legislation that has extraterritorial effect.

Checklist

Students should be familiar with the following areas:
- why the issue of jurisdiction is of importance to the international community;
- the territorial principle of criminal jurisdiction, objective and subjective theories of territorial jurisdiction;
- the *Lotus* case, the 'effects' doctrine and the application of the effects doctrine to civil law;
- the nationality principle of criminal jurisdiction;
- the protective principle of criminal jurisdiction;
- the universal theory of criminal jurisdiction;
- the passive personality theory of criminal jurisdiction; and
- anti-trust laws, restrictions of restraints of trade, price fixing and the extension of civil jurisdiction.

Question 23

An analysis of modern national codes of penal law and penal procedure, checked against the conclusions of reliable writers and the resolutions of international conferences or learned societies, and supplemented by some exploration of the jurisprudence of national courts, discloses five general principles on which a more or less extensive penal jurisdiction is claimed by States at the present time.

(Dickinson, *Introductory Comment to the Harvard Research Draft Convention on Jurisdiction with Respect to Crime 1935* (1935) 29 AJIL Supp 443.)

Discuss the nature of the 'five general principles' to which Dickinson refers.

Answer plan

This is a dream of an examination question to any student of international law. No doubt students will have been given notes outlining each of the principles in turn, which they will recall and reproduce in their answer. The skill is to perform that task better than the majority of their peers. It should be recalled that, if asked a question involving criminal jurisdiction (as the reader will see below), it is inevitable that examination candidates will have to refer to more than one of the principles of jurisdiction. As a consequence, all of them must be learnt and understood.

Note the following elements in the answer:
- definition and meaning of jurisdiction;
- the Harvard Study of 1935;
- the territorial principle; the rationale for such a principle; the extension of the principle;
- the nationality principle;
- the protective principle;
- the universal principle; and
- the passive personality principle.

A key distinction that should be made when examining the topics is the distinction that can be made between the jurisdiction to *enforce* and the jurisdiction to *prescribe*. A State may prescribe, that is, make laws that affect individuals within foreign jurisdictions. Yet, unless those same individuals enter the custody of the State whose criminal laws have been violated, that State has no effective jurisdiction to enforce.

Answer

Jurisdiction has been described as meaning 'the power of a sovereign to affect the rights of persons, whether by legislation, by executive decree, or by the judgment of the court'.[1] The capacity to exercise this power is a key element of State sovereignty. As the arbitrator, Max Huber, stated in the *Island of Palmas Arbitration* (1928): 'Territorial sovereignty ... involves the exclusive right to display the activities of a State.' This activity can be viewed in two ways. In one sense, the law produced by the organs of the sovereign State, subject to waivers it has itself made, is the exclusive system of legal rules obeyed within that jurisdiction. Such rules – again, subject to self-imposed waivers – bind both its own subjects and any other citizens who enter within its territorial boundaries.[2] The other aspect of jurisdiction is that a State's legal organs can produce law claiming to have effect not merely intraterritorially, but extraterritorially too. However, whilst no external restraint can be imposed upon the extent of intraterritorial law making, extraterritorial law produced by States can be exercised only as far as international law confers a State with that capacity. Why has the international community placed restrictions on the extranational application of national laws?

The answer to this question was made clear in the 1935 Harvard Study into extraterritorial criminal jurisdiction. It stated that:

> In exercising such jurisdiction ... States became increasingly aware of the overlappings and the gaps which produced conflicts [between two or more States demanding to prosecute the same criminal] and required co-operation. In the 19th century, with increasing facility for travel, transport and communication ... the problems of conflict between different national systems became progressively more acute.

It was because of such overlaps and gaps in jurisdiction that the Harvard Study (1935) set out to determine, by the explanation of State practice, the bases upon which States had claimed extraterritorial criminal jurisdiction. Though this study has no binding effect upon any State, it is nevertheless of considerable authority. This is because its findings were the result of the thoroughness with which it had examined State practice, which may reflect rules of customary international law.

The first of the general principles tested by the committee was the most traditional' and that most deeply rooted in international law – that of territorial jurisdiction. Under this principle, a State can base its exercise of jurisdiction upon the location of the act of the offending party. Normally, the conduct of this party both begins and ends within the borders of the State bringing the prosecution. This authority allows the State to penalise its own citizens and those citizens of any other State within its borders, unless they have specifically been granted immunity.

The rationale for the principle was touched upon by the writers of the Harvard Draft. The territorial State has the most powerful interest in bringing a prosecution for breach of its laws. It has the best facilities for doing so and the best system of law enforcement trained to apply those rules within the jurisdiction. In short, it is more convenient that criminal offences should be dealt with by that State whose social system is most greatly effected by the crime committed.[3] The UK has traditionally maintained the policy of denying to States the right to exercise over non-nationals criminal jurisdiction which cannot be based upon the territorial principle (see *Treacy v DPP* (1971)). However, with the development of international travel, crime, too, began to cross borders. As a consequence, the problem arose of the law enforcement agencies in the UK being reduced to a state of impotency in case of cross-border crime (for example, where the crime in question had been begun abroad and completed within foreign State X or, vice versa, where the crime had begun in State X and be completed in the UK). In order to deal with this new problem, English legislation was passed which altered the traditional approach to territorial jurisdiction. For example, with regard to the counterfeiting of currency, the UK will exercise its criminal law so as to punish a crime begun within the UK but completed abroad.[4] Section 3(2)(3) of the Criminal Justice Act 1993 allows for jurisdiction with regard to extraterritorial conspiracies and attempts. This will apply, with regard to a list of offences, despite no criminal act being committed within the UK and irrespective of whether or not the defendants are British nationals (*R v Sansom* (1991)).

Thus, a State has its jurisdiction defined primarily, although by no means exclusively, territorially. It has been shown how territorial jurisdiction, in order to meet the needs of crime prevention in a world in which travel is common, has itself transcended borders. With regard to non-territorial jurisdiction, the distinction needs to be made between the jurisdiction to enforce law and the jurisdiction to prescribe law. With regard to a crime that occurs within its territorial jurisdiction, a State can clearly perform both functions. However, whereas it is true that a

State may not enforce its law within the territory of another State, it may still legally prescribe for activities which occur abroad. This extension from territorial jurisdiction to what has been called 'personal' jurisdiction was also outlined in the Harvard Draft. The most obvious example of personal jurisdiction is based upon the nationality or active personality principle. Under this principle, a State has jurisdiction with regard to any crime that has been committed outside its territorial boundaries by an individual who is its national at the time when either the offence was committed or when that person was prosecuted or punished (*Blackmear v United States*).

This principle can also apply to crimes committed by individuals who would otherwise be classed as aliens but who can be assimilated as nationals for the purpose of criminal jurisdiction. For example, foreign members of the crew of a merchant ship registered in the UK come under British criminal jurisdiction under ss 686 and 687 of the Merchant Shipping Act 1894. Aliens who owe allegiance to the Crown are also assimilated for the purposes of committing such offences as treason, even though those crimes may have been committed abroad (see *Joyce v DPP* (1946)). However, the UK has outlined self-imposed limits to its exercise of jurisdiction based upon this principle. In para 58 of *British Practice in International Law* (1967), it was stated that such jurisdiction should only be exercised by the State of which the offender is a national if the exercise of that jurisdiction does not cause an interference with the legitimate affairs of other States. Further, that State must refrain from causing its national to behave in a manner contrary to the law of that foreign State. In addition, when applying this principle, there is the necessity of establishing the validity of the nationality of the criminal. If there is no 'genuine link' between the criminal and the State claiming nationality, then the claim of jurisdiction would not meet the requirements of international law.[5]

The third principle of criminal jurisdiction listed by the authors of the Harvard Draft is known as the 'protective principle'. Under this, a State has personal jurisdiction to prescribe law in respect to criminal acts committed without its territory by an alien, which threaten the territorial integrity, security or political independence of that State. The Commentary to the Harvard Research Draft Convention justified this principle because of the 'inadequacy' of most national legislation punishing offences of this type. The UK has not traditionally adopted this principle when unaccompanied by other jurisdictional elements such as nationality or a form of allegiance linking the accused to the State claiming jurisdiction. However, there are still examples of its suggested use in both case law[6] and statute.[7] For example, under the Criminal Jurisdiction Act 1975, courts of Northern Ireland are given jurisdiction over listed offences committed in the Republic of Ireland.

The 'universal principle' was also referred to in the Harvard Draft. In rare instances, personal jurisdiction has been claimed with regard to crimes committed outside the territorial boundaries of a State by an alien when the crime committed is one against the law of nations. In such an instance, any State may exercise jurisdiction over such crimes. Examples include crimes that harm diplomats, war crimes and genocide. A striking example of jurisdiction gained under the universal principle for the crime of genocide can be found in the case of *Attorney General of Israel v Adolf Eichmann* (1961). Crimes committed outside the jurisdiction of any State may come within this principle, most famously piracy *jure gentium*, aircraft hijacking (*Yunis v Yunis* (1991)).

Lastly, there is a fifth and highly contentious principle upon which jurisdiction can be based, notably the 'passive personality principle'. Under this principle, the right of jurisdiction occurring outside the State's territorial boundaries is based upon the nationality of the victim rather than of the perpetrator of the crime (see the *Cutting* case (1886)). This principle would allow the prosecution of persons who harm the citizens of the State bringing the prosecution anywhere in the world. As a consequence of the alarming way in which this would allow for the expansion of jurisdiction, this principle has not secured general acceptance. Indeed, although in 1935 the Harvard Draft scholars discovered over 20 States that adopted this principle, they did not include it within the final draft. They noted that the principle had been 'vigorously opposed in Anglo-American countries'. Moreover, the principle was rejected by all six dissenting judges of the Permanent Court of International Justice in the *Lotus* case (1927). At best, State practice would seem to indicate that this basis for jurisdiction should not be used unless another principle is applicable.

In conclusion it can be seen that the primary basis for criminal jurisdiction is based upon the territorial principle. This allows for both jurisdiction to enforce and jurisdiction to prescribe laws. However, there are instances where States will base their jurisdiction to prescribe upon other grounds, namely, the nationality of criminal (or, more controversially, of the victim); protection of the State; or protection of the international community.

Notes

1 Mann, 'The Doctrine of Jurisdiction in International Law', Hague Recueil, Vol III (1964).
2 See the decision of Marshall CJ given for the US Supreme Court in *Schooner Exchange v McFaddon* (1812).
3 See the Report of the Sub-Committee of the League of Nations Committee of Experts for the Progressive Codification of International Law (1926) on Criminal Competence of States in Respect of Offences Committed Outside their Territory.
4 See the Geneva Convention for the Suppression of Counterfeiting Currency 1929 as incorporated in the UK legislation by the Counterfeit Currency (Convention) Act 1935 c 25 s 1(1).
5 For discussion of what 'genuine link' actually means, see the ICJ decision in the *Nottebohm* case (1953).
6 *Joyce v DPP* (1946); *Naim Molvan (Owner of Motor Vessel Asya) v AG for Palestine* (1948).
7 Under the Exchange Control Act 1947, aliens who commit currency offences abroad can be prosecuted.

Question 24

Barnaby Brown is a Anrovian citizen taking a holiday in Bioconda. He travels there on board a cruise ship, the *May Bride*, registered in Cantata. Whilst on board the cruise ship, he becomes involved in a heated dispute with a fellow passenger. Brown ended the argument by smashing all the windows in the disputant's cabin.

Whilst in Bioconda, Brown sent an e-mail to the Anrovian Head of State, Mr Hamish, which attempted to blackmail the

Anrovian Head of State. Brown threatened to distribute, via the internet, doctored photographs of Mr Hamish 'giving the impression that the said leader is committing a sexual act with a rent boy'. Brown states that any distribution of the computer generated pictures would be confined to Bioconda. Brown stated that he would carry out his threat unless he were paid 3,000,000 Anrovian dollars. The source of these threats was subsequently discovered by the Anrovian police.

Upon what basis might the Anrovian authorities claim jurisdiction?

Answer plan

This question requires a good understanding of, and an ability to apply, the different principles of criminal jurisdiction. The reader will notice also a crossover with the topic usually given the appellation 'the Law of the Sea'.

Students should note the following points:

- the criminal activity of Brown whilst aboard the *May Bride*; territorial jurisdiction;
- application of the nationality principle of criminal jurisdiction;
- Anrovia's exercise of criminal jurisdiction with regard to the photographs on the objective territorial principle;
- invocation of the nationality principle with regard to the illicit photographs;
- possible application of the protective principle; and
- possible application of the passive personality principle.

It will be noted by the reader the some of the principles of jurisdiction are relied upon as supplemental. They are utilised to reinforce the legal argument for criminal jurisdiction that is primarily based upon a much more widely accepted principle.

Answer

The Anrovian authorities should be advised to examine a number of the traditional bases whereby States have exercised criminal jurisdiction for offences committed outside their immediate territorial boundaries. The principles of jurisdiction based upon territoriality, nationality, protection and passive personality will be examined in this answer.

The first issue raised in this question concerns the criminal activity of Brown whilst aboard the *May Bride*. If the cruise ship had just left port when the incident occurred, then Anrovia might still be able to allow its municipal laws to govern such illegal activity based upon the territorial principle of jurisdiction. The vessel might still be within Anrovian territorial waters. Article 3 of the 1982 Convention on the Law of the Sea establishes that all States have the right to establish the breadth of the territorial sea up to a maximum of 12 nautical miles from the baselines. The UK has chosen to adopt a 12 nautical mile limit in the Territorial Sea Act 1987, as has the United States, under Proclamation No 5928 of 1988. If the vessel in question is passing through this territorial sea after having left the internal waters of Anrovia, then Anrovia may act in a manner prescribed by its laws with regard to arrest or investigation. Moreover, under Art 27(1) of the 1982 Convention, jurisdiction may be exercised, *inter alia* '(b) if the crime is of a kind likely to disturb the peace of the country or the good order of the territorial sea'. Acts of manslaughter (*R v Anderson* (1868)) or murder (*Wildenhus* case (1887)) and possession and conveyance of illicit drugs (*Pianka v The Queen* (1979)) were held to have permitted jurisdiction. In the latter case, the Privy Council stated that '... the provisions [of Art 19] should receive a liberal construction'.

It could be contended, however, that a distinction might be made between the breaking of windows aboard the *May Bride* and the criminal acts formerly mentioned. The criminal action on board the *May Bride* would be unlikely to be of such menace so as to permit the exercise of jurisdiction under Art 27(1)(b). Moreover, it would not give the authorities jurisdiction if the *May Bride* had passed out of Anrovian territorial waters. However, if Anrovian law is similar to British law, there is another path the prosecuting authorities could pursue based not upon the territorial principle of jurisdiction, but on that of nationality.

Under the Merchant Shipping Act 1995, s 281 (formerly within s 686(1) of the Merchant Shipping Act 1894), the British authorities would have jurisdiction over Brown, despite the vessel being registered in Anrovia. This section, applying the nationality principle, gives English courts jurisdiction where any person is charged with having committed any offence '... if he is a British citizen ... on board ... any foreign ship to which he does not belong ...'. Section 686(1) of the Act of 1894 was construed in *R v Kelly* (1982) so as to give the British authorities jurisdiction to hear charges under the Criminal Damages Act 1971 for damage committed whilst aboard a North Sea ferry, registered in Denmark. If Anrovia had a similar provision within its legislation, then, should Brown return to Anrovia, charges could be pressed against him for criminal damage.

After Brown arrives in Bioconda, he is informed that he is wanted by the Anrovian police for criminal offences. It might be contended that Anrovia could exercise criminal jurisdiction based upon the objective territorial principle. By this principle, the State in which the criminal act is concluded can exercise criminal jurisdiction should the accused come legally into the hands of their enforcement officers. This doctrine was expressed by Holmes J in *Strassheim v Daly* (1911) thus:

> Acts done outside a jurisdiction, but intended to produce and producing detrimental effects within it, justify a State in punishing the cause of the harm as if he had been present at the effect, if the State should succeed in getting him within its power.[1]

It is to be noted that mail frauds have been held to have been triable in that State where the letter was received, even though it had been sent from outside the country. This rule has been justified in the common law on the theory that the mailing and receipt of the letter is a continuous act, whereas in civil law systems it has been justified on the theory of protection of public services. Could not the sending of a threatening e-mail be likened to mail fraud? Further, under British law, criminal jurisdiction based upon the objective territorial principle might also be exercised under the powers given by ss 1–3 of the Criminal Justice Act 1993.

The nationality principle of jurisdiction might also be invoked. Anrovia might have legislation, as many States do, giving it the power to exercise prescriptive jurisdiction over its nationals who commit crimes abroad.[2] Under the UK's Treason Act of 1351, the crime of treason could be committed 'within or without the realm' by a citizen who owed allegiance to the Crown. Might it be possible that Brown's attempted blackmail was deemed to be treasonable under Anrovian law? With regard to English law, this matter arose in the case of *Joyce v DPP* (1946). The accused had been responsible for pro-German propaganda broadcasts during the Second World War which had been, in part, designed to weaken the morale of the British populace. In the House of Lords, Lord Jowitt LC stated that:

> No principle of comity demands that a State should ignore the crime of treason committed against it outside its territory. On the contrary, a proper regard for its own security requires that all those who commit the crime, whether they commit it within or without the realm, should be amenable to its laws.

In response, it might be contended, perhaps rightly, that Brown's activities could not be correctly classified as treasonable in any sense that the word 'treason' is now understood, particularly when it is considered that Brown never carried out his threat. On this basis, it could be argued that a distinction might be made between *Joyce* and the present case. However, Anrovia might reject this approach. It might contend that a threat to the Anrovian Head of State is an equivalent to a threat against Anrovia itself. As such, its claim to jurisdiction might supplement its reliance on the objective territorial principle and the nationality principle by invoking the protective principle.

Under the protective principle, a State may claim jurisdiction over its own citizens, as well as citizens of other nations, for their extraterritorial conduct (*US v Pizzarusso* (1968)). In this instance, this principle might prove particularly useful to the Anrovian authorities. The threatened distribution of pictures in Bioconda might not constitute an act which would legitimise the use of the territorial principle of exercising jurisdiction under Anrovian law. However, the protective principle differs from the territorial principle in that the effects of Brown's conduct, or threatened conduct, would not have to be felt within Anrovia. In *US v Pizzarusso*, a citizen of Canada made fraudulent statements to obtain a visa whilst at the United States consulate in Montreal. In the court's judgment, it was stated that:

> ... the objective principle [which requires that the effects of the crime be directly felt within the territory] is quite distinct from the

protective theory. Under the latter, all the elements of the crime occur in the foreign country and jurisdiction exists because these actions have a 'potentially adverse effect' upon the security or governmental functions ... And there need not be any actual effect within the country as would be required under the objective territorial principle.

Hence, by applying such a principle, the Anrovian court, at some future date, could also assess the criminality of the threatened distribution of the photographs in Bioconda. Whilst the Anrovian authorities would be advised to utilise this principle, they should note that is disputed whether it can be relied upon as the sole basis for jurisdiction.

Lastly, jurisdiction might also be claimed based upon the much criticised passive personality principle. This principle would permit jurisdiction over individuals, be they foreign nationals or otherwise, when their actions affect, not the national territory, but subjects of the State asserting jurisdiction, wherever they might be. It is a natural corollary of the rule that any State is permitted to protect its own citizens abroad, and is postulated upon the view that, if the offender's State fails to punish him, that of the victim may do so. Such legal retribution would be in the interests of justice and in pursuance of the right of protection. Could it not be contended that, in this instance, it is the Anrovian Head of State who is the victim of the crime and that at least part of that crime was committed against him upon foreign soil. The response to this might be that the passive personality principle is still highly contentious, certainly as a sole basis for jurisdiction. Some of the judges on the PCIJ in the *Lotus* case expressed the view that international law does not permit any assertions of jurisdiction exclusively on this basis.

In conclusion, it can be seen that, should Mr Brown re-enter Anrovian jurisdiction, there could arguably be grounds upon which he could be charged for offences committed off the shores of Anrovia.

Notes
1 Note also the decision of the House of Lords concerning a criminal conspiracy carried out overseas in *DPP v Doot* (1973).

2 See, for example, *Re Gutierrez; Public Prosecutor v Antoni.*

Question 25

Captain Horatio Craddock was the captain of a ship, *The Mad Crad*, which constantly sailed 15 miles from the coastline of the island of Newmonia. *The Mad Crad* operated as a pirate radio station and broadcast popular music and news. Captain Craddock had Lumbagan nationality and *The Mad Crad* flew the Larungitian flag. The broadcasting equipment is registered in Tonsolitis. The dictatorial government in Newmonia strongly objected to the broadcasts from the vessel and believed them to be a violation of Newmonian sovereignty.

The Mad Crad also serves a trading vessel, its goods being slaves. The slaves are bought in Typhoidia and sold in Halitosis. To remedy this problem, Newmonia passed the Anti-Slavery Act, giving it extraterritorial jurisdiction over those involved in the slave trade wherever they may be in the world.

The Newmonian navy boarded *The Mad Crad* and arrested its crew. They discovered that Captain Craddock was not aboard the ship. He had taken a trip to the State of Alopecia.

Some weeks later, Captain Craddock had his slumber disturbed by two men in black. These gentlemen smothered his face with chloroform, nailed him into a wooden case, and transported him by ship back to Newmonia.

An extradition treaty exists between Newmonia and Alopecia for crimes such as slavery. Further, a term of this treaty specifically prohibits any abductions of suspects outside the terms of the treaty.

Captain Craddock stands trial in a Newmonian court.

Advise Captain Craddock.

Answer plan

Once again, in order to answer this question, the student will need to have some knowledge of the Law of the Sea. Any examination candidate should expect such crossover in examination topics. This is one of the factors that makes 'question spotting' such a hazardous undertaking.

The student should note the following:
- the legality of the boarding of the vessel in order to make an arrest with regard to the radio broadcasts. Can Newmonia – or any other State – exercise criminal jurisdiction on the high seas in this way?;
- whether the Anti-Slavery Act extends jurisdiction so as to allow the Newmonian navy to board *The Mad Crad*;
- slavery as a universal crime;
- the consequences that might spring from illegally obtaining custody; and
- whether Newmonia would still be able to maintain its claim.

Perhaps the most difficult part of this question concerns the decisions in which courts have determined that they do or do not have the right to try a case where custody had been obtained illegally. Faced with the seemingly inconsistent case law, good students can use this to their advantage and distinguish one case from another as best they can.

Answer

In this essay, consideration will be given to the following three questions. First, can *The Mad Crad* be boarded by the Newmonian navy, and the crew arrested, for the illegal broadcasting upon the high seas? Secondly, can a similar arrest take place for slavery under the Anti-Slavery Act? And thirdly, will the means whereby Captain Craddock's custody had been obtained mean that he should not stand trial in Newmonia for any crime?

The first issue concerns the legality of the broadcasts from *The Mad Crad* and the question of which State might have jurisdiction over Craddock. Craddock's vessel is broadcasting from outside Newmonian territorial waters. By Art 3 of the 1982 Convention on the Law of the Sea, States have the right to establish the breadth of the territorial sea up to a maximum of 12 nautical miles from the baselines. As a consequence, the primary basis upon which the Newmonian authorities would claim to exercise jurisdiction would be that of the objective territorial principle. That is, that although the broadcasts where made outside Newmonian territory, they had a criminal effect within that territory.

The allocation of radio frequencies is a matter governed by international law. It is the responsibility of the International Telecommunications Union to carry out such a function, and its national members consent to be bound by its decisions. Traditionally, problems emerged over the policing by States of the illegally used frequencies. If foreign ships were broadcasting on illegal frequencies and in international water, as in the instant case, the countries to which the broadcasts are directed might not have had jurisdiction, except with regard to broadcasts by their own nationals (and even in this instance, enforcement of the law would depend upon a State's own national re-entering the territorial jurisdiction). As a consequence, in 1965, the Council of Europe sponsored the European Agreement for the Prevention of Broadcasting Transmitted from Stations outside National Territories. Under this agreement, the parties undertook to legislate so as to prohibit the establishment of 'pirate' stations by, and in collaboration with, their own nationals. The UK introduced the Marine Broadcasting (Offences Act) 1967 in order to implement the terms of this treaty. Article 109 of the 1982 Law of the Sea Convention provides that all States should co-operate in the mission to rid the seas of pirate radio stations. Under Art 109(3), any person engaged in pirate broadcasting can be prosecuted by the flag State of the vessel (in this case Larungitis), the State in which the broadcasting equipment is registered (in this case Tonsolitis), the State of which the 'pirate' is a national (in this case Lumbago) or by any State which receives the transmissions or which has its authorised communications hampered by the illicit signals. In this case, that would allow Newmonia to exercise jurisdiction over Craddock and his crew. Paragraph 4 of this article states that: 'On the high sea, a State having jurisdiction in accordance with para 3 may, in conformity with Art 110, arrest any person or ship engaged in unauthorised broadcasting and seize the broadcasting apparatus.' Article 110 gives a warship which encounters a foreign vessel on the high seas no justification for boarding unless there are reasonable grounds for suspecting that '(c) the ship is engaged in unauthorised broadcasting and the flag State of the warship has jurisdiction under Art 109'. Thus, in the instant case, there are potentially five States that, under international law, would be permitted to have criminal jurisdiction over Captain Craddock as a result of his illegal broadcasts.

The second issue concerns the Anti-Slavery Act passed by Newmonia. Could they legitimately extend their jurisdiction in this way in order to defeat slavery? Article 110(1)(b) of the Law of the Sea Convention 1982 permits a ship to be boarded on the high seas when there are reasonable grounds for suspecting that it are engaged in such traffic. Further, the extraterritorial nature of Newmonia's legislation could be justified on the basis that slavery has come to be regarded as a crime of universal jurisdiction. A crime which allows for exercise of universal criminal jurisdiction is one concerning which there is 'universal' agreement on the evil of the crime committed and that, as a consequence, the perpetrators of which are not just the criminals of one State, but of the entire international community. As such, any State which obtains custody of such a criminal can enforce the law of its forum upon him. Slave trading would appear to be one of the crimes that has achieved universal status. To quote from the reporter's notes to the Third Restatement of US Foreign Relations Law (1987):

> Slavery and the slave trade are forbidden by international law, both as a matter of customary law and as general principles common to major legal systems. Slavery is outlawed by the constitutions or laws of virtually all States ... The Universal Declaration of Human Rights declares that slavery and the slave trade shall be prohibited in all their forms.

Article 4 of the Universal Declaration of Human Rights states:

> Slavery has been condemned and declared illegal by unanimous resolutions of the United Nations and other international bodies ... The report of the International Law Commission ... cites slavery as an example of an international crime. Slavery and slave trade are also offences *subject to universal jurisdiction to prescribe and adjudicate* ...[1] [emphasis supplied].

It could be argued, therefore, that the terms of the Newmonian statute extending its criminal jurisdiction with regard to slavery are legitimate in international law. Moreover, its power to board *The Mad Crad* and arrest its captain and crew are legal.

The third issue concerns the method by which Captain Craddock was brought into Newmonian custody. As Craddock was supposedly guilty of a universal crime, Alopecia should have been diplomatically encouraged either to put Craddock on trial itself for committing such offences or it should have extradited him under the terms of its extradition treaty with Newmonia. There is little question that the means by which custody was obtained was a breach of international law, in particular, Art 2(4) of the UN Charter (see *Nicaragua v US* (1986)). The only claim by way of defence to this charge might be that Newmonia was acting under self-defence (as permitted – in certain circumstances – by customary international law and Art 51 of the UN Charter). Craddock might be advised that, given the way in which his custody has been obtained (by a breach of due process of law), the court should refuse to try him. However, the accused should be informed that past cases illustrate that each case concerning whether or not a court could try the case in circumstances where the accused was illegally obtained has turned on its individual facts. In the case of *US v Toscanino* (1975), the defendant was an Italian citizen resident in Uraguay. He was abducted from his home by Uruguayan police, passed to Brazilian police (who tortured and sedated him), and then put into the hands of the US Drug Enforcement Administration. The accused claimed that US officers had taken part in the torture and abduction. The appellate court stated that:

> ... we view due process as now requiring a court to divest itself of jurisdiction ... where it has been acquired as the result of the government's *deliberate, unnecessary and unreasonable* invasion of the accused's constitutional rights[2] [emphasis supplied].

However, in the subsequent case of *US ex rel Lujan v Gengler* (1975), it was stated that the determination in the *Toscanino* case concerning due process only applied where extreme measure (for example, torture) had been used against the accused. Arguably, the decision of the Supreme Court in *US v Alvarez-Machain* (1992) could be distinguished from the present case. The latter case turned on a strict interpretation of the United States-Mexico extradition treaty. Rehnquist CJ, in delivering the opinion of the majority of the court, stated that Art 9 of that treaty does not purport to specify the only way in which one country may gain custody of a national of the other country for the purpose of prosecution. 'Thus, the language of the treaty ... does not support the proposition that the treaty prohibits abductions outside its terms.' However, as the question makes clear, this would not apply in the instant case, for there is clear language in the Newmonian-Alopecian extradition treaty forbidding such forms of extradition.

In other jurisdictions, there has been similar inconsistency of approach. In *R v Horseferry Road Magistrates Court ex p Bennett* (1994), however, Lord Griffiths, on the question of illegal abduction, stated:

> ... if it comes to the attention of the court that there has been a serious abuse of power it should, in my view, express its disapproval by refusing to act upon it ... If a practice developed in which the police or prosecuting authorities ignored extradition procedures and secured the return of the accused by a mere request to police colleagues in another country they would be flouting the extradition procedures and depriving the accused of the safeguards built into the extradition process for his benefit.

A similar position was adopted by the *South African Supreme Court in State v Ebrahim* (1991).

Whilst this might bring some comfort to Captain Craddock, he should be advised that State practice would indicate that one factor might seriously militate against his avoiding the jurisdiction of the court. For, as Higgins makes clear, much can turn upon the nature of the crime. Arguably, when the crime is one of a universal nature, such as the trading in slaves, which is triable by any State which currently has custody, the courts might ignore the means whereby that custody was obtained. The most well known example of this being the case of *Attorney General of Israel v Adolf Eichmann* (1961).

In conclusion, international law would, it is to be contended, allow for the arrest and detention of the captain and crew of *The Mad Crad*. It is further to be suggested that Captain Craddock, standing trial for, in part, traffic in slaves, should be advised that he might not be able to rely on the argument of failure of due process of law in order to evade punishment.

Notes
1 See *Nicaragua v US* (1986).
2 Contrast this case with that of *Ker v Illinois* (1888) and *Frisbie v Collins* (1952).

Question 26

In what way has the United States extended its civil jurisdiction? What has been the international response to the US action?

Answer plan

Most students welcome the chance to answer any question on criminal jurisdiction, but pale at the prospect of answering any question on the extension of civil jurisdiction. In order to answer any such question, it is essential to understand the legal and historical reasons for the claims of such jurisdiction. Any study will have to focus on the US judicial decisions based upon anti-trust legislation and the reaction to that legislation by foreign States. Mention also needs to be made of more recent legislation in which the US has attempted to use economic pressure, applied extraterritorially, to influence the conduct of foreign affairs by foreign States.

The following approach is suggested:
- a discussion on the extraterritorial nature of the 'effects' doctrine;
- the effects doctrine and the judicial reaction to US anti-trust legislation;
- the modification of US policy in the 1970s, in which considerations of 'balance', reasonableness' and 'comity' were introduced into judicial decision making;
- a recent return to the traditional approach to be observed in case law;
- further statutory attempts to extend US civil jurisdiction; and
- reaction from other States: blocking legislation and judicial decisions; whether the EU has adopted the US approach.

Clearly, any 2.1 answer on this topic will require a good knowledge of US and UK municipal law as well as the two key decisions made by the European Court of Justice.

Answer

In this essay, consideration will first be given to the history of the way in which US legislature and courts extended US civil jurisdiction. Secondly, there will be an outline of the international response to those actions.

Under the objective territorial principle, a State could have jurisdiction when a crime had begun within a foreign State (for example, a gun fired over the border) but it was concluded (that is, involving the death of, or injury or damage to, a person or object) within the State seeking jurisdiction. This should be distinguished from another ground for jurisdiction that was famously referred to in the *Lotus* case (1927). The judgment of the court read:

> Crimes ... are nevertheless to be regarded as having been committed in the national territory [of the prosecuting State] if one of the constituent elements of the offence, *and more especially its effects*, have taken place there [emphasis supplied].

Upon this basis, no element of the actual crime need ever have been committed in the State wishing to gain jurisdiction, either beginning or end. All that was necessary was that the criminal activity occurring in a foreign State had some impact in a neighbouring State. As such, that neighbouring State could draft legislation prescribing laws for the States where that activity took place, laws that could be put into effect by its own law enforcement agencies. In fact, one State had done this 37 years prior to the PCIJ's discussion of the 'effects doctrine' as it became known.

In 1890, the US Congress passed the Sherman Anti-Trust Act. This made illegal any contract made in restraint of trade in the United States or with foreign nations. By its wording, the Act suggested that its provisions applied across territorial boundaries.

Monopolies, those creations that the legislation was intended to eliminate, were not confined within territorial boundaries; some 'bestride the narrow world like a colossus'. The question that arose was how the US municipal courts were going to view such extraterritorial legislation. Did it mean that international law permitted the legislature of one State to expand its powers over national boundaries so as to invalidate commercial arrangements between nationals abroad? If so, in what way did the forums and legislatures of those foreign States react to such presumption?

When cases concerning the Sherman Act and foreign dealings first began to appear before the US courts, there was a reluctance to acknowledge the extraterritorial effect of the Act. In the years immediately following the passing of the Act, the Supreme Court would not examine a foreign Act of State and would not permit Acts of Congress to have an effect beyond US borders. However, a less conservative approach was adopted in *US v American Tobacco* (1911), which concerned an agreement to allocate distribution areas between two firms within the United States. One of the firms was British, the other US. The contractual agreement was executed within the UK and was governed by English law. The 'effect' of this foreign contract was to exclude the British company from operating within the United States. The Supreme Court held that the contract was illegal. Although the Supreme Court did not claim that the Sherman Act allowed them to invalidate contracts made outside US jurisdiction, it could intervene when the consequences of the agreement were to be carried out in the United States. However, in the instant case, the result of acting in such a way defeated the entire purpose of the contract.

In 1944, such an approach was applied to a contract made outside US jurisdiction and between two foreign companies. In *United States v Aluminium Co of America* (1944), the rule was expressed thus:

> Any State may impose liabilities, even upon persons not within its allegiance, for conduct outside its borders that has consequences within its borders; and these liabilities other States will ordinarily recognise.

This forceful view was qualified by two factors. First, there had to be no question that the agreement would clearly have been unlawful had it been made within the United States. Secondly, there had to be evidence that the performance of the extraterritorial agreement would have an 'effect' upon the imports and exports of the United States. Yet despite these qualifications, the US courts showed an increasing willingness to extend US civil jurisdiction. For example, in *United States v Imperial Chemicals Ltd* (1951), the US court went beyond simply examining the consequences of non-US contracts in the United States; they now claimed that they had jurisdiction because of the presence within the United States of a foreign subsidiary. It logically followed that if the court had undisputed jurisdiction over the subsidiary, it also had jurisdiction over the parent company. The US courts were also very willing to order discovery of documents of foreign firms in foreign states (*Re Grand Jure Subpoena Duces Tecum Addressed to Canadian International Paper Co* (1947)).[1]

Perhaps in reaction to the protests of foreign States, the courts in the US tempered the rigour with which they had implemented the anti-trust legislation. *Timberlane Lumber Co v Bank of America* (1976) and *Mannington Mills v Congoleum Corporation* (1979) introduced a further test that the courts should examine whilst making a determination based upon the anti-trust legislation. The court must not only apply the *Aluminium Co* test of examining the possible 'consequences' of 'effects' of the foreign transaction; they must now, additionally, apply a 'balancing test'. In such a way, the courts seemed to enter the field of international diplomacy. Now they would balance up the rival interests of the nations concerned vis à vis those of the United States. In the *Mannington* case, some criteria were developed in order to help determine the result of this balancing act. Further, moves in this direction can be seen in the Third Restatement of Foreign Policy Relations Law (1987) which emphasises the principle of 'reasonableness' in the making of such decisions, a criterion which seems to have been given legislative support by the wording of the US Foreign Trade Anti-Trust Improvements Act 1982, which stated that jurisdiction was to be based upon 'direct, substantial and reasonably foreseeable effect'.

However, since the 1980s, the United States, both in terms of legislation and judicial decisions, seems to have retrenched its position. Even before that time, US legislation had interterritorially and extraterritorially frozen Iranian assets. In 1981 and 1982, the Export Administration Acts applied extraterritorially for equipment that was to be used on the Siberian pipeline. Perhaps most controversially, the Cuban Democracy Act of 1992, Helms-Burton[3] and D'Amato Acts of 1996 have demonstrated an increased willingness on the part of the US to achieve its foreign policy objective through extending its civil law extraterritorially. These Acts introduced penalties for foreign companies that had dealings with expropriated property in Cuba and those engaged in the development of the Libyan or Iranian petroleum industry.

Judicially, there has also been a return to the pre-*Timberlane* view. In *Laker Airways v Sabena* (1984), the view taken by the court indicated that it was not in a position to make a decision based upon diplomatic factors, such as 'reasonableness' and 'comity'. These were matters to be settled by the executive. Once the court had determined that the anti-trust legislation was applicable (that is, that it could identify 'effects'), it was bound apply it strictly. In *Hartford Fire Insurance Co v California* (1986), the majority of the Supreme Court rejected the relevance of 'comity' and 'reasonableness' in making a determination. The only question for the court was whether the foreign conduct was meant to produce, and did in fact produce, some substantial effect within the United States.

International reaction to the extension of US civil jurisdiction has been marked by judicial criticism and by blocking legislation. In reaction to the US decision in *United States v Imperial Chemical Industries* (1949), Lord Evershed MR declared his belief that the US court was improperly intruding upon the jurisdiction of foreign States (*British Nylon Spinner Ltd v Imperial Chemical Industries Ltd* (1953)). Further, the British courts have never accepted that British civil legislation could apply to any foreign dealings which might have an effect within the UK (see, for example, *Attorney General's Reference (No 1 of 1982)* (1983)). The same, however, cannot be said of the European Court of Justice, which has, both in the *ICI v Commission* case and the *Wood Pulp* case, adopted the US approach to the effects doctrine with regard to the activities agreements in restraint of trade and price fixing.

Blocking legislation has also been passed to counter the extension of US civil jurisdiction. In response to the US demand for documentation concerning foreign shipping in 1963, the representatives of 11 States concluded an agreement in London which declared the US actions to be an infringement of their countries' jurisdictions. As a consequence, Parliament passed the Shipping Contracts and Commercial Documents Act 1964. In 1980, this was extended to documentation in other areas of British commerce by the Protection of Trading Interests Act 1980.[4] In addition, under this statute, a British citizen or resident could bring an action in an English court for recovery of multiple damages which had been paid under the judgment of a foreign court. Other States have passed similar blocking legislation. For example, the Danish Limitation of Danish Shipowners' Freedom to Give Information to Authorities of Foreign Countries (1967) and the Australian Foreign Proceedings (Prohibition of Certain Evidence) Act 1976.

The European Union, in its attempt to avoid jurisdictional conflict with the United States, concluded the Agreement Regarding the Application of Competition Law, which came into effect in 1995. This only went a little way to help resolving the increasing diplomatic tensions that were a result of the expansion of the extraterritorial civil jurisdiction. A problem that was only further exacerbated by the introduction of the Helms-Burton and D'Amato Acts.

In conclusion, it can be observed that the existing position on the extraterritorial civil jurisdiction is still most unsatisfactory. It is to be hoped that disagreements will be resolved through negotiation.

Notes

1 In *Rio Tinto Zinc v Westinghouse Electric Corp* (1978), the US approach drew criticism from the UK Attorney General. He stated that 'the wide investigating procedures under the United States antitrust legislation against persons outside the United States who are not United States citizens constitute an 'extraterritorial' infringement of the proper jurisdiction and sovereignty of the United Kingdom'.
2 Note that the Restatement does not represent the view of the US Government. The Statement is completed by a team of US international lawyers.

3 At the time of writing the application of this legislation has been suspended by the US President.
4 See the reference to statute in the case of *British Airways Board v Laker Airways Ltd* (1983).

CHAPTER 8

IMMUNITY FROM JURISDICTION

Introduction

Prior to the entry into force of the State Immunity Act 1978, there was great judicial debate as to whether the so called restrictive approach to State immunity had been adopted in the UK. The traditional rule of international law was that any activity carried out under the auspices of the State was regarded as *acta imperii*. Such actions, in order to maintain comity between States, were immune from being impleaded within a municipal court. For the classic statement of this principle, see the decision of Marshall CJ in *Schooner Exchange v McFaddon* (1812). This was the position, called the doctrine of absolute immunity, adopted by British courts, and it became binding upon subsequent courts by the rule of *stare decisis*.

However, following the Second World War, States increasingly began to intervene in industry. There seemed to be no reason why these commercial activities should continue to be protected by State immunity. For example, if a nationalised industry could enter into contracts, why should it not be capable of being sued for breach of contract if it refused to honour its contractual obligations? Consequently, most jurisdictions began to change their policies on State immunity. They abandoned the view of absolute immunity and adopted that of restrictive immunity. A distinction was introduced between *acta imperii* and activities *acta jure gestionis*. The latter activities were deemed essentially commercial in nature, and so would not benefit from the protection that State immunity afforded.

In the UK, however, the matter was still entirely governed by the common law. The common law still adhered to the absolute view. In 1972, the Crown signed and later ratified the European Convention on State Immunity which allowed for the adoption, in stated circumstances, of the restrictive approach. The treaty provisions were not to become part of English law until the passing of the enabling statute, the State Immunity Act 1978. Were the English courts to turn a blind eye to the change in international law regarding immunity, a change that had been adopted by the Crown? If they were to follow the rule of *stare decisis*, they answered that they had no choice but to do so (with the exception, after the Practice Statement of 1966, of the House of Lords). However, in the famous case of *Trendtex Trading Corporation Ltd v Central Bank of Nigeria* (1977), the Court of Appeal refused to be bound by past authorities and adopted the restrictive approach. Although this decision was thought to have been made *per incurium* (see Donaldson J in *Uganda (Holdings) Ltd v Government of Uganda* (1979)), the Court of Appeal later re-asserted the standing of its earlier decision (see *Hispano Americana Mercantil SA v Central Bank of Nigeria* (1979)). Approval of this approach was made by the House of Lords in *I Congreso del Partido* (1978).

To those students who have read Chapter 3 of this book, the *Trendtex* discussion should be familiar. It is mentioned again because the candidate may get a question concerning the development of the law of the restrictive approach, for which discussion a knowledge of the authorities will be vital.

On this topic, questions may also be asked concerning diplomatic immunity. In order to answer such questions, students should be familiar with the key provisions of the Diplomatic Privileges Act 1964.

In answering a problem question, for example, the following issues should normally be considered, in the order given:
- the historical development of State immunity and the change from the absolute to the restrictive approach;
- the State Immunity Act 1978 and what count as commercial transaction;
- the waiver of immunity;
- diplomatic immunity: the Vienna Convention on Diplomatic Relations 1961 and the Diplomatic Privileges Act 1964; and
- waiver of diplomatic immunity.

IMMUNITY FROM JURISDICTION

Checklist

Students should be familiar with the following areas:
- acts *jure imperii*;
- acts *jure gestionis*;
- the nature of commercial acts;
- the legal position on the employment rights of diplomatic staff;
- what diplomatic premises are protected by immunity;
- the legal position of diplomatic baggage; and
- waiver of diplomatic immunity.

Question 27

The premises of the mission shall be inviolable.

(Vienna Convention on Diplomatic Relations 1961, Art 22(1).)

How true is this statement?

Answer plan

This question clearly concerns an aspect of State immunity – that of diplomatic immunity. To answer any such question, the examination candidate must have an understanding of, first, the Vienna Convention on Diplomatic Relations 1961; secondly, the additional elements that were added when the Diplomatic Privileges Act 1964 transformed such rules into English law; and thirdly, authority that has emerged since the entry into force of the above legal provisions which demonstrate the way in which their terms should be construed.

Issues that will be considered include:
- the historical position with regard to the inviolability of diplomatic premises;
- the current treaty and statute law on inviolability;
- judicial interpretation of Art 22 of the Vienna Convention;
- whether demonstrations outside the embassy violate the rule of inviolability; and

159

- whether premises are inviolable if a crime is committed upon them.

It should be pointed out that, to answer such a question well, a knowledge of British, foreign and ICJ decisions will be necessary.

Answer

This essay will outline the way in which international law has determined the inviolability of diplomatic missions. However, as will be shown, such inviolability does not mean that the embassy and embassy staff are totally immune in all circumstances from the law of the receiving State.

Customary international law long recognised the inviolability of diplomatic premises. The immunity of the official residence (or domicile) is known as the *franchise de l'hôtel*. Prior to the 19th century, the theory of the extraterritorial nature of the embassy gave rise to an exaggerated notion of the rights attaching to it. This, in turn, led to diplomatic premises being exploited. Some became a bolt hole for those who wished to avoid the penalties of the municipal law to be applied outside the embassy walls.[1] This traditional theory has now been abandoned. In *Radwan v Radwan* (1972), Cumming-Bruce J quotes and adopts the words of JES Fawcett:

> ... there are two popular myths about diplomats and their immunities which we must clear away: one is that an embassy is foreign territory, and the other is that a diplomat can incur no legal liabilities in the country in which he is serving ... The building occupied by a foreign embassy and the land on which it stands are part of the territory of what we call the receiving State: it is therefore under the jurisdiction of that State.

Thus, modern international law draws a distinction between the territory of the receiving State on which the sending State's mission stands, and the sending State's primary jurisdiction and control over the members of the mission and their activities in the embassy.

However, although the theory of extraterritoriality had been jettisoned in the 19th century, customary international law still extended the privilege of immunity to the minister's person, and this personal immunity was extended to his domicile. This would include his official residence, outbuildings and modes of transport used for diplomatic purposes. As a consequence, such areas could not be entered by the police or other municipal public officials exercising their duties. This rule of customary international law was reasserted by Art 22 of the Vienna Convention on Diplomatic Relations 1961. Subject to s 3 of the Diplomatic Privileges Act 1964, the 1961 Convention had the force of law within the UK (see Sched 1 of the statute). Such premises are regarded as the property of the sending State and are regarded as being inviolable. The rationale for the need for inviolability can be found in the preamble to the Vienna Convention on Diplomatic relations, namely, it is 'to ensure the efficient performance of the functions of diplomatic missions as representing States'. This is sometimes referred to as the functional necessity theory.

The concept of inviolability has been variously defined. It has been expressed as 'the right of the sending State to have its diplomatic premises, its diplomatic personnel and all official records and communications safeguarded against interference of any sort'. Although imprecise, this view has been taken to imply that immunity exists 'from all interference, whether under colour of law, or right, or otherwise, and connotes a special duty of protection, whether from such interferences or from mere insult on the part of the receiving State'. Further, Art 30 states that the private residence of a diplomatic agent shall enjoy the same inviolability and protection as the premises of the mission. Intervention by the authorities would be legalised if the ambassador had given his consent (for example, in *Fatemi v United States* (1963)).

The text of Art 22 discloses two elements to diplomatic inviolability that have to be observed by the receiving State. First, the receiving State is obliged to prevent its agents from entering the premises for any official purpose whatsoever (para 1). Secondly, the receiving State is duty bound to take all appropriate steps to protect the premises from any invasion or damage, and to prevent any disturbance of the peace of the mission or impairment of its dignity (para 2). The receiving State must, in order to satisfy this obligation, take special measures *over and above* those it takes to discharge its general duty of ensuring order.[2]

This duty imposed upon the receiving State under Art 22(2) was emphasised by the International Court of Justice in 1980. The United States Embassy at Teheran, its consulates at Tabriz and Shiraz having been occupied by militant student demonstrators and diplomatic and consular personnel taken hostage. This occupation took place with the initial acquiescence and later support of the Iranian Revolutionary Government. The seizure was motivated by American gestures of friendship to the deposed former Shah of Iran. The students subsequently discovered documents which the Iranian government later published to support its allegation that American diplomatic premises had for many years been a 'centre of espionage and conspiracy' by 'people [who] hatched plots against our Islamic movement' and who therefore 'do not enjoy international diplomatic respect'.

The United States brought suit against Iran in the ICJ in the *Case Concerning United States Diplomatic and Consular Staff in Tehran* (1980). The court held that:

> ... the action required of the Iranian government by the Vienna Conventions and by general international law was manifest. Its plain duty was at once to make every effort and to take every appropriate step to bring these flagrant infringements of the inviolability of the premises, archives and diplomatic and consular staff of the United States Embassy to a speedy end, to restore the consulates at Tabriz and Shiraz to United States control, and in general to re-establish the status quo and to offer reparation for the damage.

Does this mean that the municipal authorities, in order to maintain the 'peace' and 'dignity' found in Art 22(2), have to suppress all demonstrations that take place *outside* the diplomatic premises? Unfortunately, these words are not defined in the convention and were not discussed in the ILC commentary. There is little evidence of pre-convention State practice in relation to demonstrations outside, or criticism directed to, diplomatic missions. The Harvard Draft Convention on Diplomatic Privileges and Immunities 1932 required the receiving State to '... protect the premises acquired or used by a mission or occupied by a member of the mission against any invasion or other act tending to disturb the peace or dignity of the mission or of its personnel'. In the commentary which accompanied that draft, it was proposed that the special duty of protection included protection against crowds or mobs collected in the environs of the premises for the purposes of expressing abuse, contempt or disapproval of the sending State or its mission.[3]

British State practice would not seem to extend the concept of inviolability to protect diplomatic missions from expressions of public opinion. In its report on the 1984 Libya People's Bureau incident, in which shots were fired from the Bureau upon peaceful demonstrators outside the premises, the House of Commons Foreign Affairs Committee stated:

> Our view is that, although the 'peace of the mission' may not be entirely identical to the Queen's peace, the receiving State's duty to protect the peace of the mission cannot be given so wide an interpretation as to require the mission to be insulated from expressions of opinion within the receiving State. Provided always that work at the mission can continue normally, that there is untrammelled access and egress and that those within the mission are never in fear that the mission might be damaged or its staff injured, the requirements of Art 22 are met. A breakdown of the public order outside mission premises would put in jeopardy the fulfilling of obligations under Art 22, an orderly expression of opposition to the policies of the sending State cannot, of itself, do so.[4]

The Committee reviewing the Libyan People's Bureau incident examined two conflicting opinions about the duty of the receiving State. Professor G Draper expressed the view that allowing demonstrators to form up behind barriers in the immediate frontage of the Libyan mission premises was incompatible with Art 22. However, the Head of the Diplomatic Service, Sir Anthony Acland, considered it essential that demonstrations be adequately controlled and policed so that there 'is no damage done physically or otherwise to the mission or the people within it'. With reference to the demonstrations which had been permitted to take place outside the People's Bureau by the British authorities, he stated: 'I do not think, in that case, the peace of the mission within the mission or the impairment of its dignity really applied, this country having the tradition of freedom of demonstration.' The committee would appear to have adopted the view of the Head of the Diplomatic Service. The White Paper accepting the committee's report and recommendations was subsequently published by the UK government. On the question of the permissibility of demonstrations outside diplomatic missions, it said (para 85(g)):

> The government accepts that demonstrations outside diplomatic missions should be allowed so long as they do not imperil the safety or efficient work of the mission.[5]

This approach was consistent with that taken in *R v Roques* (1984). Here, anti-apartheid protesters who had demonstrated on a pavement immediately outside the South African Embassy in Trafalgar Square were charged with obstructing a police officer. On the basis that the demonstration was in breach of the Diplomatic Privileges Act 1964, which it was the duty of the police to apply, the officer made use of his power to arrest. The charge was later dismissed in the Bow Street Magistrates' Court on the basis that impairment of the dignity of the mission 'required abusive or insulting behaviour, and that political demonstrations do not themselves amount to such'.

What might happen if a crime had been committed within embassy premises? In such an instance, would the diplomatic premises still be inviolable? Despite the internationally accepted view that diplomatic premises are inviolable, it has also been established that such premises must not be used in a manner incompatible with the functions of a mission (see Art 41(3) of the Vienna Convention). State practice seemed to indicate that, although the inviolability of diplomatic premises was, in theory, absolute, States did in fact reserve a right, in the most extreme cases, to enter those premises. This was on the condition that there was strong proof that embassy personnel or others in the building were violating their duties under Art 41 of the 1961 Convention. For example, in 1973, the Pakistani authorities forced entry into the Iraqi embassy and discovered large supplies of arms and ammunition. They had earlier requested to enter embassy property but this had been refused. The ambassador and attaché were thereupon declared *persona non grata*. If a criminal act has been committed within the house of an envoy by a person who lacks personal immunity from municipal jurisdiction, then that criminal must be surrendered to the municipal authorities (the *Nikitschenkoff* case (1867) supports this view). Moreover, a member of the diplomatic mission cannot legally seize a national from his own State who is in the receiving State.[6]

Thus, it can be seen that, although the Vienna Convention does guarantee the inviolability of diplomatic missions, that does not mean that the mission shall be immune from peaceful protest. Nor does it mean that the mission might never be used in a manner incompatible with its function.

Notes

1 For the expression of this fiction, see Grotius, *De Jure Belli ac Pacis Libri Tres*, Bk II, ch XVII–IV-7.
2 See the Draft Commentary to Art 22 produced by the International Law Commission in its commentary (1958) YBILC II, p 95
3 'A similar duty would seem to exist to protect such premises against so called "picketing", this being an act tending to disturb the peace and dignity of the mission.'
4 See First Report from Foreign Affairs Committee (1984), paras 73–105; UKMIL, BY (1984), pp 459, 471–72; Cameron (1985) 34 ICLQ 610–14.
5 Cmnd 9497, Misc No 5 (1985) and see Higgins, 'UK Foreign Affairs Committee Report on the Abuse of Diplomatic Immunities and Privileges: Government Response and Report' (1986) 80 AJIL 135 and Higgins, 'The Abuse of Diplomatic Privileges and Immunities: Recent United Kingdom Experience' (1985) 79 AJIL 641, pp 650–51.
6 If the *Sun Yat Sen Incident* (1896) is any guide, the local authorities will insist upon the right to intervene to preserve the ordinary liberties of persons without the realm. In this case, a Chinese forcibly detained in his embassy applied for habeas corpus. However, the matter was ultimately taken up diplomatically. Despite protests that the embassy was Chinese territory, Sun Yat Sen's release was secured.

Question 28

Mr Anthony, Mr Bobby and Mr Snodgrass are employed by the Slappian Embassy in London. Under a contract drawn up in London, they are employed by the Embassy to give demonstrations of native Slappian dancing at functions organised by Embassy's Tourist Section.

Mr Anthony and Mr Bobby are both Slappian nationals and Mr Snodgrass is a British citizen with a passion for Slappian culture. They contract out their services to perform at culture festivals. The British Foreign and Commonwealth Office had not been informed about the employment of the three dancers. Their contracts of employment were made in London. After one performance, Mr Bobby is stopped by the police who reasonably suspect that he is driving with an excess of alcohol in his bloodstream. When stopped by a police officer, he refuses to take a breathalyser test. In Slappia, British diplomats are required by law to undergo tests if they are believed to be driving after consuming any alcohol.

In August 1997, all three men (the dancers) were dismissed from their employment. They wished to take their case before an industrial tribunal claiming unfair dismissal.

Technocap, a British firm, entered into an agreement with Slappia to produce postman's hats. The felt part of the hat was to be produced in the UK and the peak put on in Slappia. Slappia refused to pay for the hats when they are supplied.

Answer plan

As in the last question, here, a reasonable knowledge of the Vienna Convention and the Diplomatic Privileges Act is essential. However, in addition, examination candidates will be expected to understand the basic principles of the State Immunity Act 1978. They will, predictably, be required to know the authority on all these documents in order to enable them to construe the key sections of such Acts. In particular, with regard to the State Immunity Act 1978, they will be required to be able to make a distinction between acts *de jure imperii* (those acts of a governmental character) and those acts *de jure gestionis* that are purely matters of commercial activity.

The following approach is suggested:
- consider whether the breathalysing of Mr Bobby can legally be done;
- consider whether 'the dancers' can successfully bring their case for unfair dismissal;
- consider the importance of nationality and whether the fact that the Foreign and Commonwealth Office has not been informed about the dancers' employment matters; and
- consider whether Slappia can be impleaded for breach of its contract with Technocap.

Remember that whenever you cite the relevant statute or refer to the relevant authorities, always relate them to your current question by analogy.

Answer

This essay will examine the issues regarding the breathalysing of Bobby; the possibility of impleading the Slappian Embassy before an industrial tribunal; the possibility of impleading the Slappian State for being in breach of contract.

The first issue to be discussed is the breathalysing of Bobby. Section 2(1) of the Diplomatic Privileges Act 1964 (DPA) states that 'Schedule 1 to this Act (being articles of the Vienna Convention on Diplomatic Relations signed in 1961) shall have the force of law in the United Kingdom'. Article 29 of the Vienna Convention on Diplomatic Relations 1961 (reproduced in Sched 1 of the statute) states:

> The person of a diplomatic agent shall be inviolable. He shall not be liable to any form of arrest or detention. The receiving State shall take all appropriate steps to prevent any attack on his person freedom or individual dignity.

This begs two questions. First, would Mr Bobby qualify as a 'diplomatic agent' for the purposes of the statute? Secondly, would being stopped to be breathalysed constitute a breach of Art

29? The phrase 'diplomatic agent' is defined in Art 1(e) as 'the head of the mission or a member of the diplomatic staff of the mission'. Article 1(d) states that 'members of the diplomatic staff' are 'members of the staff of the mission having diplomatic rank'. Thus, if it can be established that Mr Bobby has such rank, he may be entitled to the immunity granted by Art 29. It would further appear to be the case, as reported in Hansard, that the scope of Art 29 would be wide enough to include immunity from a breathalyser test or other such medical examination to determine alcohol level.[1] However, it is to be noted that in this instance there is no reciprocal treatment of British diplomatic staff in Slappia. Section 3 of the DPA refers to restrictions on privileges and immunities. It states that:

> If it appears to Her Majesty that the privileges and immunities accorded to a mission of Her Majesty in the territory of any State, or to persons connected with that mission, are less than those conferred by this Act on the mission of that State or on persons connected with that mission, Her Majesty may, by Order in Council, withdraw such of the privileges and immunities so conferred from the mission of that State or from such persons connected with it as appears to Her Majesty to be proper.

As a consequence, if such an Order in Council had been drafted with regard to Slappia, it could result in Mr Bobby being deprived of the immunity afforded by Art 29.

The second issue concerns the attempt of the three dancers to bring their cases of unfair dismissal before the industrial tribunal. This will require examination of the law on State immunity. The general rule as to State immunity is found in s 1(1) of the State Immunity Act 1978 (SIA): 'A State is immune from the jurisdiction of the courts of the United Kingdom except as provided in the following provisions of this Part of this Act.' By the general interpretation section of the Act (s 22(1)) 'court' is defined as including 'any tribunal or body exercising judicial functions'. Moreover, s 4(6), headed 'Contracts of Employment', states that 'proceedings relating to a contract of employment' include 'proceedings between the parties to such a contract in respect of statutory rights or duties to which they are entitled or subject as employer or employee'. Thus, the industrial tribunal in this question would be a court for the purposes of this Act. This section is intended to qualify the immunity created by s 1 with regard to contracts of employment. It establishes that:

> A State is not immune as respects proceedings relating to a contract of employment between the State and an individual where the contract was made in the United Kingdom or the work is to be wholly or partly performed there.

If the statute stopped here, the three dancers might be capable of bringing their cases before the industrial tribunal for unfair dismissal. However, there are legal barriers to the dancers bringing their action. First, s 4(2) disapplies this section when '(a) at the time when the proceedings are brought the individual is a national of the State concerned'. In this instance, both Mr Bobby and Mr Anthony are Slappian nationals. On this count, they would thus be prevented from bringing their proposed action. Yet this provision is, in turn, subject to sub-s (3), which provides:

> Where the work is for an office, agency or establishment maintained by the State in the United Kingdom for *commercial purposes*, sub-ss (2)(a) and (b) above do not exclude the application of this section unless the individual was, at the time when the contract what made, habitually resident in that State [emphasis supplied].

It is clear that, in this instance both, Mr Anthony and Mr Bobby resided in the UK when the contract of employment was signed. The question that should next be addressed is whether the tourist section of the Embassy was maintained by the Slappians for 'commercial purposes'? The relevant provisions here are ss 17(1) and 3(3) of the 1978 Act. Section 17(1) states that 'commercial purposes' means 'purposes of such transactions or activities as are mention in s 3(3) above'. Section 3(3) states that 'commercial transaction' means (*inter alia*):

> (a) any contract for the supply of goods and services; ...
>
> (c) any other transaction or activity (whether of a commercial, industrial, financial, professional or other similar character) into which a State enters or in which it engages otherwise than in the exercise of sovereign authority.

In order to determine whether the activity of the Embassy's tourist section would constitute a 'commercial transaction' under the Act, it is necessary to examine the way in which that section has been construed by case law. The issue of distinguishing acts *jure imperii* (of a government character), from those *jure gestionis* was examined by the House of Lords in *I Congreso del Partido* (1981), by the Court of Appeal in *Littrell v United States of America (No 2)* (1993), and, more recently, in the Employment Appeal Tribunal in *Egypt v Gamal-Eldin* (1995). In the latter case, Mummery J states that the approach in *Littrell* is correct. That approach is:

> ... to inquire whether an activity is commercial or in exercise of sovereign authority, [it] involves looking at all the circumstances in relation to the activities and their context and then [considering] all the factors together. No one factor is in itself determinative in characterising the activity, the identity of those who deal with it, and the place, in order to resolve the question.

He found, after examining the relevant circumstances, that the employees of the Egyptian medical office of the Egyptian Embassy were not engaged in 'commercial purposes' under s 4(3) of the 1978 Act. This was so despite the fact that the office made commercial contracts for its medical services. Following this case, it could be contended that Mr Anthony and Mr Bobby would fail in bringing their action before the tribunal.

Yet what of Mr Snodgrass, a British citizen, who wishes to bring his case before the industrial tribunal? If he was capable of surmounting the legal obstacle of s 4, he fails to clear that of s 16(1) of the SIA which provides that:

> This part of the Act does not affect any immunity or privilege conferred by the Diplomatic Privileges Act 1964 ... and – (a) s 4 above does not apply to proceedings concerning the employment of the members of a mission within the meaning of the convention scheduled to the said Act of 1964 ...

Article 1 of the said convention provides a number of definitions of what 'members of the mission' means. Article 1 states (*inter alia*):

> (c) 'members of the staff of the mission' are the members of the diplomatic staff, and the administrative and technical staff of the mission ...

(f) the 'members of the administrative and technical staff' are the members of the staff of the mission employed in the administrative and technical service of the mission.

This would also prove to be an additional bar to an action by Mr Anthony and Mr Bobby. Yet with regard to Mr Snodgrass, could it not be argued that he was not, in the truest sense, 'a part of the mission'? Mr Snodgrass was a British citizen. Could it not be suggested that the ordinary meaning of the word, not defined by the treaty (or by the DPA), referred to a body of persons sent to a foreign country to serve their home government? If so, then Mr Snodgrass could pursue his claim unfettered by the 1964 Act. Such a contention was put forward and then rejected by the Court of Appeal in *Ahmed v Government of the Kingdom of Saudi Arabia* (1995). As Peter Gibson LJ states:

> However, [counsel for the plaintiff] recognises from the convention [that is, Art 39(1) of the Vienna Convention on Diplomatic Relations 1961] itself, if nowhere else, that members of the mission cannot be limited to those who enter the United Kingdom by reason of being sent from the State in question: they include those who are already in the United Kingdom and whose appointments are notified to the Foreign and Commonwealth Office (Art 39).

Further, as Browne-Wilkinson J stated in *Sengupta v Republic of India* (1983):

> ... s 16(1)(a) operates to exclude jurisdiction over the claims relating to the employment not only of diplomatic staff but also of lower grade administrative, technical and domestic staff *irrespective of their nationality* [emphasis supplied].

In the *Ahmed* case, Peter Gibson LJ respectfully agreed with this statement and further noted that their was no reference to nationality being a test as to who was a member of a mission in Art 1 of the Vienna Convention.

However, Mrs Ahmed, the plaintiff in the *Ahmed* case, was in a similar position to that of Mr Snodgrass to the extent that her appointment had not been reported to the Foreign and Commonwealth Office as required by Art 39(1) and thus, also, by English law. In response to this, Peter Gibson LJ states:

If authority were needed for the proposition that membership of a mission for the purposes of the convention is not dependent upon notification to the Foreign and Commonwealth Office, it is to be found in the decision of this court in *R v Secretary of State for the Home Department ex p Bagga* (1991).

The third issue concerns the dishonoured contract and the question of whether Slappia could claim State immunity with regard to its contract with Technocap. The relevant section of the SIA is s 3, which states: '(1) A State is not immune as respects proceedings related to (a) A commercial transaction entered into by the State ...' Commercial transactions are defined by sub-s (3)(a) as 'any contract for the supply of goods or services'. It could be contended that, once it is established that the agreement between Technocap and Slappia did constitute such a contractual arrangement, Slappia could be impleaded for breach of contract. Authority on this can be found in the case of *Commissioners of Customs and Excise v Minister of Industries and Military Manufacturing* (1992), in which a British company was under contract 'to supply component parts of a supergun' to Iraq. As this was a 'supply of goods or services' under s 3(3)(a), the defendant could be impleaded, and a confiscation order was made by the High Court.

If there is doubt as to whether the agreement constituted a 'commercial transaction' under sub-s (3), which, it is contended, would be unlikely, Technocap might be advised to place reliance on s 3(1)(b). This section states that 'an obligation of the State which, by virtue of a contract (whether a commercial transaction or not), falls to be performed wholly or partly in the United Kingdom cannot clothe a State act with immunity'. As part of the hats Technocap are producing is made in the UK, their contract would fall under this sub-section.

In conclusion, it can be seen that, first, unless an Order in Council has been made in response to the Slappian treatment of British diplomats in that receiving State, Mr Bobby can most probably rely upon the terms of the Diplomatic Privileges Act 1964 (which incorporated Art 29 of the Vienna Convention of Diplomatic Relations 1961) to allow him to escape any tests for alcohol in his bloodstream. Secondly, because of the terms of the Acts of 1964 and 1978 referred to above, it is contended that the

IMMUNITY FROM JURISDICTION

dancers would be unable to implead the Slappian Embassy in an English tribunal. Lastly, based upon a construction of the 1978 Act, Slappia, it is contended, would be prevented from claiming State immunity in its action with Technocap because of the commercial nature of the transaction involved.

Notes
1   Hansard, HC, Vol 101, col 64.

Question 29

In August 1995, Spinlandia is invaded by Revoltia. On the instructions of the Revoltian High Command, the Revoltian State Airline (RSA) requisitioned all seven civil airliners belonging to Spinlandiaflot. In September of that year, the Revoltian High Command, through legislation, dissolved Spinlandiaflot and legally transferred all of its assets to the RSA. The airliners were removed from Spinlandia and flown to Revoltia. Following the legislation coming into force, the RSA incorporated the airliners into its own fleet and painted them with its livery.

Spinlandia is later liberated by the Coalition of the Forces of Freedom. Following the liberation, the Spinlandian Foreign Office serves a writ upon the RSA seeking the return of the seven airliners and damages.

The matter is to be resolved through an application of English law.

Discuss.

Answer plan

The State Immunity Act 1978 adopted, in set circumstances, what is known as 'the restrictive approach to sovereign immunity'. However, there was still room for judicial wrangling as to which activities that might be carried out by a separate entity, be it an airline or the police force of a State, would be essentially governmental in nature. What criteria would be applied by the courts in making such a determination? To answer this question, examination candidates must understand more than just the terms of the 1978 Act; they must also be very familiar with the cases in which that Act has been construed.

The following matters should be discussed in the essay:
- s 14 of the State Immunity Act 1978;
- whether the relevant actions are *acta jure imperii* or *de jure gestionis*;
- an examination of authority;
- the 'governmental character' of the action of requisition;
- the consequences that would follow from the Revoltian legislation that would legally transfer the assets to RSA.

If students have enough time, they might also consider discussing the reasoning behind the dissenting judgments in the *Kuwait Airlines v Iraqi Airways* (1995) of Lord Mustill and Lord Slynn of Hadley.

Answer

In this answer, consideration will be given to whether the Revoltian State Airline (RSA) could escape liability for its actions in an English court.

RSA should be advised to claim that its acts could not be impleaded in a English court because its actions were protected by State immunity. In particular, the RSA should refer to s 14 of the State Immunity Act 1978. The 1978 Act was passed, at least in part, to give effect to the European Convention on State Immunity of 1972. Chapter 1 of the Convention is entitled 'Immunity from Jurisdiction' and contains a number of articles setting out circumstances in which 'a contracting State cannot claim immunity from the jurisdiction of a court of another contracting State'. Section 14 of the Act is concerned, first, to define, for the purposes of English law, what is a State, and second, to give effect to Art 27 and the 'entities' contemplated in that article. Section 14(1) of this Act states that: '(1) the immunities and privileges conferred by this Act apply to any foreign or Commonwealth State other than the United Kingdom'; and references to a State include references to (*inter alia*) '(c) any department of that government, but not to any entity (hereafter referred to as a "separate entity") which is distinct from the executive organs of the government of the State and capable of suing or being sued'. Sub-section (2) then states that:

> A separate entity is immune from the jurisdiction of the courts of the United Kingdom if, and only if:
>
> (a) the proceedings relate to anything done by it in the exercise of sovereign authority; and
>
> (b) the circumstances are such that a State ... would have been so immune.

Therefore, in order to claim State immunity, RSA (the 'separate entity') would have to establish that its activities possessed the character of government acts. Such acts of governmental authority are referred to as acts *jure imperii*. Acts not of this character, acts which are as commercial in nature, are referred to as acts *de jure gestionis*.

Lord Goff of Chieveley, in *Kuwait Airways v Iraqi Airways* (1995), suggested that:

> ... in construing this section, the logical answer would appear to be first to apply the condition in s 14(2)(a), which would have the effect of excluding *acta jure gestionis*, with the practical effect that questions relating to commercial transactions should not arise under s 14(2)(b).

His Lordship further stated that, when determining whether an act had been carried out by a separate authority under s 14(2)(a), it would be appropriate to examine English authorities relating to the distinction between *acta jure imperii* and *acta de jure gestionis*.

In *Playa Largo (Owners of Cargo Lately Laden on Board) v I Congreso de Partido (Owners)* (1981),[1] Lord Wilberforce described the *Claim against the Empire of Iran* case, decided by the Federal Constitutional Court of the German Federal Republic. According to Lord Wilberforce, this was a case of 'great clarity' which contained 'an instructive view of the law of State immunity over a wide area'. His Lordship cited the following from that case:

> As a means of determining the distinction between acts *jure imperii* and *jure gestionis*, one should rather refer to the nature of the State transaction or the resulting legal relationships, and not to the motive or purpose of the State activity. It thus depends on whether

the foreign State has acted in exercise of its sovereign authority, that is in public law, or like a private person, that is in private law.

Lord Wilberforce stated that, in considering whether or not State immunity should be granted, the court should consider whether the relevant acts should:

> ... be considered as fairly within an area of activity, trading or commercial, or otherwise of a private law character, in which the State has chosen to engage, or whether the relevant acts should be considered as having been done outside that area, and within the sphere of governmental or sovereign activity.

In the *Kuwait* case, the conclusion that Lord Goff draws from his analysis of the authorities is as follows. In order that one may determine what constitutes an act *jure imperii*, the issue is whether the act in question is 'of its own character a governmental act, as opposed to an act which any private citizen can perform'.[2] It follows from this that, when the act is of a separate entity (for example, an airline, as in the *Kuwait* case and in the present question), it is not enough just to ask whether the entity is acting at the behest of the State. Such an act need not automatically possess the character of a governmental act. Lord Goff continues: 'To attract immunity under s 14(2), therefore, what is done by the separate entity must be something which possesses that character.' Without such a character, 'the mere fact' that the reason and motive for the act was to benefit the State will not be sufficient to enable the separate entity to claim immunity under s 14(2) of the 1978 Act. Lord Goff refers to the persuasive authority of *Arango v Guzman Travel Advisors Corp* (1980), in which the national airline of Dominica was claiming State immunity in response to an action by a passenger. Judge Reavley, delivering the judgment of the court, stated that, as the airline, in following government orders to re-route, was acting merely as an arm of that government, it was entitled to State immunity. That would be so as the liability arose from the airline carrying out a governmental function.

In the *Kuwait* case, the Iraqi Minister of Transport, following the invasion of Kuwait, ordered the Director General of Iraqi Airways Company Limited (IAC) to take control of the 10 passenger aircraft belonging to the plaintiff in that case, the Kuwait Airways Corporation. The IAC followed this order and transferred the airliners to Iraq. The IAC was a body owned and controlled by the State. It did, however, engage in commercial activity as a passenger airline. The question arose whether it should be considered as a 'separate entity' acting in a private capacity, and thus not entitled to State immunity under s 14. Following authority, the House of Lords decided that the acts carried out by the IAC in taking the aircraft constituted an exercise of governmental power by the Iraqi State, thus entitling the actions of the IAC to State immunity. As Lord Goff said:

> I am satisfied that, in so acting, IAC was not just doing a job of work, but was closely involved with the State of Iraq ... On this basis, I am of the opinion that the IAC, in so acting, was acting in the exercise of sovereign authority.[3]

Following this authority, it could equally be contended that RSA could avoid being impleaded for the requisition of the airliners by claiming State immunity.

The second issue concerns the Revoltian legislation which dissolved Spinlandiaflot and transferred all of its assets to the RSA. Could the RSA, in these circumstances, claim State immunity? If one is bound by the *Kuwait* decision, the answer, it is contended, would be in the negative. Following requisition of the Kuwaiti airliners, the Iraqi government passed RCC Resolution 369. This dissolved the Kuwait Airways Corporation and transferred all of its assets to the IAC. The majority of the House of Lords (Lord Mustill and Lord Slynn of Hadley dissenting) found that, after the resolution came into force, the actions were no longer protected by State immunity: they were no longer done in sovereign authority but were pursuant to the Iraqi legislation which had transferred the aircraft to the IAC. Lord Goff addressed the question of whether property first acquired in a manner protected by State immunity could, given a change of circumstances, cease to be so protected. He stated:

> I, for my part, cannot see that the characterisation as an act *jure imperii* of the earlier involvement by the entity in the act of seizure can, on the facts of the present case, be determinative of the characterisation of subsequent retention and use of the property by the State entity following the formal vesting of the property in the entity of a legislative act of the State.

In conclusion, it can be seen that, when construing the State Immunity Act 1978 in the light of relevant authority, it can be contended that the initial act of requisition by the RSA would be protected by State immunity. However, this protection would cease once the Revoltian government had transferred the airliners to it by legislation.

Notes

1 In this case the House of Lords considered the doctrine of sovereign immunity at common law, the relevant events having occurred before the 1978 Act came into force. See also the opinion expressed by Lord Diplock in *Alcom Ltd v Republic of Colombia* (1984).
2 See also *Littrell v USA (No 2)* (1994) and *Propend Finance Pty v Sing* (1997).
3 Note that Lord Goff also states that the IAC are protected by state immunity not only or their actions in the original seizure but also for their acts (ie, flying to Iraq, maintenance), between the original seizure and RRC 36.

CHAPTER 9

THE LAW OF THE SEA

Introduction

The law of the sea has always been an integral part of public international law. It is, therefore, also an important section of any public international law syllabus, although its actual weighting within the syllabus may vary. A thorough understanding of the background and principles developed in the law of the sea is important for at least two main reasons:

(a) it is an important area of substantive rules within public international law, regulating most, if not all, of humankind's activities within the vast maritime arena that is the world's ocean space, variously described as comprising up to 71% or even three-quarters of the earth's surface; and

(b) because of its long and vivid association with the historical development of public international law, it is often possible to find very useful examples within the treaty, customary, case law and other important events in the law of the sea which provide us with a better understanding of general issues arising in public international law, for example, the relationship between customary and treaty sources of international law. Also, knowledge of various treaty, customary and case law authorities in the law of the sea often proves useful in providing illustrative examples of, and insights into, the development of public international law generally.

The major development in the law of the sea in recent times is the entry into force of the 1982 UN Convention on the Law of the Sea (1982 UNCLOS), which ostensibly provides for a comprehensive legal regime governing most, if not all, maritime activities undertaken in ocean space. All students must be aware of this important achievement by the international community of States, not just in terms of its implications for the law of the sea but also in terms of its wider impact on the international legal system. For example, the negotiations for the 1982 UNCLOS represent the first major exercise involving the participation of many newly independent, developing countries as sovereign and equal States in the reshaping of a very important part of public international law.

Despite the fact that, to date, there are at least 123 States party to the 1982 UNCLOS, questions can still be asked about the universal applicability of its provisions, especially among States that have yet to ratify, accede to, or otherwise formally accept the convention. The United States is a prime example of a non-party State to this convention. Also, many of the provisions contained in the 1982 UNCLOS are vague or ambiguous in their wording, and this will surely give rise to disputes over their interpretation and implementation by States.

Both essay and problem questions are prevalent in the law of the sea. Generally speaking, they fall into several different categories:

(a) there are questions that focus on what is the applicable law as between different sources of treaty or customary law, depending on the legal status of the 1982 UNCLOS in relation to any particular State, for example, whether it has signed, ratified or acceded to the convention;

(b) assuming that the 1982 UNCLOS is applicable to the States concerned, there are questions that require the student to examine various provisions within the convention, with a view to forming an opinion or answering a problem concerning the right balance between potentially conflicting uses of the seas, such as where allegedly excessive coastal State regulation of foreign flagged fishing activities may impinge on a claimed freedom of navigation of these fishing vessels in the exclusive economic zone; and

(c) there are questions that combine law of the sea issues with other areas of public international law, such as State responsibility (see Chapter 10) and the international protection of human rights (see Chapter 12).

Checklist

When answering questions on the law of the sea, students should bear in mind the following points:
- despite the entry into force of the 1982 UNCLOS and its large number of party States, it should not be assumed that the provisions of the convention are the only applicable law. General customary international law and the four 1958 Geneva Conventions may still have a part to play in the determination of the applicable law, especially in problem questions;
- the 1982 UNCLOS represents the codification of a combination of already existing customary international law and progressive development of new subject areas in the law of the sea. All these provisions were agreed as part of a 'package deal' using an innovative, consensus based approach during the negotiations, which thereby did away with the need for a majority vote on the individual acceptance of the provisions as part of the convention;
- the 1982 UNCLOS also attempts to achieve a balance between the increased sovereignty, sovereign rights and jurisdiction of the coastal States and the traditional rights and freedoms of the maritime States, especially the freedom of navigation;
- as a general rule, the jurisdiction of a coastal State diminishes as we move further away from the coastline, to be replaced by flag State jurisdiction, especially over shipping vessels exercising their right of innocent passage within the territorial sea of the coastal State and freedom of navigation in the exclusive economic zone and high seas;
- now that the 1982 UNCLOS is in force, the focus of contemporary debate has moved from academic speculation to analysis of actual State practice, whether such practice is in conformity with the provisions of the 1982 convention, and the possible implications if it is not.

Question 30

Does the 1982 UN Convention on the Law of the Sea represent a new consensus under customary international law regarding the rights and duties of all States in relation to major maritime activities?

Answer plan

This is a fairly open ended essay question that invites the student, first, to discuss issues arising from the legal status of the 1982 convention, and secondly, to attempt to distinguish between different areas of the convention where the balance of rights and duties appears to be accepted in State practice, and where they have not, in relation to any of the major maritime activities, space and time permitting.

Among the major maritime activities alluded to here are navigation, fishing, offshore oil and gas development, marine scientific research, pollution of the marine environment, and the laying of submarine pipelines and cables.

The student should select a few examples from amongst the important maritime activities above and proceed to examine the relevant provisions of the convention and compare these with previous and current State practice in relation to these activities. The student should come to a conclusion on whether this State practice reflects the consensus achieved in the convention, and, if it does not, where the new balance appears to lie between coastal, maritime and other user States.

Answer

The 1982 UN Convention on the Law of the Sea (1982 UNCLOS) entered into force with effect from 16 November 1994, with the passage of one year from the deposit of 60th instrument of ratification (that of Guyana), as provided for under Art 308(1) of the convention. The convention was the product of at least nine years of negotiations (1973–82) between representatives of at least 150 States. Furthermore, negotiations proceeded on the basis of a 'package deal', whereby all the participating States agreed, at least implicitly, that they would have to accept compromises concerning some of their perceived national maritime interests in order to pave the way towards the universal acceptance of the convention as a whole.

The 'package deal' approach agreed at the negotiations was underpinned by the (then) innovative method of securing acceptance of individual provisions of the proposed draft convention by consensus rather than by the usual majority voting procedure. Despite the fact that this process was undermined late in the day by the USA, which insisted on a vote for the final act of the convention, the consensus approach has now been utilised in many more multilateral treaty making exercises, especially in the field of the environment. Both the 'package deal' approach and the acceptance of the provisions of the convention by consensus are further underpinned by the provision in Art 309 of the convention prohibiting reservations or exceptions made against the convention.

A further point that must be noted in this context is the numerous and wide ranging formal acceptances to the convention, whether by signature and ratification, or accession, according to Arts 305–7. To date, there are at least 123 State parties to the convention out of an international, world community of States numbering about 180.

The above points and facts allow us to make certain conclusions as to whether the 1982 UNCLOS represents a consensus under customary international law as well as conventional international law. Arguably, the fact that so many States have not just participated, but have now, also, accepted the convention, coupled with the use of the 'package deal' and consensus approach in securing initial acceptance of the convention, suggest that the requisite elements of customary international law (namely, State practice and *opinio juris*) are present. This enables us to conclude that the convention as a whole has found its way into acceptance by States as a body of customary rules of international law too, and is therefore binding on all States, with the exception of those very few States that are able to fulfil the conditions in order to qualify for 'persistent objector' status.

Ranged against this initial conclusion, however, is the argument that, both during and after the negotiation process, many States held the opinion that the exercise they were undertaking involved, in part only, the codification of already accepted rules of customary or conventional law (in the form of the four 1958 Geneva Conventions).

Other provisions of the draft convention were regarded as crystallising the progressive development of certain new areas of the law of the sea. Examples of these include the transit passage regime through straits utilised for international navigation (Part III of 1982 UNCLOS), which came about due to the extension of territorial seas by many littoral straits States to 12 nautical miles, thereby leaving no more high seas strips in the middle of straits which are less than 24 nautical miles wide. The provisions for protection of the marine environment (Part XII) provide another example of the progressive development of the law of the sea which was crystallised by the convention, albeit not necessarily having been fully accepted as part of customary international law during the negotiation process of the convention.

We can now proceed to a discussion of the regulation of certain major maritime activities under the convention, with a view to assessing whether the provisions of the 1982 UNCLOS have been implemented by States in their practice on the law of the sea, thereby attempting to confirm or disprove the claim that the convention represents a consensus in customary, as well as conventional, law. Three areas will be examined here: (a) the innocent passage of foreign warships through the territorial waters of a coastal State; (b) the rights and obligations of coastal States in relation to the fisheries resources in their exclusive economic zones and beyond into the high seas; and (c) the exercise of enforcement jurisdiction by the coastal State over marine pollution offences committed by foreign flagged vessels.

In respect of the first issue, it should be noted that this was a major bone of contention during the negotiation process for the 1982 UNCLOS. Many Group of 77 countries (composed mainly of newly independent, developing countries) and communist States, such as the People's Republic of China (PRC) and (at least initially) the (then) Soviet Union were ranged against the major maritime and naval powers such as the USA, UK and France in denying the latter States the right of their warships to innocent passage through the objecting States' territorial waters without the requirement of prior permission and authorisation or, at least, prior notification of such passage. Only an eleventh hour compromise was able to prevent the negotiation process breaking down irretrievably. As it stands now, Art 14 of the 1982 UNCLOS allows the right of innocent passage through territorial waters for 'ships of all States', under the sub-section heading of 'Rules Applicable to all Ships', and therefore does not explicitly provide that the right is accorded to warships. Numerous examples of State practice (mainly from developing countries, but also from newly industrialised States, such as the Republic of (South) Korea, and even from industrialised States, such as Denmark and Sweden) require either prior notification or permission for the passage of warships through their territorial waters. Despite the repeated protests and assertions by maritime States to the contrary, these States persist in their legislative requirement, if not actual enforcement, of their incompatible domestic laws requiring such prior notice or authorisation. Thus, this issue may be held up as one area where State practice as a whole is not in conformity with the consensus that appeared to have been agreed in the 1982 UNCLOS.

In the second example, too, discrepancies in the manner in which coastal States have legislated on the sovereign rights they have been given under Art 56 of Part V of the 1982 UNCLOS suggest that the consensus that was achieved is breaking down in actual State practice. Many coastal States have legislated to put into effect their sovereign rights over the fisheries within their claimed exclusive economic zones (EEZ) without the corresponding obligations (for example, to determine the total allowable catch, their own harvesting capacity, and provision of any surplus fishery resources to distant water fishing States), as required under Arts 61(1) and 62(2) respectively of the 1982 UNCLOS. Perhaps more importantly, three worrying trends may be observed. First, coastal States are not taking into account the rights of landlocked and geographically disadvantaged States (under Arts 69 and 70 respectively) to participate in the exploitation of surplus fishery resources in their EEZs. Secondly, certain domestic legislation by coastal States in some cases effectively denies the right of freedom of navigation to foreign flagged fishing vessels traversing their EEZs or territorial waters, despite the fact that these fishing vessels may only be using these waters in transit to their final destinations, and not to fish. Thirdly, at least three States (Canada, Argentina and Chile) appear to be ready to enforce their fisheries conservation measures on a unilateral basis even beyond the limits of their 200 nautical mile exclusive economic and fishery zones. The arrest and detention by Canadian fishing authorities of the *Estai*, a Spanish flagged vessel fishing in the North Atlantic just beyond the limits of the 200 nautical mile Canadian exclusive fishing zone, is a case in point, and is currently before the International Court of Justice for adjudication.

Finally, a number of diverse States, in terms of their level of economic development and geography, such as the USA, Malaysia and the People's Republic of China, have provided, within their domestic legislation, enabling powers to enforce their marine pollution laws against foreign flagged merchant vessels on the basis of strict liability, contingent on the mere presence of a certain amount of pollution. However, under the provisions of Art 56(1)(b) of the convention, read together with Art 220, such an exercise of enforcement jurisdiction in all but the more serious of marine pollution incidents is not permitted.

In conclusion, therefore, it may be submitted that, despite the consensus approach utilised during the negotiations and agreement of the 1982 UNCLOS, and the delicate initial balance thereby achieved between States with vastly different maritime interests at stake, the actual wording of the convention is being undermined at various points, mainly by coastal States' practice exhibiting signs of the phenomenon called 'creeping jurisdiction'. If this phenomenon continues unchecked, it will eventually threaten to unravel the very consensus that was so painstakingly built up during the long years of treaty negotiation. On the other hand, however, many of the alleged coastal States' abuses of their maritime jurisdictions, particularly where they have been held to impinge upon long established freedoms of the seas, (for example, the freedom of navigation), have been the subject of protest both by immediately affected and other third party States, thus ensuring that a new rule of customary law does not evolve in a way which threatens to undermine the consensus achieved in the 1982 convention.

Question 31

The Republic of Sunshine Islands are a group of four islands located about 300 nautical miles west of Australia in the Indian Ocean. East and West Island are the largest, each being about 2,000 square miles in size and 50 nautical miles apart. Both these main islands have substantial, locally based fishing industries and an increasing tourist trade centred upon cruise ships operating out of Perth, Australia.

South Island, which is only 500 square miles in size, is located about 120 nautical miles due south of West Island. Thirteen nautical miles immediately to the north of East Island is Awesome Rock, an uninhabited piece of granite which soars more than 100 feet above the surface of the ocean. A navigation light has been placed on Awesome Rock by the Republic of Sunshine Islands' Ports Authority.

The newly elected President of the Republic has indicated that she wishes to make a proclamation that includes the following measures:

(a) the drawing of archipelagic straight baselines around the outer limits of the four islands, including Awesome Rock, so as to be able to declare the Republic of Sunshine Islands an archipelagic State;
(b) limitations on the freedom of shipping by foreign flagged vessels within the newly established archipelagic waters of the Republic;
(c) the establishment of an 18 nautical mile territorial sea, a six nautical mile contiguous zone, a 200 nautical mile Exclusive Economic Zone (EEZ), and a 350 nautical mile continental shelf; and
(d) a complete prohibition on the entry of any foreign flagged fishing vessels within the newly established EEZ of the Republic.

The Republic has signed, but not yet ratified, the 1982 United Nations Convention on the Law of the Sea (UNCLOS) and acceded to the 1969 Vienna Convention on the Law of Treaties.

Advise the President of the international legal issues that would arise from her proclamation.

Answer plan

This problem question seems complex because of its length and the need for a certain amount of geographical awareness. In fact, the general public international law (mainly within the law of treaties) and law of the sea issues to which it gives rise are straightforward and easily derived from a reading of the relevant provisions of the Vienna Convention on the Law of Treaties 1969 and the 1982 UNCLOS combined with some knowledge of archipelagic State practice in the law of the sea to date.

First, the student should begin by writing a few lines on what is the applicable or binding international law on the Republic of Sunshine Islands; that is, whether it is the 1982 UNCLOS or customary international law with the aid of Art 18 of the 1969 Vienna Convention, or whether, for the purposes of this problem, conventional and customary international law should be regarded as one and the same.

Secondly, the student would be well advised to attempt a quick sketch of the geography of the Sunshine Islands archipelago, including the coastline of western Australia, 300 nautical miles away from East Island.

Thirdly, by reading the problem carefully, the student should be able to identify the following issues:

- whether the geography of the Republic of Sunshine Islands qualifies it to be included within the legal definition of an archipelagic State under Part IV of the convention, such that it can draw archipelagic straight baselines enclosing the archipelago, paying special attention to the limits within which the ratio of water to land need to be (Art 47(1)), and the maximum length of the archipelagic straight baselines (Art 47(2));
- whether Awesome Rock can be included within the definition of an island (Art 121(3)), such that it can be utilised as basepoint from which to draw archipelagic straight baselines enclosing it within the proposed archipelagic State of the Republic of Sunshine Islands; and
- whether the other measures within the President's proposed proclamation are in conformity with the relevant provisions of

the 1982 UNCLOS or customary international law, should these be adjudged to be different legal regimes.

Answer

The first issue that needs to be addressed in advising the President about the legality (or otherwise) of her proclamation on behalf of the Republic of Sunshine Islands is to consider which is the applicable source of public international law binding upon the Republic in relation to law of the sea questions generally. The question here is whether the Republic is bound by the provisions of the 1982 UNCLOS, despite having signed the convention, but not formally having ratified it. Under Art 18 of the Vienna Convention on the Law of Treaties 1969, which the Republic has ratified and by which it is therefore bound, a State is obliged to refrain from acts which would defeat the object and purpose of a treaty which it has signed but not yet ratified, even prior to its entry into force. Arguably, therefore, the fact that the Republic has signed the treaty, which has entered into force and now has more than 120 State parties, would suggest that its provisions are binding upon the Republic, at least in so far as the Republic is unable to act in a manner that would defeat the object and purpose of the 1982 UNCLOS.

On the other hand, it may be argued that this question is redundant, because all the provisions of the 1982 UNCLOS represent codified rules of customary international law of the sea. This is not necessarily true, however, in respect of certain parts of the 1982 UNCLOS, which are arguably the result of the crystallisation of the progressive development of customary rules, rather than merely already accepted customary rules. This is especially so in the case of the archipelagic State regime, which was included in conventional law for the first time only in the 1982 UNCLOS, having not been accepted during the negotiations to the four 1958 Geneva Conventions on the Law of the Sea.

Assuming the provisions of the convention are binding upon the Republic under customary law, if not conventional law as well (except where there are areas of wide divergence between conventional and customary law), we can now examine the different proposed measures in the President's proclamation and whether they conform with the relevant provisions of the 1982 UNCLOS.

First, it is important to consider whether the geography of the Republic of Sunshine Islands qualifies it to be included within the legal definition of an archipelagic State under Art 46 of Part IV of the convention, such that it can draw archipelagic straight baselines enclosing the archipelago, paying special attention to the limits within which the ratio of water to land needs to be (Art 47(1)), and the maximum allowed length of the proposed archipelagic straight baselines (Art 47(2)).

Before considering this question, however, the status of Awesome Rock must be clarified in order to see whether it can be included within the definition of an island (Art 121) such that it can be utilised as basepoint from which to draw archipelagic straight baselines, enclosing it within the proposed archipelagic state of the Republic of Sunshine Islands. Under Art 121(3), rocks that cannot sustain human habitation do not qualify as islands in the sense of being able to generate 200 nautical mile (nm) exclusive economic zones (EEZs) or continental shelves. This does not appear to preclude Awesome Rock from being utilised as a basepoint from which to draw archipelagic straight baselines, but it is doubtful whether it can be used to claim anything more than a 12 nm territorial sea and 24 nm contiguous zone.

Returning to the issue of whether the proposed archipelagic straight baselines fulfil the strict requirements laid down under Art 47 of the convention, it would seem that the water to land ratio achieved when drawing these baselines around all four islands and rocks is within the limits provided; but unless the Republic acts cleverly in terms of the number of straight baselines it draws around the islands concerned, it will not be able to fulfil the requirement that less than 3% of the number of its baselines are more than 100 nm long each, up to a maximum of 125 miles. In any case, the longest baseline (that between South Island and East Island) will almost certainly be more than 125 nm, and therefore in breach of the uppermost limit provided under the 1982 UNCLOS. It is important to note, however, that the specific limits provided in the 1982 UNCLOS have been violated by more than a few archipelagic States to date (most notably, by Indonesia and the

Philippines), although such errant State practice has led to protests by many of the major maritime States, such as the USA.

Next, we must consider whether other measures within the President's proposed proclamation are in conformity with the relevant provisions of the 1982 UNCLOS or customary international law, should these be adjudged to be different legal regimes.

Although the regime of archipelagic waters applies within the archipelago, and the sovereignty of the archipelagic State extends to these waters under this regime (Art 49), nevertheless, a right of innocent passage for ships of all States continues to be provided under Art 52. Under Art 19, this means that passage is to be considered 'innocent' so long as it is not prejudicial to the peace, good order or security of the coastal State. Such a right would appear to be violated should the restrictions on shipping proposed by the proclamation be anything more than setting down the criteria for when passage is rendered non-innocent according to Art 19(2), or be temporary in nature (Art 52(2)).

Furthermore, while the outer limit of the contiguous zone is correctly set at 24 nm (Art 33(2)), the proposed limit for the territorial waters, at 18 nm, is beyond the norm of 12 nm prescribed by the convention (Art 3). The Republic would be in clear breach of the convention, and arguably of customary international law, if it legislated, maintained and enforced this 18 nm territorial sea upon foreign flagged vessels, especially warships exercising the right of freedom of navigation beyond the prescribed 12 nm limit. With very few exceptions, all of which have been the subject of vigorous protests by many maritime States (and not merely by the major naval powers), State practice in relation to the outer limits of the territorial waters has respected the 12 nm requirement. Therefore, in this issue, there is very little discrepancy between the provisions of the convention and actual State practice, such that it is possible to State unequivocally that the Republic is bound to respect the 12 nm territorial sea limit under either conventional or customary rules, whichever is deemed to apply.

With respect to the proposed 200 nm EEZ and 350 nm continental shelf, both of these zones may be claimed providing that the relevant provisions of the convention (that is, Parts V in relation to the EEZ and Part VI in relation to the continental shelf) are adhered to. For example, Art 57 allows a 200 nm EEZ to be claimed, in which the Republic has sovereign rights, certain jurisdictions and duties provided under Art 56. In relation to the continental shelf, however, the right to claim this zone is inherent, that is, it cannot be lost to the claim of another State, even if it is unclaimed (Art 77(3)). The situation is different when it comes to the outer limits of the continental margin which can also be claimed as part of the continental shelf of any coastal State (Art 76(1) and (3)). Thus, although the Republic has sovereign rights over the natural resources of the seabed and subsoil of the continental shelf, at least up to a distance of 200 nm, any claim to a distance further than this has to meet the specific technical criteria laid down in Arts 76(4)–76(7). These requirements, however, do allow for the possibility of the outer limits of a coastal State's continental shelf to reach up to 350 nm. Information on how this criterion has been fulfilled for continental shelf limits which are beyond 200 nm are required to be submitted to the Commission on the Limits of the Continental Shelf (Art 76(8)) and deposited with the Secretary General of the UN (Art 76(9)).

More importantly though, the enforcement of the proposed complete prohibition on the entry of foreign fishing vessels into the Republic's EEZ would be regarded as a serious violation under the conventional and even customary international law on this issue. This is because the sovereign rights and jurisdiction provided to coastal States generally, and to the Republic specifically in this case, do not extend in any way to allow restrictions on the freedom of navigation provided to all vessels, without exception, within the EEZ. This is clear from Art 58(1) of the convention and relevant State practice. Again, where such practice has not been in conformity with this general right, available to all types of ships, it has been the subject of vigorous and sustained protest on the part of many other States in the international community.

In conclusion, therefore, it is noted that several of the proposed measures included in the President's proclamation are likely to lead to diplomatic protests by other States should they not be amended to be more compatible with the acceptable norms provided under both conventional law (in the form of the 1982 UNCLOS) and customary international law. Even where it may be possible to point to some discrepancies between the provisions of the 1982 UNCLOS and current State practice, the President would be well advised to implement the 1982 UNCLOS regime, as the Republic is, in any case, bound by its signature to the convention not to act in a manner that would defeat the object and purpose of the 1982 UNCLOS. Finally, it should be noted that, if the Republic proceeded to ratify the 1982 UNCLOS with these proposed measures still in force in the form they are now in, it would lay itself open to any number claims against its interpretation of the various 1982 UNCLOS provisions under Part XV, which provides for the dispute settlement mechanism of the convention (Arts 279–99).

Question 32

'The traditional balance of rights between coastal State and flag State jurisdiction over maritime activities has been maintained with the recent entry into force of the 1982 UN Convention on the Law of the Sea (UNCLOS).'

Discuss the above statement in relation to such important maritime activities as shipping and fishing.

Answer plan

This is a relatively simple essay question, which invites the student to conduct a balanced analysis of the various relevant provisions of the 1982 Convention related to the maritime activities mentioned. This kind of question is usually asked in undergraduate public international law courses that do not emphasise or spend as much time on the subject of the law of the sea as perhaps others do.

It is important not to merely engage in a dour recital of the provisions of the convention, even if these are relevant to the issues at hand. Although the language adopted by the convention is often vague and ambiguous, it is still possible to discern where the true balance between the two ostensibly competing coastal and flag State jurisdictions lies. Some effort should therefore be made at interpreting the various provisions in order to come to conclusions as to where the balance may lie in respect of these maritime activities.

Some knowledge of State practice in relation to the regulation of these activities, in order to illustrate whether the balance that was achieved in the treaty provisions has been maintained in the 'real' world, would be very usefully employed.

Answer

It is fairly clear that the coastal States were the 'big winners' of the nine year long negotiation exercise between 1973 and 1982 that spawned the 1982 UN Convention on the Law of the Sea (UNCLOS). As we shall see below, in many aspects of the new law of the sea, the coastal States were able to gain much in the form of new and extended sovereign rights and jurisdictions over a range of maritime activities which hitherto would have fallen solely within the domain of flag State jurisdiction.

This is especially true in relation to the sovereign rights and jurisdictions that coastal States can now exercise within the context of the exploration and exploitation of marine living resources, such as fisheries and the protection of the marine environment from vessel source pollution. In general, it may be argued that coastal States' rights and jurisdictions have grown under the provisions of the convention in both quantitative and qualitative terms.

This growth can be said to be quantitative in the sense that the geographical scope of coastal States' sovereign rights and jurisdictions has now increased considerably. A good example would be the breadth of the territorial waters that they can now claim, that is, up to 12 nm (Art 3), as compared to the previously accepted custom of only three nm. For most foreign flagged merchant vessels, this may not result in much change in their daily operations, as these will not be hindered whether they sail through the territorial sea under the right of innocent passage or in the exercise of freedom of navigation. However, for foreign flagged warships, whose status in terms of navigational rights through territorial waters is ambiguous under both customary and conventional law, this difference may prove crucial in terms of whether it is required to provide notice of its passage through a wider territorial sea than when it was exercising freedom of navigation through high seas. Article 17 appears to safeguard the right of innocent passage for ships of all States, under the subheading entitled 'Rules Applicable to all Ships', but this interpretation of the relevant wording was hotly contested during the 1982 UNCLOS negotiations, and many different States still purport to require some form of prior notification or authorisation, and even permission, before allowing the innocent passage of foreign warships through the territorial waters. It is therefore uncertain whether the proposed balance between the extended sovereignty over a wider belt of territorial waters provided for coastal States, and continuing safeguards for the navigational rights of all ships, and foreign warships especially, has been adhered to in actual State practice.

This problem is exacerbated in the case of straits used for international navigation which are less than 24 nm in width. The extension of coastal States' territorial waters to 12 nm means that all such narrow straits, or those parts of straits which are less than 24 nm, wide ostensibly fall within the territorial waters of the littoral straits States. High seas corridors through these straits, which previously provided naval vessels from all States complete freedom of navigation, were now possibly subject to the regime of innocent passage. Part III of the 1982 UNCLOS recognised this problem and provides for a new transit passage regime for such straits used for international navigation, with s 2 of Part III dealing with transit passage (Arts 37–44). Transit passage for these purposes means the freedom of navigation and overflight for all ships and aircraft for the purpose of continuous and expeditious transit of the strait concerned (Art 38), subject to certain duties in relation to the exercise of this right (Art 39). This right of transit passage appears to safeguard the right of freedom of navigation that had previously existed in the high seas corridors through these straits. However, many littoral straits States have signified their opposition to the right of transit passage through these straits.

In 1971, for example, a joint statement by Indonesia and Malaysia, with Singapore taking note of the situation, attempted to deny that the Straits of Malacca, the second busiest strait in the world after the English Channel, was subject to this regime.

Although this statement was ultimately to no avail, nevertheless it serves to show that the new balance of rights and duties provided by the 1982 UNCLOS in relation to these extensions to coastal States' jurisdictions has not always been supported in subsequent State practice in these areas. Indonesia has also, on at least one occasion recently, initiated a temporary closure of certain straits through its archipelago which are used for international navigation, apparently going against the express injunction on suspension of transit passage by States bordering these straits (Art 44).

Another example of the quantitative increase of coastal States' sovereignty and jurisdiction concerns the increased distance of the fisheries jurisdiction of the coastal State from around 12 nm or so in the late 1960s and early 1970's, under customary international law, to an accepted limit of 200 nm under both customary and conventional law by the time UNCLOS was opened for signature on 10 December 1982, with many States having already provided for the exercise of such jurisdiction in their national legislation, even before the final agreement was made allowing for the extension of coastal States' fisheries jurisdiction to 200 nm in the form of the EEZ under Part V of the convention.

Perhaps even more important than the quantitative increase in the sovereign rights and jurisdictions over fisheries and other natural resources within the 200 nm EEZ is the qualitative increase in coastal States' jurisdiction over such activities, particularly fishing. Apart from exercising almost sole discretion over the right to provide access to surplus fisheries resources within its own EEZ (Arts 61 and 62(2)), the coastal State can require that nationals of other States fishing in its EEZ shall comply with conservation and other measures including those concerning the licensing of fishermen, fishing vessels and equipment (Art 62(4)(a)), species to be caught and quotas for each species (Art 62(4)(b)), fishing seasons, areas and types of vessel and gear used (Art 62(4)(c)), the age and size of fish (Art 62(4)(d)), and information on the vessels themselves (Art 62(4)(e)). All of these amount to a significant reduction in the flag State's jurisdiction over its own registered fishing vessels that operate in the EEZs of other States, in favour of the coastal State jurisdiction.

In conclusion, therefore, it is possible to state that, while the provisions of the 1982 UNCLOS certainly attempt to maintain the balance between coastal and flag State jurisdiction in the case of navigation through territorial waters and international straits, the provision of new sovereign rights and jurisdictions over fishing activities in particular have created a new balance in this area, which is heavily tilted towards the coastal State, both in quantitative and qualitative terms.

Question 33

The Kingdom of Mungo and the Republic of Jerry are neighbouring coastal States, located adjacent to one another. As a consequence of recent developments in the law of the sea, both these countries have each claimed a 200 nautical mile (nm) Exclusive Economic Zone (EEZ) and 250 nm continental shelf for themselves. Both countries have ratified all four of the 1958 Geneva Conventions on the Law of the Sea. In addition to this, Mungo has also ratified the 1982 UN Convention on the Law of the Sea (1982 UNCLOS). Jerry, on the other hand, has signed, but not yet ratified, the 1982 Convention.

In early 1994, Tom a national of the Republic of Jerry, who owns and captains a fishing boat registered with, and flying the flag of, the Kingdom of Mungo, was caught fishing without a licence outside the 200 nm Jerry EEZ, but within the limits of the 250 nm Jerry continental shelf. Tom's fishing boat, the *Maria del Mar*, was arrested at the scene and towed back to a port in Jerry, where it was impounded by the Jerry fishing authority and put up for sale by auction. Tom is detained by the same authority and forced, after many hours of severe interrogation and veiled threats against the safety of his family (who still live in Jerry), to confess to the charge that he had been fishing without a licence within the 200 nm Jerry EEZ, rather than outside of it. Tom is then sentenced to five years' imprisonment, without leave to appeal.

Discuss the international legal issues that are raised by Tom's case.

Answer plan

This is perhaps the most complex, and therefore the most difficult, of the problem essay questions in this chapter, due to a number of reasons:

- first, this problem does not merely raise issues in respect of the law of the sea. Familiar questions in relation to the applicable sources of international law, whether customary or conventional, and the international law of treaties (specifically Art 18 of the 1969 Vienna Convention) are coupled with issues arising from State responsibility (see Chapter 10) and possibly even international human rights law (see Chapter 12);
- secondly, within the law of the sea itself, the issues raised by problem require some extensive analysis of the 1982 UNCLOS, especially Part V on the EEZ.

In this problem, the relevant issues may be discussed in this order:

(a) first, there should be a determination of whether the States of Mungo and Jerry are bound on these issues by customary international law, the four 1958 Geneva Conventions, or the 1982 UNCLOS, or a combination of any of these sources of the law of the sea;

(b) secondly, assuming that the applicable source of international law in relation to a coastal State's rights and duties within its EEZ is either covered by Part V of the 1982 UNCLOS or customary international law in accordance with Part V of the 1982 UNCLOS, a detailed analysis should be conducted of Part V, to see whether Jerry has the jurisdiction to arrest, impound and auction Tom's boat, the *Maria del Mar*;

(c) thirdly, should Jerry have acted beyond its rights and jurisdictions under the 1982 UNCLOS in respect of Tom's boat, then the possibility of Mungo making a claim, on the basis of State responsibility, for the arrest and disposal of the *Maria del Mar* should be raised. A possible complication here is Tom's continuing nationality with Jerry, which may negate the *locus standi* for Mungo's claim; and

(d) fourthly, does the Jerry authority's treatment of Tom amount to a breach of Jerry's international obligations for the protection of the human rights of its own citizens. If this is the case, then to whom is the duty owed under international law: Tom? – or

Mungo? – or even to the international community of States as a whole?

Answer

Before we begin our analysis of the international legal issues raised by this problem, it should be noted that it does not merely raise issues in respect of the law of the sea. Familiar questions in relation to the applicable sources of international law, whether customary or conventional, and the international law of treaties, specifically Arts 18 and 30 of the Vienna Convention on the Law of Treaties 1969; are coupled with issues arising from State responsibility and possibly even international human rights law.

The position in relation to the applicable source of the law of the sea as between Mungo and Jerry is provided by Art 30(4)(b) of the Vienna Convention, which is widely regarded as embodying the position under customary international law in this respect. This states that, as between a State party to both treaties and a State party to only one of the treaties, the treaty to which both States are party governs their mutual rights and obligations. Thus, it would appear to be the case that, at least in respect of international treaty law, it is the relevant provisions of the 1958 Conventions that are applicable to both these States. This position, however, creates a dilemma because the legal question which has arisen here relates to the limits of the exercise of enforcement jurisdiction on the part of the coastal State within its exclusive economic zone (EEZ), a maritime zone of jurisdiction which is not provided for anywhere within the four 1958 Geneva Conventions.

Any such legal question will need to answered by recourse to the legal regime for the EEZ as established under customary international law; the 1982 Convention itself having not yet entered into force in early 1994. (The 1982 UNCLOS entered into force for its State parties on 16 November 1994, one year after the deposit of the 60th instrument of ratification, that of Guyana, in accordance with Art 308(1).) The circumstances under which the EEZ regime developed in custom (that is, mainly through widespread State practice during the negotiations towards the 1982 UNCLOS, between 1973 and 1982), which eventually provided for the inclusion of this new *sui generis* legal regime of the EEZ, suggests that many of the provisions in Part V of the 1982 UNCLOS are, in fact, in accordance with the customary legal regime on the EEZ. This enables us to apply these provisions as between Mungo and Jerry, unless certain specific customary rules are deemed to have developed in a different way within State practice accepted as law.

Another reason why the application of the 1982 UNCLOS is appropriate in these circumstances is the fact that, under Art 18 of the 1969 Vienna Convention, both Jerry (under Art 18(a)) and Mungo (under Art 18(b)) appear to be under an obligation not to defeat the object and purpose of a treaty which they have signed and ratified prior to its entry into force. This obligation would clearly seem to apply in these circumstances in relation to the 1982 UNCLOS.

Having determined that the applicable source of the law of the sea between Mungo and Jerry is the 1982 UNCLOS, a detailed analysis needs to be conducted of Part V on the EEZ, to determine whether Jerry has the jurisdiction to arrest, impound and auction Tom's boat, the *Maria del Mar*.

Article 56(1) provides Jerry with sovereign rights for the purpose of exploring and exploiting the living and non-living natural resources of the 200 nm EEZ that it can claim under Art 57. Articles 61 and 62 of Part V further provide for the coastal State's conservation and management duties. In particular, Art 62(4) expressly requires the nationals of other States fishing in the EEZ to comply with the laws and regulations established by the coastal State in relation to nearly all aspects of such fishing activity, from the licensing of fishermen (Art 62(4)(a)) to enforcement procedures (Art 62(4)(k)). Article 73(1) confirms this enforcement jurisdiction on the part of the coastal State (subject to certain conditions on the prompt release of vessels and their crews (Art 73(2)), no imprisonment or corporal punishment penalties for the violations of fisheries laws (Art 73(3)), and notification of the flag State (Art 73(4)).

Thus, it would appear that the sovereign rights accorded to Jerry under the EEZ legal regime both under conventional and customary international law include the possibility of the exercise of enforcement jurisdiction in the case of non-compliance with its fisheries conservation and management laws by foreign nationals.

However, the legitimacy of the Jerry authority's arrest of the *Maria del Mar* is complicated by at least one major difficulty: the fact that it took place in the high seas beyond the 200 nm Jerry EEZ, albeit within the 250 nm Jerry continental shelf. Under Art 116, all States have the right for their nationals to fish on the high seas subject certain conditions (Art 116(a)–(c)) and the duty to conserve the living resources of the high seas (Art 117). Thus, the exercise of Jerry's EEZ authority outside the Jerry EEZ, in absence of any multilateral or bilateral treaty arrangements providing for such enforcement jurisdiction, is arguably in breach of international law, which provides that such jurisdiction can only be exercised by the flag State of the fishing vessel concerned.

On the other hand, a further complication in this respect is the fact that Tom, the owner and captain of the fishing vessel concerned, is a Jerry national. The question arises of whether the Jerry fishery authority can enforce any fishing laws applicable to their own fishermen as their flag State, both within and beyond the Jerry EEZ, on Tom as well. The answer to this question would appear to be in the negative, as Tom's boat, the *Maria del Mar*, is registered with, and flies the flag of, Mungo. However, the relevant provisions of the 1982 UNCLOS (Arts 62(4) and 117) are ambiguous in this respect, as they do not distinguish adequately between the nationality of individual citizens and vessels flying the flag of the State concerned.

Yet another complication may arise if Tom had been fishing for sedentary species as defined by Art 77(4) in Part VI on the continental shelf and not included in Part V on the EEZ. Article 77(1) provides the Jerry with sovereign rights for the exploring and exploiting of such species. Thus, Jerry's sovereign rights over these living natural resources on the seabed may provide it with the requisite enforcement jurisdiction within the 250 nm Jerry continental shelf in which Tom was indeed arrested. This scenario seems less plausible, though, when we consider the later actions of the Jerry fishery authority in getting Tom to confess to fishing within the 200 nm Jerry EEZ.

Should Jerry have acted beyond its rights and jurisdictions under the 1982 UNCLOS in respect of Tom's boat, then the possibility of Mungo making a claim on the basis of State responsibility for the arrest and disposal of the *Maria del Mar* is raised. A possible complication here is Tom's continuing nationality with Jerry, which may negate the *locus standi* for Mungo's claim. On the other hand, however, Mungo may be able to claim nationality over Tom's boat as it is registered with, and flies the flag of, Mungo. Under Art 91 of the 1982 UNCLOS, ships have the nationality of the State whose flag they are entitled to fly, provided there is a genuine link between the State and the ship concerned.

The required elements for State responsibility on the part of Jerry for the arrest of the *Maria del Mar* consist of a breach of an international obligation binding upon Jerry, whether by act or omission, attributable to the State of Jerry, which has a negative impact upon Mungo's rights, although not necessarily resulting in actual damage. It would seem from the above discussion of the facts of this case that Jerry has fulfilled all these criteria, in the sense that: (a) the arrest was beyond the 200 nm Jerry EEZ limit and therefore illegal; (b) the arrest by the Jerry fishery authority is definitely attributable to the Jerry State; and (c) Mungo has suffered the loss of one of its registered vessels. The *Chorzow Factory* case (1928) is but one among many cases that provide recognition of the requirement to make reparations for the breach of an international obligation giving rise to State responsibility.

Finally, did the Jerry fishery authority's treatment of Tom amount to a breach of Jerry's international obligations for the protection of the human rights of its own citizens. If this is the case, then to whom is the duty owed under international law – Tom? – or Mungo? – or even the international community of States as a whole?

It should be noted that one of the greatest developments in public international law since the Second World War is the recognition by States of their international legal obligation to ensure the protection of the individual human rights of their citizens, often from themselves. This represents a unique development in public international law in the sense that it provides the possibility of the enforcement of an individual's human rights against his or her own State, and therefore constrains the notion of absolute sovereignty of a State within its own territorial jurisdiction.

Such obligations can now be found in both treaty and customary international as well in as other non-binding, but highly influential instruments, such as the 1948 Universal Declaration of Human Rights. The Universal Declaration provided the impetus for the acceptance of human rights as part of customary international law and was recognised as such by a US court in the case of *Filartiga v Peña-Irala* (1980). It also spawned more comprehensive treaty regimes such as the International Covenant on Civil and Political Rights (ICCPR) 1966, which entered into force in 1976 and now has at least 132 party States (as at 1 January 1996).

Unlike the Declaration, however, the ICCPR 1966 is a legally binding treaty, and party States are legally bound to give effect to its provisions. Although it is not known whether Jerry or Mungo are bound by its provisions, it is at least arguable that, given the fundamental nature of its provisions and the large number of States party to it, the ICCPR is binding upon both these States under customary international law. In particular, Art 9(1) of the ICCPR provides for the right to liberty, and its corollary, the right to be free from arbitrary arrest or detention. This obligation may have been breached by Jerry in respect of Tom's apparently false imprisonment in contravention of its fisheries laws, itself a possible breach of Art 73(3) of the 1982 UNCLOS, which requires that penalties for such contravention do not include imprisonment or corporal punishment.

Furthermore, should both Jerry and Mungo have agreed on a reciprocal basis to submit to the procedure for inter State complaints under Art 41 of the ICCPR, it may be open for Mungo to bring such an inter State complaint against Jerry for its treatment of Tom.

In conclusion, there are several possible legal bases for State responsibility on the part of Jerry for its treatment of Tom and the *Maria del Mar* which may be claimed by Mungo, as well as the possibility of Tom receiving some form of legal redress from Jerry itself for the manifestly unjustifiable manner in which he has been treated.

CHAPTER 10

STATE RESPONSIBILITY

Introduction

Almost by definition, questions of State responsibility arise whenever a State is alleged to be in breach of an international legal obligation that applies to that State. In reality, however, as one might expect in an international community of ostensibly sovereign and equal States, few States are inclined readily to accept the notion of responsibility for their actions when they are alleged to have negatively affected the rights of another State. It should therefore be no surprise to any student of public international law that this subject is among the more complex in the field of public international law generally. Almost every aspect of the general rule that a breach of an international obligation binding upon a State gives rise to the international responsibility of that State has been challenged at one time or another.

Another clear indicator of the difficulties to which the issue of State responsibility gives rise lies in the lack of any successful attempt so far to codify this particular area of public international law. The various rules that have thus far been deemed acceptable by States are to be found solely in within the domain of general or customary international law.

Mention should always be made of the draft articles on State Responsibility that have been developed over a number of years by the International Law Commission (ILC), the august body charged with the task of promoting the progressive codification of international law. However, the fact that the draft articles that have thus far been developed have still not been found to be agreeable among States, such that the ILC can proceed to the next stage of proposing the articles in the form of a draft convention for consideration by the international community of States, is an eloquent testimony to the problems that beset this area of public international law. While they serve as a useful reference point, perhaps in the same vein as judicial decisions and the writings of eminent publicists, as a subsidiary means of determining the law (Art 38(1)(d) of the Statute of the International Court of Justice 1945), it is currently not possible to attribute anything further in the way of a legal imperative to the ILC draft articles.

In the face of such complexity, and arguably uncertainty, in this area of public international law, students should be clear in their minds of the parameters of the discussion and the broad issues that continuously arise, rather than becoming confused with the more sophisticated nuances of the academic debate in this area, and thereby miss the wood for the trees.

In line with the above point, it is important to note that State responsibility issues can arise in any situation where the rights of one State are negatively affected by the acts or omissions of another State. This is most clearly seen in a case where activities within one State cause transboundary environmental damage or harm in the territory of another State. Such claims of transfrontier environmental harm, however, are notoriously difficult to prove. Indeed it may be said that the whole area of international environmental treaty law has grown from the difficulty of attributing State responsibility to actions or omissions by one State which have harmful or damaging impacts on the environment of another State. (See Chapter 11, International Environmental Law.)

Checklist

When answering questions on the international law of State responsibility, students should note the following points:
- because issues of State responsibility arise whenever there is an allegation of a breach of an international obligation, such issues may crop up in nearly any problem question where such a claim can be justifiably made;
- the various elements that comprise the rules on State responsibility are, in each case, subject to challenge as to their possible interpretation. This is a consequence of the failure thus far of any codification exercise in this subject;
- conversely, there are numerous case law examples that a student can utilise in order to support one type of interpretation or another in any particular situation;

- the student must be familiar with the main elements that are required to establish international responsibility, *viz*, an illegal act or omission of a binding legal obligation, attributable to the State, which gives rise to consequent liability to provide either reparation or some other form of satisfaction to the injured State; and
- Finally, the student should be aware that, although the vast majority of case law involving issues of State responsibility concern either the ill treatment of foreign nationals or their property, or the expropriation of said foreign owned property, usually by some expropriation or nationalisation exercise on the part of the host State, these are not the only types of headings under which claims that may give rise to international responsibility can be made.

Question 34

John is a citizen of Capitalia. He lives in mineral rich Neocolonia, where he owns a house and is the managing director of TINCO (NC), a company that mines tin. TINCO (NC) is a wholly owned subsidiary of TINCO Limited, a Capitalian company whose capital assets and main source of income consist only of TINCO (NC) and its earnings.

Until recently, Neocolonia was ruled by a repressive military junta. A revolution took place in 1990, bringing to power a revolutionary government committed to restoring traditional values and national pride.

During the revolution, a crowd of pro-revolutionary supporters attended a mass meeting at which one of the revolutionary leaders called on them to demonstrate their commitment to the revolution 'by attacking all aspects of the collapsing, corrupt regime and its foreign supporters'. Immediately, groups of the supporters, inspired by the fervour of the moment, went out and damaged much foreign property, including the headquarters of TINCO (NC), which were set on fire by a petrol bomb.

Two weeks after the new revolutionary government came to power, police came to the new premises to which TINCO (NC) had temporarily moved with the archives of the company that had been saved from the fire. They arrested John and seized and evacuated the building.

John was treated well but held in solitary confinement for four days without any charge being brought against him, before being deported to Capitalia, after sustained diplomatic protests from the Capitalian government that he be released. He was not allowed to take any personal belongings or property with him. Upon enquiring as to what would become of his house, he was informed that, due to its pleasant location, one of the revolutionary leaders, together with her family, had occupied it in the name of the new revolutionary government. A Neocolonian revolutionary government decree also declared that all shares in TINCO (NC) were now the property of the recently established Natural Resources Development Organisation.

Your services have been retained as the legal advisor to John and TINCO Limited. They seek your advice on the violations of international law for which Neocolonia may be held responsible, and what remedies may be available to them.

Answer plan

This problem question concerns the two main areas that have traditionally raised issues of State responsibility: the ill treatment of foreign nationals or their property (usually individuals); and the expropriation (or nationalisation) of foreign owned property (usually companies). The international case law on State responsibility is replete with examples on both these issues. It is important here to choose cases which are pertinent to the situations of John and TINCO Limited, rather than adopting a 'scatter gun' approach to the problem.

Attention should also be paid to the criteria that need to be fulfilled in relation to any claim of international responsibility on the part of a State. These criteria encompass the following questions:
- whether the alleged breach of an international obligation is binding on the State concerned. A related question to this is whether a requirement of culpa or fault is attached to the notion of what constitutes a breach of an international

obligation. Opinion has traditionally been divided on this issue, but recent writing and the ILC draft articles appear to be moving to the notion that fault is not required, and therefore responsibility is allocated on the basis of risk, rather than fault. In other words, an objective rather than subjective test seems to be preferred, although this is by no means certain in its application;
- whether the act or omission which allegedly violated an international obligation is attributable to the State concerned. This issue is especially pertinent here in relation to whether the activities of the 'pro-revolutionary supporters' may be attributable to the new revolutionary government for the purpose of any claim to State responsibility on behalf of John or TINCO Limited;
- whether, if the alleged breach is proven and attributable to the State concerned, reparation in the form of compensation or some other form of satisfaction is required; and
- whether, if there is an alleged expropriation of a foreign company's property or assets, compensation for this expropriation should be forthcoming, and whether this compensation needs to meet an international minimum standard or conform to the prevailing standard for national treatment of the expropriating country.

Answer

This problem question concerns the two main areas that have traditionally raised issues of State responsibility: the ill treatment of foreign nationals or their property (in this case, John); and the expropriation (or nationalisation) of foreign owned property (in this case, TINCO Limited).

Taking John's case first, the main issue is whether the Capitalian government is able to make a claim against the new Neocolonian revolutionary government on John's behalf, under the doctrine of State responsibility, for his ill treatment at the hands of the Neocolonian police force and the loss of his house, other property and personal belongings.

As John is a citizen of Capitalia, there should be no problem in Capitalia making a claim on his behalf on the basis that

Neocolonia owes Capitalia an obligation under international law to ensure the protection of foreign nationals and their property from harm and non-interference within Neocolonian territory. It should be noted, however, that the *Nottebohm* case (1955) appears to require a 'genuine link' between the person claiming the nationality of the protecting State and the State concerned for the purpose of claiming protection under international law, although the *Flegenheimer Claim* (1958) casts doubt on the extent of this requirement to show a 'genuine link', and the presumption of this requirement is therefore uncertain.

On the basis of the facts laid out, there can be no doubt that the general rule requiring the protection of a foreign national's physical well being and property has been breached in this situation. The question is whether the new Neocolonian revolutionary government is responsible for the acts of its police force in their ill treatment and deportation of John, and for the act of the revolutionary leader in appropriating John's house in Neocolonia. In both instances, much case law exists to suggest that the principle of attributability of their actions to the Neocolonian State is fulfilled. Any act or omission of an organ of a State is to be attributed to that State so long as the organ was acting in that capacity at the time of the act or omission. In the *Youmans Claim* (1926), even soldiers who were alleged to have acted *ultra vires* of their own orders in killing three US nationals were held to have given rise to the international responsibility of their State (Mexico). In *Yeager v Iran* (1987), on facts very similar to the treatment of John in this case, Yeager was detained by so called 'revolutionary guards' whose actions were alleged not to be attributable to the new government of Iran. Nevertheless, Iran was held internationally responsible and obliged to pay compensation both for the loss of his personal property and even loss of salary due to his expulsion. In John's case, therefore, the actions of both the police and the revolutionary leader, as recognised organs of the new revolutionary government, would appear to give rise to international responsibility on the part of Neocolonia.

Such international responsibility for a breach of an international obligation gives rise to the secondary obligation to make reparation for the breach, and this has been confirmed both in the case law (*Chorzow Factory (Merits) (Jurisdiction)* (1928)) and Part II of the ILC draft articles on State responsibility.

Turning to TINCO Limited, the issue of whether the actions of the crowd of pro-revolutionary supporters, urged on by a revolutionary leader, give rise to Neocolonian State responsibility in damaging the headquarters of TINCO (NC), its subsidiary in Neocolonia, is more difficult to answer. The case law suggests that, where the foreign national has suffered harm or loss to his property at the hands of private persons with no ostensible connection to a government organ, and which cannot be shown to give rise to the responsibility of the authorities concerned, then a lack of protection cannot be established. The *Noyes Claim (US v Panama)* (1933), and to a certain extent the *Home Missionary Society Claim* (1920), which both concerned loss of life and damage to property by local people rather than State officials, would tend to support this conclusion. Even more pertinent are the cases of *Short v Iran* (1987) and the *United States Diplomatic and Consular Staff in Tehran* (1980), in which it was held that the acts of the supporters of a revolution (as opposed to its agents) cannot be attributed to the government, just as the acts of supporters of an existing government are not attributable to the government. Thus, it may be difficult for Capitalia to claim State responsibility on the part of Neocolonia for the damage sustained by TINCO Limited, through its subsidiary TINCO (NC), due to the actions of a rabble.

On the other hand, in respect of the expropriation by the new Neocolonian Natural Resources Development Organisation of all TINCO (NC) shares through a Neocolonian revolutionary government decree, it would seem that TINCO Limited has a better case for claiming that this expropriation, if adjudged lawful, provides Capitalia with a claim for appropriate compensation on TINCO Limited's behalf. Although there are still circumstances whereby an expropriation is considered unlawful, for example, where it is obviously undertaken for private gain rather than public purposes, or is inherently discriminatory against the nationals of particular State only, as in the case of *BP v Libya* (1974), the act itself is now considered as a right inherent in sovereignty, and, therefore, *prima facie* lawful, provided the conditions established by international law are met.

Furthermore, the requirement of compensation is now regarded as a corollary to the lawful exercise of a State of the expropriation of foreign owned property or other assets, such as shares. It is supported by numerous examples of case law and several important and well supported UN General Assembly resolutions, which, though, in themselves, not legally binding, nevertheless appear to be evidence of what is accepted by States as the position under customary international law. Among these General Assembly resolutions are the 1962 Resolution on Permanent Sovereignty over Natural Resources (Resolution 1803 (XVII)), the 1974 Declaration on the Establishment of a New International Economic Order (NIEO) (Resolution 3201 (S-VI)), and the 1974 Charter of the Economic Rights and Duties of States (Resolution 3281 (XXIX)).

These General Assembly resolutions affirm the legality of expropriation, but, more controversially, the ones agreed later (in 1974) provide that the standard by which to measure the compensation that is required to be paid is solely by reference to national law, that is, attempting to implement a so called national standard of treatment. This view is fiercely opposed by many Western industrialised countries which demand the standard of compensation to be of an international minimum standard. This is perhaps the most relevant issue in relation to TINCO Limited, as it appears that the expropriation itself is not unlawful given that it is for public policy purposes under the ambit of the Natural Resources Development Organisation, and, from the facts, there is no evidence of any discrimination against Capitalian nationals *per se*. However, international responsibility may arise on the part of the Neocolonian revolutionary government should it fail to provide adequate compensation for the expropriation of the TINCO (NC) shares, as this may be seen to be an unlawful expropriation, as was the case in *Starrett Housing Corp v Iran* (1983).

Therefore, the issue here turns on whether the appropriate standard of compensation to be applied is that of an international minimum standard or the national treatment standard, which would usually result in a lower amount of compensation. Many industrialised countries still favour the so called 'Hull formula' that compensation must be 'prompt, adequate and effective'. In practice, however, national courts and international tribunals have reached sensible compromise solutions about the levels of compensation, rather than fully adopting one or the other of the two opposing standards. For example, in the *Southern Pacific Properties (Middle East) Ltd v Arab Republic of Egypt* case (1993), the arbitral tribunal held that 'fair' compensation was required for lawful compensation.

Finally, both John and TINCO Limited need to be advised about the important initial requirement of the exhaustion of local remedies for any claims they may wish to make against the State organs and individuals in Neocolonia before representations are made to the Capitalian government to take up claims for State responsibility on their behalf against the Neocolonian revolutionary government at the international plane. Failure to do so may result in the claims by the Capitalian government on their behalf being rejected by the international tribunal or commission established to hear these claims on the grounds of non-exhaustion of local remedies. This is exactly what occurred in the *Ambatielos Arbitration (Greece v UK)* (1956), where the deemed failure of the individual claimant, a Greek national, to exhaust the local remedies available to him through the British municipal judicial system was held to result in the rejection of the claims at the international level brought on his behalf by Greece.

Question 35

Under what circumstances does international law recognise a right of States to espouse claims of their nationals whose economic interests have been harmed in another State?

Answer plan

This is a fairly straightforward essay question on State responsibility that focuses on the specific issue of harm to the economic interests of foreign nationals.

The economic interests and activities of foreign nationals abroad can usefully be divided into two different categories for the purposes of this essay:
(a) the first category covers the economic interests and activities of individuals within a foreign country, which may be harmed due to the action of some State organ. In these circumstances, subject to the general rule requiring the exhaustion of local remedies, claims can arguably only be made once a defect in

the foreign administrative machinery or judicial system has been identified, such that the individual is not able to gain adequate redress for the perceived harm or damage to his or her economic interests;
(b) the second category deals with the issue of foreign investment, either by foreign companies in establishing local subsidiaries within another country, or through foreign ownership of shares in local firms or local subsidiaries of foreign companies. In these circumstances, again subject to the general rule on the need to exhaust local remedies, the issue may well be one of the appropriate compensation to be paid should a lawful expropriation exercise be carried out by the host State.

Some discussion should also be entered into about the nature of the economic or property interests which may give rise to a claim should they be harmed or damaged in any way.

Answer

In so far as the harm to the economic interests of their nationals in another State amounts to violations of international obligation, international law certainly recognises that a State may espouse claims of State responsibility against that other State on behalf of its nationals. These claims, however, are subject to the fulfilment of a certain number of specified criteria under the doctrine of State responsibility, and it is to a discussion of these criteria that we must turn in answering this question.

Before we enter into this discussion, it may be useful to define the circumstances under which claims on behalf of a national may be made by a claimant State against another, respondent State under the international law of State responsibility. First, a breach of an obligation binding on both the States concerned which results in some negative impact or denial of the rights of claimant State must be present. This denial of the claimant State's rights is usually in the form of some injury or loss to the person who is a national of the claimant State, or to his property or economic interests.

Another important area deals with the loss of some economic interests on the part of the claimant State's nationals, whether they be individuals or companies, in the form of their ownership of property, shares or other assets affected by a lawful expropriation or nationalisation exercise within the respondent State. This latter area is technically not an issue of State responsibility, but merely one of assessing the right amount of compensation for the lawful expropriation of property or other economic interests.

Secondly, this breach must also be attributable to an organ of the respondent State in order to sustain a claim under State responsibility. In addition to these two major elements of State responsibility, certain other requirements also need to be met, for example, that local remedies in the respondent State have been exhausted (*Ambatielos Arbitration* case (1956)), and the link between the claimant State and the nationals on whose behalf it purports to be acting is genuine (*Nottebohm* case (1955)).

The economic interests and activities of foreign nationals abroad can usefully be divided into two different categories for the purposes of this essay:

(a) the first category covers the economic interests and activities of individuals within a foreign country, whether persons or companies, which may be harmed due to the action of some State organ. In these circumstances, subject to the general rule requiring the exhaustion of local remedies, claims can arguably only be made once a defect in the foreign administrative machinery or judicial system has been identified such that the individual is not able to gain adequate redress for the perceived harm or damage to his or her economic interests; and

(b) the second category deals with the issue of foreign investment, either by foreign companies in establishing local subsidiaries within another country, or through foreign ownership of shares in local firms or local subsidiaries of foreign companies. In these circumstances, again subject to the general rule on the need to exhaust local remedies, the issue may well be one of the appropriate compensation to be paid should a lawful expropriation exercise be carried out by the host State. This is technically not an issue of State responsibility *per se* any longer, as the concept of expropriation itself is lawful provided it is accompanied by appropriate compensation. However, should the expropriation be carried out in an unlawful manner, then the issue of whether State responsibility arises returns. An expropriation may be deemed unlawful due to at least four reasons: (i) lack of a public purpose; (ii) discrimination against the nationals of one State (*BP v Libya* (1974)); (iii) breach of treaty obligation (*Certain German Interests in Polish Upper Silesia* case (1926)); and (iv) the failure to provide any compensation or inadequate compensation.

Focusing on the first category, that of individuals within a foreign country, the combination of the twin requirements of a breach or violation of international law and the need to exhaust local remedies suggests that the mere loss of, or harm to, the economic interests of the individual does not give rise to any possible claim by the national's State on the basis of State responsibility on the international plane. Thus, State responsibility only arises where there is a further denial or wrongful treatment of the foreign national concerned such that he, she or it cannot obtain the requisite legal redress for the loss or harm that has been sustained using the usual domestic administrative or judicial remedies available.

However, should such a situation arise, it may be seen that international law allows the property and economic interests to be the part of the claim for reparations under the doctrine of State responsibility. For example, in the case of *Yeager v Iran* (1987), once it was held that Iran was responsible under international law for the unlawful expulsion of the claimant, then reparations in the form of compensation were provided, not just for the loss of personal property left behind when he was unlawfully expelled, but also for his loss of salary – clearly a purely economic interest which was nevertheless negatively affected by his expulsion. On the other hand, in a case involving a fellow employee of BHI, an American company, that of *Rankin v Iran* (1987), once it was held that his evacuation was not as a result of an unlawful expulsion, his claim for either loss of personal property or salary was dismissed.

Moving to the second category, that is the issue of foreign investment in the form of the property and assets of subsidiary companies and shares in these or other local firms, in *Starrett Housing Corp v Iran* (1983), the effective deprivation of the use, control and benefits of the claimant American company's property rights in a subsidiary company was held to amount to an unlawful expropriation under international law, not merely of property rights in the subsidiary, but also contractual rights that were not able to be exercised upon its expropriation. This case, therefore, also provides for an argument to the effect that claims under State responsibility can include not just property, but other economic rights too.

The issue of whether the shareholders of an expropriated company, as opposed to the company itself, may be able to rely on the State of their nationality to make a claim for the international responsibility on the part of the expropriating State is considerably more uncertain. In the *Barcelona Traction* case (1970), an attempt by Belgium to bring a claim against Spain for alleged injuries suffered by a Canadian registered company on the grounds that the majority of the shareholders in the company (about 88%) were Belgians was rejected, as the rights of the company were to be regarded as separate from those of the shareholders, despite the fact that any damage suffered by the company might impact negatively on the value of the shareholding. However, it is apparently not the case that the ICJ was denying a claim based on economic interest, but merely noting that the rightful claimant State in this case could only be Canada, as the State of registration of the company concerned. Furthermore, if a separate and exclusive right of the shareholders is allegedly damaged, then the State of nationality of the shareholders may be able make a claim on their behalf under State responsibility. The only ways in which the State of nationality of the shareholders could otherwise make a claim for damage suffered by the company itself is: (a) if the company itself no longer exists; or (b) if the State of nationality of the company is incapable (as opposed to unwilling) to make a claim; or (c) if it is the State of nationality of the company that caused the harm or injury in the first place.

In conclusion, therefore, international law clearly recognises the right of States to espouse claims of their nationals whose economic interests have been harmed, but only when a breach of international law has occurred in relation to the harm caused to these interests such that it may give rise to international responsibility on the part of the State which has harmed these economic interests.

Question 36

Jones is a citizen of Mainland. He is an expert in the archaeology of Outland. On one of his regular visits to Outland, he is arrested, accused and convicted of espionage. The only evidence against him is a signed confession to the crime. Jones claimed in court that the signature on the confession is merely a crude attempt to copy it from his passport. He further argues that the charges against him are wholly imaginary. In finding him guilty, the court dismisses his allegations concerning the falsification of his signature and the imaginary nature of his crimes as defamatory of the State and sentences him to life imprisonment, without leave to appeal against sentence. The court also orders the confiscation of his property, which includes some very expensive equipment used for his archaeological work in Outland.

Two years later, after much diplomatic pressure from the Mainland government, Jones is released. He feels that he has been treated most unjustly and seeks your advice on what possible legal remedies may be available to him.

Assuming that neither Mainland nor Outland is party to any international human rights treaty, what legal advice would you give Jones?

Answer plan

This problem question deals mainly with the frequently occurring situation involving State responsibility, namely the ill treatment of foreign nationals and their property and other economic interests.

As such, it allows the student to elaborate on all the basic requirements for a claim of international responsibility, as well as to enter into an extended discussion of some of the more interesting points on the specific duty of protection over foreign nationals.

The answer should begin with a rundown of all the main elements of the doctrine of State responsibility before drawing out the issues raised in the problem and commenting on them with a view to ascertaining whether they strengthen or weaken the case on behalf of Jones.

The questions raised by this problem are as follows:
- whether there has been a violation of an international legal obligation, in the sense of a breach of the duty to protect Jones from ill treatment by organs of the State, and the nature and the extent of this duty under customary international law;
- whether the violation is attributable to Outland, which owes to the States of all the foreign nationals within its territory, a duty to protect foreign nationals from ill treatment;
- whether the secondary requirements of Jones's nationality to Mainland, and the exhaustion by Jones of local remedies within Outland, are satisfied in order to ensure that Mainland can legitimately claim a right of protection on the basis of nationality over Jones, such that it can claim international responsibility on the part of Outland for its ill treatment of Jones and his property;
- whether there are any defences that Outland may be able to argue to mitigate, or even to negate, its international responsibility for the ill treatment of Jones;
- whether reparation in the form of compensation, or some other type of satisfaction, is required once international responsibility has been established; and
- when assessing the amount of compensation that must be paid, what standard should be applied in assessing whether Jones's ill treatment amounts to State responsibility: an international minimum standard or a national standard of treatment.

Answer

As neither Mainland nor Outland is party to any international human rights treaties, Jones must argue that his rights are protected under customary international law, both in relation to any claim made on his behalf by Mainland in respect of State responsibility, and by Jones himself against Outland for its violation of his rights. On the evidence before us, it would seem that Jones has a much better case under customary international law if Mainland were prevailed upon to take up a claim of international responsibility against Outland on his behalf.

Several questions may be raised in respect of the claim for international responsibility made by Mainland against Outland.

First, has there been a violation of an international legal obligation in the sense of a breach of the duty to protect Jones from ill treatment by organs of the State? What is the nature and the extent of this duty under customary international law?

In so far as his conviction was based only on the allegedly falsified confession, it would appear that various State organs of Outland have been at least negligent in their treatment of Jones. However, the burden of proving this alleged lack of proper protection afforded to a foreign national on the part of Outland is one which Jones, and by extension Mainland, as the State making the claim under international law, have to fulfil. In the *Rankin v Iran* case (1987), for example, in respect of the claimant's allegation of illegal expulsion, it was held that a claimant alleging expulsion has the burden of proving the wrongfulness of the expelling State's action; in other words, that it was arbitrary, discriminatory, or otherwise in breach of the State's international obligations

This was also held to be the case in the *Neer Claim* (1926), where it was stated that, in order to constitute an international delinquency, the treatment of a foreign national should amount to an outrage, bad faith, wilful neglect of duty, or to an insufficiency of governmental action so far short of international standards that every reasonable and impartial person would readily recognise its insufficiency. However, such insufficiency could arise from the deficient execution of an intelligent law. The *Roberts Claim* (1926) provides further evidence in favour of a rule requiring an appropriate standard for the administration of justice to be maintained by the legal system of the host State to a foreign national. In the *Roberts Claim*, it was held that the unusually long period of detention without trial and general ill treatment of the claimant gave rise to the international responsibility of Mexico. In the light of these analogous cases, it can be seen that Jones's, and by extension Mainland's, rights were clearly violated under international law by the maladministration of the Outland criminal justice system.

A further issue which may arise concerns the standard of treatment that a foreign national can reasonably expect in the host country. It is submitted here that, in the great majority of awards, as exemplified by the *Neer Claim* (1928), support the view that international law requires States to treat foreign nationals according to an international minimum standard rather than a national standard of treatment akin to that meted out to their own citizens. Therefore, Jones could reasonably have expected to be treated by the State organs of Outland to an international minimum standard.

Secondly, is the violation attributable to Outland, which owes to the States of all the foreign nationals within its territory a duty to protect foreign nationals from ill treatment? Since the violation appears undoubtedly to have been perpetrated by the recognised State organs of Outland – namely the law enforcement and judicial authorities of Outland – in the absence of any special circumstances or times of emergency, such as during an internal civil war or a period of great revolutionary foment, these actions must be considered to be imputable or attributable to Outland for the purposes of any claims of international responsibility against it. Cases such as *Rankin v Iran* (1987) and *Short v Iran* (1987), however, suggest that a general policy encouraging discrimination and ill treatment of foreign nationals is insufficient in itself to be a violation of international law attributable to the State.

Thirdly, are the secondary requirements of Jones's nationality to Mainland and the exhaustion by Jones of local remedies within Outland satisfied in order to ensure that Mainland can legitimately claim a right of protection on the basis of nationality over Jones, such that it can claim international responsibility on the part of Outland for its ill treatment of him and his property? Although the facts of the present case do not allow us to come to a conclusion on these important procedural questions, it is important to note that there is a general need to ascertain that Jones is, in fact, allowed to draw on the protection of Mainland by virtue of his nationality. Although the *Nottebohm* case (1955) suggests that a genuine link between the national and his or her State must be established, this requirement has since been disproved in other cases such as the *Flegenheimer Claim* (1956) and *Salem* (1932). Nevertheless, it is still a procedural requirement that needs to be fulfilled in order for a claim to be made under international law

Fourthly, are there any defences that Outland may be able to argue that mitigate, or even negate, its international responsibility for the ill treatment of Jones? International law recognises that there are circumstances precluding wrongfulness which may allow Outland to claim a valid defence to a charge of unlawful conduct on the part of its State organs, such that it incurs international responsibility. Articles 29–34 of Part I of the ILC draft articles on State responsibility (which are indicative, but not yet ascertained to be a source of customary international law), list a number of these defences, including: (a) the consent of the potential victim State to the commission of an otherwise unlawful act (Art 29); (b) situations where the alleged act violating an international obligation is a legitimate counter measure (Art 30); (c) *force majeure* or some unforeseen event making it materially impossible for the respondent State to fulfil the international obligation allegedly violated (Art 31); (d) State necessity (Art 33); and (e) lawful self-defence (Art 34). None of these defences, however, would seem to fulfilled on the facts of this case.

Finally, are reparations required in the form of compensation, or some other type of satisfaction, once international responsibility has been established? And in assessing the amount of compensation that must be paid, what standard should be applied in assessing whether Jones's ill treatment amounts to State responsibility: an international minimum standard or a national standard of treatment? It is now well established, both in the *Chorzow Factory* case (1928) and incorporated in Part II of the ILC draft articles, that a breach of an international obligation gives rise to a secondary obligation to make reparations, in the form of compensation or some other type of satisfaction. Such reparation can take many forms, but by far the most common is monetary compensation for the loss or injury suffered. In Jones's case, though, he may consider making a claim for reparation in the form of restitution of property unlawfully taken by requiring the return of his very expensive and presumably highly specialised archaeological equipment (as long as it has remained undamaged, of course).

The issue of whether there is an international minimum standard or a national standard of treatment arises again in assessing the amount of compensation that must be paid to Jones for his ill treatment. In this case, the situation is unclear with most arbitral awards attempting to steer a middle ground between the two ends of the spectrum and award a fair amount of compensation to the individual claimant.

Question 37

The population of the State of Arcadia is divided: 80% are of Arcadian origin and 20% of Bognian origin. All are Arcadian citizens. Arcadian and Bognian are separate languages. Last year, there were broadcasts on Arcadian state run TV which denounced 'Bognian vermin who infect decent Arcadian women with AIDS'. There were outbursts of violence between the two communities. These were suppressed by the police. Reports from reputable NGOs have called into question both the impartiality of the police, 98% of whom are of Arcadian origin, and the degree of force used.

The State of Bognia is adjacent to Arcadia. In November 1996, Charlie, a citizen of Bognia, visited his aunt Doris in Elleville, Arcadia. On 12 November, there was a traditional Arcadian parade in Elleville, whose population is mostly of Bognian origin, commemorating the Arcadian defeat of Bognian armies in 824 AD. This parade is always a source of tension between the two communities. On this occasion, 500 police were on duty, and some 50,000 marchers were expected. Arcadians of Bognian origin were advised to stay indoors.

Charlie was not aware of the advice, and went to buy his aunt a bunch of flowers. He was hit on the head by a brick thrown by a marcher of Arcadian origin. The brick had actually been thrown at the window of the florist's shop, which was run by an Arcadian of Bognian origin. While Charlie was on the ground, bleeding profusely, an Arcadian policeman hit Charlie several times with his truncheon, and kicked him out of the way of the marchers. A passer by took Charlie to the local hospital. Four doctors refused to treat him because he was 'Bognian AIDS-infected vermin'. Several hours later, Charlie received emergency treatment from another doctor. The delay in receiving treatment meant that his injuries had more serious consequences than would otherwise have been the case.

Upon his return to Bognia, Charlie sought the advice of the Bognian government in bringing a claim against Arcadia. Arcadia has ratified no human rights treaties.

Advise the government of Bognia.

Answer plan

This problem question raises certain basic issues of the international law on State responsibility, with a focus on a few of the constituent element of responsibility, particularly those concerning the attributability or imputability of actions by individuals to the State in terms of fulfilling claims for State responsibility.

The answer should begin by drawing out the main elements required in order to give rise to a possible claim of State responsibility, before entering into an extended discussion of the issue of attributability or imputability of the actions of individuals to a State. This discussion should encompass the various problems thrown up by the issue of attributability or imputability of individual action on behalf of a State organ.

Among these problems are:

- situations where the exact connection between the individual who perpetrated the loss or injury concerned and the State organ he or she is supposed to represent is unclear;
- the alleged infraction was undertaken in a manner which was *ultra vires* of the actual authority given to the individual by the State organ concerned; and
- the actions of the individuals alleged to have caused the loss or injury are nevertheless argued to be in fulfilment of the standard of care expected of a host State.

Answer

The question to be answered here is whether Bognia has a valid claim under international law against Arcadia under State responsibility on behalf of Charlie, a Bognian citizen. The international law of State responsibility, in its most basic version (which commands general agreement), considers that, if a State violates an international obligation, it bears responsibility for that obligation. Where a State is deemed to have violated such an international legal obligation, this gives rise to apparently serious consequences for it under the international law of State responsibility.

This much is clear from the International Law Commission's (ILC) draft articles on State responsibility, which attempt to codify public international law in this important issue area. Article 1 of the draft articles states that, 'Every internationally wrongful act of a State entails the international responsibility of that State'. Article 3(b) further provides that there is an internationally wrongful act of a State when its 'conduct constitutes a breach of an international obligation of the State.' The conclusion that may reasonably be drawn, upon reading these draft articles in tandem, is that Bognia can claim international responsibility on the part of Arcadia should Bognia be able to show that Arcadia has acted, or omitted to act, in breach of its international obligations towards Bognia in respect of the injuries that Charlie suffered while he was in Arcadia.

This conclusion is strengthened by the recognition of a more general trend which is evident within the ILC draft articles towards an objective formulation of the secondary rule providing for State responsibility. In this respect, it is important to note that the rules of public international law on this issue have moved away from a historical requirement (pre-Second World War) to prove fault as a basis for international responsibility, to the position that States should be responsible for their actions independently of fault. The main reason for dispensing with the need to prove fault is the absence of adequate procedures to establish it. Thus, increasingly, responsibility for result became the accepted form of responsibility for wrongful actions, although not for omissions. Adopting this test in relation to Charlie's injuries, it may be possible to impute international responsibility on the part of Arcadia without needing to show fault on the part of any of the Arcadian authorities actually responsible for his injuries.

This objective definition of a breach of obligation giving rise to State responsibility throws up several different kinds of questions regarding the nature and scope of State responsibility for the violation of an international obligation, the most important of which is: what constitutes a violation of an international obligation? This question can itself be divided into several different component questions, such as: (a) what exactly is the nature of an international obligation such that violation of it may give rise to State responsibility?; (b) can such a violation occur by way of an omission as well as an act on the part of the State?; and (c) is every violation, whether by act or omission of a State, deemed to give rise to responsibility under international law?

The ILC draft articles on State responsibility attempt to provide answers to some of these questions. Article 3, for example, provides that an internationally wrongful act occurs when conduct constituting a breach of an international obligation (whether in the form of an act or omission), and such acts and omissions are attributable to the State. Most publicists on the international law of State responsibility have taken their lead from these points by focusing upon the actions of a State, specifically on what amounts to an internationally wrongful act. This mode of analysis has traditionally taken two approaches: the first concentrating on the attributability of the actions of an individual or group to the State, and the second on the standard of due diligence to be applied in order to ascertain when exactly responsibility arises for the omissions of a State.

This problem raises issues for Bognia which are squarely in the realm of the first issue stated above, namely the attribution of the actions of an individual or group to a State organ in such manner that it may give rise to State responsibility for actions which have caused loss, injury or damage. Various problems are thrown up by the issue of attributability or imputability of individual action on behalf of a State organ.

First, there are situations where the exact connection between the individual who perpetrated the loss or injury concerned and the State organ he or she is supposed to represent is unclear. This is the case here in relation to Charlie, as his actual injury was caused by what appears to be the actions of a private citizen of Arcadia in the form of one of the marchers. However, this initial injury was no doubt exacerbated by the further injuries inflicted upon him by the actions of the policeman and the omissions of the four doctors who refused to treat him. The initial incident, grievous as it was, may not necessarily give rise to questions of

State responsibility in itself, but the latter two events clearly involve issues of the attribution of these individuals – the policeman and the doctors – to the State of Arcadia for purposes of State responsibility.

Focusing on the first incident, this may not necessarily give rise to questions of State responsibility in itself, unless Charlie is unable to obtain adequate redress in the Arcadian judicial or administrative system, such that this may give rise to an issue of the maladministration of justice, which, in turn, provides the grounds for a claim of State responsibility. This was the issue, for example, in the case of *Janes Claim* (1926), where the murderer of an American citizen was notorious within the local district but never apprehended. The omission of the Mexican authorities in not taking the proper steps to apprehend the slayer of Janes was held to give rise to international responsibility on the part of Mexico.

In the aftermath of the Islamic revolution in Iran, a number of cases arose between the USA and Iran concerning this type of issue. For example, in the *US Diplomatic and Consular Staff in Tehran* case (1980) (before the International Court of Justice), it was held that the actions of the militant students who had acted on the exhortations of their supreme religious leader in taking possession of the US Embassy in Tehran by force were nevertheless not to be regarded as actions of official agents or representatives of the official organs of the Iranian State. Nevertheless, the Iranian government was held to have breached its obligations to the USA by omission, through its inaction and consequent failure to take the necessary steps to prevent, deter or otherwise mitigate or stop the takeover of the Embassy. This case appears to provide Charlie with possible grounds for a claim against Arcadia on the basis of a lack of protection afforded to him by the Arcadian authorities.

However, the standard of protection that a foreign national may rely upon is not necessarily as high as one might prefer. For example, in the *Noyes Claim* (1933), it was held that the mere fact that a foreign national has suffered aggression at the hands of private persons, which could have been averted by the presence of a sufficient police force on the spot, does not make a government liable for damages under international law. There must be shown special circumstances from which the responsibility of the authorities arises: either their behaviour in connection with the particular occurrence, or a general failure to comply with their duty to maintain order, to prevent crimes or to prosecute and punish criminals. Thus, in Charlie's case, the facts do not augur well for a convincing argument on his behalf, as it appears that, for responsibility to arise in relation to his initial injuries caused by a private Arcadian citizen, these would have to be imputable to a general failure of the Arcadian public authorities to maintain order. The fact that Arcadians of Bognian origin had been advised to stay indoors arguably further reduces the standard of care to be placed upon the Arcadian authorities for responsibility for Charlie's initial injuries.

Turning now to the latter two events, these clearly involve issues of the attribution to the State of Arcadia for purposes of State responsibility of the acts and omissions of the policeman and the doctors. A distinction may be made between the policeman and the doctors, however, if it were known whether the local hospital where Charlie was taken was a private concern or a government run or supported hospital, in that it may be more difficult to attribute to the Arcadian State for the purposes of State responsibility the actions of privately employed doctors who refused to treat Charlie. Unless this is the case, though, it is arguable that the actions (beating and kicking) and omissions (refusal to treat) of both the policeman and the doctors are attributable to the State of Arcadia as giving rise to international responsibility.

One argument that may be advance by Arcadia in its defence is that the alleged infraction was undertaken in a manner which was *ultra vires* of the actual authority given to the individual by the State organ concerned. This was claimed, for example, in the case of *Youmans Claim* (1926), in which it was argued that a government is not responsible for the acts of officials committed outside of, or exceeding, the powers vested in them. However, this argument was not accepted by the claims commission in that case, and this is arguably also true for the present case involving Charlie. Thus, it would seem that Bognia is able to make a claim for international responsibility on the part of Arcadia for the actions and omissions of agents attached to its State organs even where it is alleged that the actions of these agents have exceeded their powers.

CHAPTER 11

INTERNATIONAL ENVIRONMENTAL LAW

Introduction

This chapter is devoted to a relatively new branch or area of substantive rules of public international law, namely the international law of the environment or international environmental law. As we noted previously in Chapter 10, the two traditional and main areas of substantive public international law on State responsibility are the ill treatment of foreign nationals and expropriation of foreign owned companies. The international law of the environment may be seen in this sense as a developing area of substantive rules for the protection of the environment, the violation of which may ultimately also give rise to State responsibility under international law.

As mentioned above, international environmental law is a relatively new branch of international law. Although there were already more than a few treaties and a certain amount of customary and case law on the broad subject of the environment, particularly with respect to nature conservation, for example, it is generally accepted that a truly international environmental movement, in global terms, only began in 1972 on the occasion of the Stockholm Conference on the Human Environment, which yielded the now famous Stockholm Declaration. Therefore, as mentioned earlier, much of the law is, in fact, to be found in the burgeoning number of environmental treaty regimes that either have been established, or are in the process of being established, in relation to particular environmental problems. Some of these environmental problems or threats have been around for a while and needed urgent attention at the international level. Several others, however, are of more recent pedigree, but nevertheless require prompt action. Significantly, it may be seen that the process of environmental treaty making has progressed beyond the traditional form prevalent in most international treaty making processes, incorporating many innovatory methods designed primarily to facilitate the effective implementation of these treaties. This is especially the case in respect of more recent environmental treaties and instruments.

Another important aspect of international environmental law, which contributes to its development through the treaty making process rather than the formulation of general rules of customary international law, is the specific nature of many modern environmental threats. These require detailed regulation, as opposed to broad guidelines, to combat them effectively. Explicit rules are nevertheless susceptible to simple amendment procedures when based on new scientific information accepted by treaty institutions; all of this, functioning within overall treaty regimes for protection against specific environmental threats, appears to be the accepted pattern of international environmental regulation. Also, in many cases, the need for international co-operation in the identification, monitoring and prevention or control of the environmental problem concerned, tilts the balance towards the negotiation of a treaty regime, based on the institutional co-operation that has already occurred between States, and mitigates against the usually slower accretion of *opinio juris* and States practice that give rise to a customary rule of international law. Thus, international environmental law may be said to be mainly composed of negotiated international environmental agreements on specific subjects, rather than evolving customary international rules. In other words, codified, rather than accumulated, rules prevail. It is imperative, therefore, to develop an analytical framework and criteria for the critical assessment of the effectiveness of these agreements from an institutional perspective.

International environmental agreements contain several important aspects, such as the following, non-exhaustive list which arguably aids States in their efforts to ensure the successful implementation and effectiveness of the environmental treaty regime they have established:

- definitions (of pollution or any other environmental interference);
- substantive obligations for environmental protection against the identified threat or pollution defined within the treaty;

- procedural obligations for consultation, exchange of information and research providing an objective standard for the due diligence test;
- provisions for monitoring the compliance, implementation and enforcement of the procedural and substantive obligations above;
- establishment of international institutions to govern the environmental treaty regime that has been set up;
- simplified treaty amendment procedures to aid progressive development of the regime;
- provisions for State responsibility and liability (if any) for non-compliance with the due diligence requirement, resulting in pollution damage or harm to the interests of another State or the interests of all the States within a treaty regime;
- dispute settlement procedures for the resolution of interpretation and implementation issues; and
- proposals for future action to ensure continued environmental protection from the threats identified.

The progressive development of international environmental treaties incorporating these elements is arguably the main way forward for continuing efforts to establish a truly effective system of global environmental protection under public international law.

It may also be argued that the development of environmental law at the international, European and domestic UK levels reflects the practical application of underlying general principles of law which have evolved in tandem, with rising concern over environmental degradation, and the real and potential threats of such degradation for the survival of humankind. It has been argued that a simplistic description of this relationship would view it as existing on three levels: (1) the application of specific rules; (2) based on accepted general principles; (3) which in turn reflect certain ethical values deemed important enough to be protected. A better view is that there exists a dynamic relationship between rules, principles and ethics, both as to the formulation of the law and as to its implementation and enforcement.

A non-exhaustive list of these general environmental principles would encompass the following:

(a) sustainable development;
(b) 'the polluter pays' principle;

(c) the preventive principle;
(d) the precautionary principle; and
(e) the principle of conservation of shared natural resources.

These principles initially evolved from non-binding intergovernmental declarations, such as the Stockholm Declaration 1972 and its follow up, 20 years later, in the form of the Rio Declaration on Environment and Development 1992, agreed at the UN Conference on Environment and Development (UNCED) held at Rio de Janeiro, Brazil, in June of that year. Another important, but non-binding instrument in this respect is the 1982 UN Charter for Nature, a UN General Assembly resolution. Presently, however, these principles can readily be found in many other multilateral instruments of a legally binding nature. Examples of these include: the Rio Framework Convention on Climate Change 1992, the Rio Convention on Biological Diversity 1992, the Basel Convention on the Control of Transboundary Movement of Hazardous Wastes and Their Disposal 1989, the Montreal Protocol on Substances that Deplete the Ozone Layer 1987, the Washington Convention on International Trade in Endangered Species of Wild Fauna and Flora 1973, and the London Convention on the Prevention of Marine Pollution by Dumping of Wastes and Other Matter 1972.

A traditional notion of public international law would seek to place the development of international law for environmental protection as a specific, but not entirely separate, body of international law. Within the overall context of the structure and methodology of public international law, this notion has a sound basis. For example, it may be noted that the international law for environmental protection relies on the same sources of public international law as those recognised elsewhere, in other subject areas of international law. As noted above, these are generally accepted as being those sources listed in Art 38(1) of the 1945 Statute of the International Court of Justice.

On the other hand, it is possible to discern, as with other newly evolved and developing areas of public international law, a number of aspects which are inherent to the discipline of international environmental law, as opposed to being merely international law for environmental protection.

First, keeping with the above example of recognised sources of international law, it can be seen that, in addition to the established sources of public international law, there is a further, important though, as yet not properly defined or formally recognised, source of international environmental law, namely, the so called international environmental 'soft' law, described above. The development and use of 'soft' law is by no means confined to international environmental law, as a specific branch of international law, or even to international law only, and is also present in national law. However, it has a special place in the evolution, development and continuing progress of international environmental law.

Secondly, it may be argued that, unlike more established subject areas of international law, international environmental law has relied far less on the development of specific customary rules of international law, as opposed to the development of treaty based legal regimes, often addressing specific global, regional or even bilateral environmental problems. As has been noted by a leading commentator in the field, with the exception of some of the general rules and principles, and the particular rules established by each individual treaty, there exists no 'level playing field' which subjects all States and other members of the international community to identical standards. This is not to suggest that customary rules have no place in the continuing development of international environmental law. Nor is it being argued that this, so far mainly treaty based, discipline of international environmental law is operating independently, and therefore is outside the context of the general development of customary international law on this subject. The treaty and custom nexus that underpins the development of all international law is certainly much in evidence in this area of international law too.

What is being suggested here is simply a means to a better understanding of the development of international environmental law as a separate branch of international law, albeit having the same roots, as well as providing for an initial methodology with which to examine and analyse this particular subject area of international law. In this sense, it is an attempt to describe a method by which international environmental law may be explained as a separate discipline within the general body of international law, rather than merely being a specific subject area to which this body of international rules is also applied. Environmental treaties share many of the general characteristics of other treaties, but certain special features exist, even if a standard format has not yet emerged. There are several aspects of international environmental law, especially within the environmental treaty regimes that now form much of it, that may arguably benefit from the use of such a methodology in order to explain and understand their workings.

Public international law students should therefore be familiar not only with the general principles enunciated in the relevant case law on the subject, but also where these principles have been applied in more detail in international environmental agreements. Both essay and problem questions can be found on this topic. The depth and scope of these questions, however, vary according to the time and space that is spent on the subject in the standard public international law undergraduate degree courses.

Checklist

When revising this subject for examination, the issues to note are as follows:

- international environmental law is a relatively new area of international law; it provides substantive principles for and obligations regarding the protection of various aspects of the global environment from the harmful or damaging effects of human activities;
- these substantive principles and obligations have initially developed through non-binding international instruments, and are now provided mainly in binding global and regional treaty regimes, rather than through accumulated rules of customary international law;
- where these international obligations for environmental protection relate to human activities within the territorial jurisdiction of States, they present a structural threat to the international legal system, predicated upon the notion of exclusive State sovereignty over such activities;
- in order to accommodate this perceived structural threat to one of the main tenets of public international law, international environmental treaties aim to develop co-operative regimes (which focus on the definition, evaluation, monitoring, supervision, prevention, reduction, and mitigation of

environmental threats by States), rather than providing rules of State responsibility and liability for non-compliance with international obligations;
- however, the provision of such standards of environmental behaviour for States does contribute to the development of the requirement of due diligence on the part of these States, in respect of the fulfilment of their overall legal obligation to protect the global environment, and may give rise to issues of responsibility in the event of a breach, or violation, of an international obligation resulting in massive environmental damage or pollution.

Question 38

Can the traditional sources of public international law provide the basis for the evolution of new legal principles governing the environment?

Discuss.

Answer plan

This is a fairly straightforward essay question which encapsulates the problems inherent in finding the applicable principles for environmental protection within the traditional sources of public international law.

The issue is, therefore, whether we expand the accepted categories of international law to incorporate principles currently found in non-binding 'soft' law in order to impute new obligations upon States, or whether, in fact, these obligations are still to be determined only by reference to the traditional sources of international law, specifically, treaty law within the context of environmental protection.

Thus, after a summary of the traditional sources of international law where they pertain to the environment, the discussion must incorporate references to ostensibly non-binding, but nevertheless important sources of international environmental law, such as intergovernmental declarations and UN General Assembly resolutions.

Finally, the discussion must take into account the poverty of present sources of general or customary international law, with the exception of treaty law, in respect of the provision of general principles of environmental protection and how this issue can be reconciled with the need for such principles to be applicable between States in their daily activities.

Answer

In summary, the sources of international environmental law are the same as those which are traditionally recognised by international law, namely, international treaties or conventions, customary international law, general principles of law and, as secondary sources, judicial decisions and the writings of eminent publicists. Reference is usually made to Art 38(1) of the 1945 Statute of the International Court of Justice, which lays down these generally accepted sources of international law to be applied by the International Court of Justice (ICJ) in cases that come before it.

These sources have been shown to have both advantages and disadvantages as bases for developing international law generally, and international environmental law specifically. Also, questions remain as to whether these traditional sources of international law are exhaustive in respect of new subject areas, such as international environmental law, which incorporate many different types of resolutions, declarations and other material as possible sources of law. The list of sources identified in Art 38(1) does not, however, wholly reflect the sources of obligation, broadly understood, which have arisen in international environmental law.

Each of the main sources of public international law will be considered briefly, in turn. First, international conventions or treaties, establishing rules expressly recognised by the States concerned, represent the clearest form of legal obligations between States. Secondly, customary international law, while being a significant, if not main source of international legal obligations between States generally, fulfils a largely secondary role in international environmental law. Once it has been determined that a rule of customary international law exists, then, in principle, it is binding upon all States. However, the essential role of consent in the formation of customary international law, as in all international law, has two important consequences as far as the general principle above is concerned. First, if a State persistently objects to an emerging rule of customary international law, it may not be regarded as being bound by that rule. Secondly, as a corollary to the above requirement of consent before being bound, it is unnecessary to have recourse to the general practice of States in order to create the presumption that a particular State is bound by a rule if it can be proved that the State in question has in fact consented to the rule by its own practice.

In respect of these traditional sources of international law, it is worth noting that general principles, which do not usually play a major role as a primary source of international law, are nevertheless important to the current development of international environmental law. It has been argued that this category of international legal sources should be expanded to include those principles of international law that have been recognised by the States themselves as governing relations between them, either generally or specifically. Such substantive principles include the prohibition against use of force, basic principles of human rights, the freedom of the seas, and the prevention of harm to another State's territory. The recognition of these substantive principles of international law, in addition to the more commonly accepted procedural ones, would be a useful addition to the general body of applicable international law, especially international environmental law. Such an approach has been helpful in developing international environmental law, leading to the gradual acceptance of principles of precautionary action, sustainable development, equitable utilisation of shared resources, etc. These principles, however, are often enunciated in the form of intergovernmental declarations which are codified, but without the usual signature and ratification process to confirm their consent, as in a treaty. There now exists an increasing number of these so called 'soft' law instruments. The result is some considerable uncertainty as to their validity as a primary source of international law. One argument in relation to this ambiguity has been to acknowledge the general principles laid down in these declarations as a secondary source of international law, that is, reliant on the court or any other international adjudicatory body, rather than States, to enunciate and apply by induction.

Judicial decisions and the writings of eminent publicists fulfil a similar place as a subsidiary or secondary means for the determination of international environmental law, as they do in general international law. Until very recently, it was possible to note the brevity of both these subsidiary sources as means of establishing the general principles of international environmental law. This is still the case in relation to the number of international law cases that concern the environment, leading at least one of the major commentaries on international environmental law to suggest that the impact of these cases on the progressive development of the law has been overemphasised.

The amount of literature on the subject, however, both at the general and specific levels, has burgeoned of late. In international law generally, the published works of some academic writers and reports of international codification bodies, such as the International Law Commission, have been recognised by national and international adjudicatory bodies as indicative of the *lex lata* (normative) and *lex ferenda* (prescriptive) legal aspects of a particular subject area. Their impact on the development of international environmental law, however, has yet to be felt.

Returning to the growing body of what is often known as international 'soft' law, it has been argued that 'soft' law rules are not binding *per se*, but that they play an important role, especially in the field of international environmental law. They do so in at least three ways: first, by pointing to the likely future direction of formally binding obligations; secondly, by informally establishing acceptable norms of behaviour; and thirdly, by codifying, or possibly reflecting, rules of customary international law. Examples of international environmental 'soft' law abound, not least in the form of the 1972 Stockholm Declaration on the Human Environment and the 1992 Rio Declaration on Environment and Development.

The same problem arises with respect to the legal status to be accorded to United Nations General Assembly resolutions, for example, the World Charter for Nature 1982. United Nations General Assembly resolutions on environmental subjects (as well as in other fields of international law) have also been proposed as a source of international law, in terms of their possible imputation of international legal obligations consented to by States voting in favour of such resolutions. Since membership of the UN now comprises most States constituting the international community, resolutions of the General Assembly may be argued to be generally representative of world opinion and cited as evidence of the *opinio juris* of States. In fact, however, most States do not intend their support to be taken as consent to any rule of law which the resolution may purport to lay down, and, in the absence of such intention, an affirmative vote for a resolution is merely a declaration of political intent, and not an assumption of legal obligation. Despite this and other reservations, it has been argued that, although resolutions are not *per se* binding upon States, especially those that have supported them, they may become so in the light of the subsequent conduct of these States.

The existence of international environmental 'soft' law is therefore undeniable. Less certain, however, is the place it occupies among recognised sources of international environmental law. The recognition of 'soft' law as a possible source of legal obligation in international environmental law is thus steeped in controversy.

Among the rules of customary international law which have emerged from prior State practice, international case law, intergovernmental declarations and UN General Assembly resolutions concerning the protection of the environment are: (a) no State can cause, or allow its territory to be used to cause, damage to the environment of other States; and (b) every State is under an obligation urgently to notify States at risk of having their environment adversely affected by any situation or event. The first duty – that no State shall allow its own territory to be used to cause damage to the environment of other States – is formulated in Principle 21 of the 1972 Stockholm Declaration and re-affirmed in Principle 2 of the 1992 Rio Declaration.

The duty to co-operate, which is embodied in Principle 24 of the Stockholm Declaration, also appears to have acquired the status of a customary rule of international environmental law. Other general principles of environmental law include, *inter alia*: (a) the principle of sustainable development (Principles 1, 4, 5, 7, 8 and 9 of the Rio Declaration 1992), which is defined as 'development that meets the needs of the present without compromising the ability of future generations to meet their own needs'; (b) the preventive principle (Principles 6 and 7 of the Stockholm Declaration), which requires that activity which does or will cause damage is to be prohibited or, at the very least, minimised; (c) the precautionary principle (Principle 15 of the Rio Declaration), which holds that lack of full scientific certainty shall not be used as a reason for postponing measures to prevent environmental degradation; and (d) 'the polluter pays' principle (Principle 16 of the Rio Declaration), which provides that the costs of environmental pollution should be borne by those whose activities were responsible for causing the pollution.

There are two main problems with the application of these general principles of international environmental law. First, the generality inherent in their wording makes it difficult to construe specific duties or obligations by which a State can be regarded as bound in international law. Secondly, the rules of international environmental law are largely founded on the traditional concept of prohibiting one State from causing harm to another, that is, they are predicated upon the regulation of bilateral relations between States.

What is required, however, are rules which are global in their scope, in order to protect the biosphere from environmental harm. When the problems with the environment transcend national or international boundaries, the ability of traditional sources of international law to cope is limited. Furthermore, international environmental law has to protect, preserve, and regulate those areas of the world which are outside States' territorial jurisdiction, known as the global commons – that is, the high seas, deep sea bed, atmosphere, Antarctica, outer space, etc.

The traditional framework of transfrontier pollution merely focuses on acts which take place or originate on the territory of one State and give rise to conflict between the rights of the two States. The following cases chart the development of this doctrine: the *Corfu Channel* case (1949); the *Trail Smelter* arbitration (1939–41); the *Lake Lanoux* arbitration (1957); and the *Nuclear Test* cases (1974).

In the *Corfu Channel* case, for example, it was held that every State has an obligation not knowingly to allow its territory to be used for acts contrary to the rights of other States. It is questionable, however, whether these 'rights' include environmental rights. In the *Trail Smelter* arbitration, this duty is stated more explicitly, in that no State has the right to use or permit the use of its territory in such a manner as to cause injury by fumes in or to the territory of another State.

Principle 21 of the Stockholm Declaration goes further than either of the above cases: it notes that States have the responsibility to ensure that activities within their jurisdiction and control do not cause damage to the environment of other States, or to areas beyond the limits of national jurisdiction.

It is clear from the above cases, however, that there is an inherent problem in public international law with respect to the imputation of an international obligation upon States to protect the environment, whether it is the environment of a neighbouring State or the environment as a whole, that is, the environment as an area of global commons.

This problem in international law may be contrasted with the situation in municipal or national law whereby once damage or harm has occurred, then the facts are ascertained and the relevant rule is sought to be applied. In public international law, the general nature of the applicable principles mean that, for every new dispute between States, these general principles have to be analysed carefully in order to draw out the specific rule which can then be applied to the situation at hand. The difficulty of setting down specific obligations under international law, even in respect of bilateral State responsibility and liability over transboundary environmental harm, puts into perspective the greater difficulties associated with the protection of the global environment.

There is a line of argument which points out that, if environmental protection encompasses the entire biosphere, international rules should safeguard the environment within States, even if the harmful activities produce no proven detrimental effects outside the acting State. It has been further suggested that globally oriented regulation is increasingly being included in the form of an international common law of the environment. Within this context, the doctrine of abuse of rights takes on a greater significance, because, although it recognises the exclusive territorial jurisdiction of the polluting State, it subordinates this to a superior rule of international law which forbids sovereignty to be exercised in an abusive manner. The doctrine of abuse of rights recognises that a State's territorial sovereign rights are correlative and interdependent in respect of other States' rights, and consequently, that a State's territorial sovereign rights are limited to the extent that they cannot be used in such a way as to constrain another State from exercising its own territorial sovereign rights.

A major problem occurs, however, when, in a legal dispute between two or more sovereign States, the same legal justification is invoked by both parties. This problem arose in the *Nuclear Test* cases (1974) between France, on the one hand, and Australia and New Zealand on the other. The question before the ICJ was whether France's right to conduct nuclear tests as an exercise of its sovereign right within its own territory in the South Pacific was in conflict with the rights of the applicant States to exercise their sovereignty over their territorial integrity by not allowing any extraterritorial effects from the nuclear testing to enter their atmosphere? However, this question was ultimately not decided by the court.

An important question that was also not answered by the court was whether or not the applicant countries had to show evidence that the extraterritorial effects of the nuclear testing had indeed caused harm before these effects could be deemed to have violated their territorial integrity. This question is related to another very important issue concerning state responsibility – whether material damage must be shown before the extraterritorial effects of a State's activity which is lawful *per se* can be said to be in breach of an international obligation. In other words, is a State's activity which is lawful *per se*, in the sense that it is a lawful exercise of sovereignty within its own territory, nevertheless in breach of international law, simply because it has extraterritorial effects? It would appear to be the case that, unless some form of material damage can be proven, the mere fact of a 'violation of territorial sovereignty or integrity' implicit in an action which has transfrontier effects is not sufficient to render State responsibility or liability for these extraterritorial effects (*Trail Smelter* arbitration between Canada and the United States).

It has been stated that, at the present time, international law does not allow States to conduct activities within their territories, or in common spaces, without regard for the rights of other States, or for the protection of the global environment. Given the vagaries of traditional sources of international law, with only treaties and custom said to be able to bind States to international legal obligations (and even then, only if States have either signed and ratified the treaty concerned) or by way of State practice and *opinio juris*, it is perhaps no wonder that, in the field of the environment, these traditional sources of international law are being replaced by what may be called 'international environmental regulation'. These normally take a written form. In its final form, international environmental regulation manifests itself in the form of environmental treaties. However, international environmental regulation also comes in the form of declarations of principles, guidelines, resolutions, action plans, etc, and are usually accompanied by forms of environmental institutions, whether they be bilateral joint commissions or multilateral commissions with executive bureaucracies. It can now be seen that the more successful of these principles are being put forward in the new treaties as binding obligations, thereby transcending their initial non-binding character and becoming part of international environmental law.

This is confirmed by the latest decision of the ICJ in the *Case Concerning the Gabcikovo-Nagymaros Project (Hungary v Slovakia)* (1997), where the court held, *inter alia*, that new environmental norms and standards had been developed and set forth in a great number of instruments during the last two decades. These new norms had to be taken into consideration not only when States contemplated new activities, but also when continuing with activities begun in the past. Unfortunately, this reference both to the need and acceptance of principles of environmental protection among States is somewhat undermined by the court's reluctance to provide an explicit statement of the applicable principles in this case, apart from vague allusions to the concept of sustainable development, to be achieved through (a) the integration of environmental considerations in development projects; (b) a precautionary approach based on the preventive principle, taking into account the often irreversible character of environmental damage; and (c) nature conservation.

Question 39

Scourge plc are a large, multinational conglomerate based in Switzerland and specialising in the management of large development projects all over the world, especially in developing countries. These projects mainly concern the setting up and running of heavy industries, such as the manufacture of steel products, the car making industry, the construction of offshore oil and gas extraction equipment, and the petrochemical industry.

As a result of the increasing number of international environmental regulations affecting Scourge plc's activities and concerns expressed by several prominent environmental non-governmental organisations (NGOs), the Managing Director of Scourge plc has hired you as a consultant to advise on the environmental principles that you would recommend Scourge plc to apply in its guidelines for project management activities all over the world as best practice.

In preparing this legal opinion, analyse the legal status under public international law of each of the environmental principles you have identified as applicable to Scourge plc's activities, and provide examples of them in various international instruments.

Answer plan

This problem question initially provides the student with an opportunity to conduct a short examination of an inherent problem regarding the implementation and enforcement of public international law, that is, the fact that, in general, it only binds States to international obligations as between themselves.

Despite their non-binding nature on the part of Scourge plc, it is in its interests to incorporate these principles of environmental law within its own best practice guidelines in order to ensure that it does not fall foul of most countries' environmental legislation where these purport to implement the environmental principles accepted at the international level.

The following discussion should therefore focus on the legal status of important principles of environmental law, providing examples of their implementation and interpretation in various international environmental agreements.

The question is which of these principles may be considered applicable as part of general or customary international law on the part of the majority of States in the world, thereby being the most useful principles for inclusion in the Scourge plc's guidelines on best practice for its activities all around the world.

Answer

This problem question allows us to conduct an initial examination of an inherent problem regarding the implementation and enforcement of public international law, that is, the fact that, in general, it only binds States to international obligations as between themselves. Traditionally, it is well known that public international law is the system of law governing States alone as the only entities capable of possessing international legal personality. The possession of international legal personality was, to a large extent, dependent upon the ability of a State to show evidence of its sovereignty over a specific piece of land territory and the human population within this territory. State sovereignty over territory and population, as well as the activities undertaken within the State, meant that States were the supreme entities under international law. However, in recent years, this paradigm has come under increasing pressure from a variety of new international factors, all of which play an increasingly important role in international affairs, but whose international legal status has not yet been clarified. Among these new international entities are global and regional intergovernmental organisations (IGOs) such as the United Nations, the European Union, international non-governmental organisations (NGOs) in the fields of human rights and environmental protection (such as Amnesty International, Greenpeace, Friends of the Earth, World Wide Fund for Nature), and transnational or multinational companies (TNCs or MNCs), such as Royal Dutch Shell, Microsoft, Coca-Cola, Nestlé, Novartis, Unilever, etc.

While the IGOs have begun making inroads towards being accepted as having partial international legal personality, for example, in terms of their participation in multilateral conventions (with the acceptance of States), the other two types of international entities – the NGOs and TNCs/MNCs – have not yet been accorded such international legal status. Both these new types of international entities have important reasons for being given at least partial international legal personality. In the case of the human rights and environmental protection NGOs, this is in order to give the views of their constituencies an airing in the international arena, in order that the issues raised are accepted by States as requiring urgent action. In the case of the TNCs and MNCs on the other hand, this is due to a perception of the need for greater controls to be put into place in respect of the global activities of these economically powerful and politically influential entities, which, when left unchecked, have allegedly had destabilising effects on many developing countries in particular.

Although Scourge plc itself is not bound to apply any of the environmental principles that may be identified, nevertheless it may be required to do so either by the national legislation of any of the countries, whether developed or developing, which are party to a binding international environmental agreement, or EU legislation implementing the international obligations that it has accepted. Therefore, it is in Scourge plc's interests to incorporate these principles of environmental law within its own best practice guidelines prior to being required to do so by national or EU legislation.

The following discussion will focus on the legal status of important principles of environmental law, providing examples of their implementation and interpretation in various international environmental agreements. The question is which of these principles may be considered applicable as part of general or customary international law on the part of the majority of States in the world, thereby being the most useful principles for inclusion in the Scourge plc's guidelines on best practice for its activities around the world.

Within this context, it is important to note, too, the rise of environmental NGOs, such as Greenpeace, Friends of the Earth and the World Wide Fund for Nature (WWF), and the consequent part they have played in raising public consciousness over environmental issues at the international, national and local levels.

The most significant of these non-binding instruments, in terms of the principles of international environmental law which it purports to set down, is the 1992 Rio Declaration on Environment and Development. The Rio Declaration represents an important step in the process begun by the Brundtland Commission towards the legal recognition of the concept of sustainable development, representing, as it does, a series of compromises between developed and developing countries and a balance between the objectives of environmental protection and economic development.

Sustainable development

Defined simply, 'sustainable development' is the general principle that the anthropocentric development and use of natural resources must take place in a sustainable manner. At the international level, the 1987 Brundtland Report of the World Commission on Environment and Development (WCED) defined 'sustainable development' as 'development that meets the needs of the present without compromising the ability of future generations to meet their own needs'. It is alluded to, without actually being defined, in Principles 1, 4, 5, 7, 8 and 9 of the Rio Declaration 1992.

Sustainable development is arguably the most important general principle of environmental law. Indeed sustainable development may be seen as the guiding principle in the evolution of environmental law at all three levels of international, European and domestic UK law. This is because, in its broadest sense, the principle encompasses not merely the legal, but also the economic and political fields. The successful application of this principle would require not merely legal measures, but also economic and policy instruments in order to bring it about. Perhaps even more importantly, any human activity deemed useful, but which affects in a detrimental manner the environment in which we all live, may be required to fulfil the criterion of sustainability in the sense that such activity may not be allowed to reduce the capacity of the environment to ensure its continued usefulness for that and other human activities.

The recognition of the broad nature and application of the principle or concept of sustainable development, in terms of the various disciplines it covers, does raise questions concerning its progressive development as a general legal principle of environmental law. For example, at the international level, can it be said that it is specific enough in its formulation to be capable of creating legal obligations between States? One might argue that the function of general legal principles does not necessarily include the formulation of legal rights and duties, but merely guides the policies and actions of the authorities involved. Nevertheless, it is important to know exactly how far individuals and other entities, such as Scourge plc, are legally required to implement the principle of sustainable development in their daily activities. This will certainly differ from State to State, and especially between developed and developing countries, both in terms of the standard of its implementation and scope of its application. Best practice would therefore suggest that Scourge plc implements the highest standards available which do not entail excessive costs, the so called BATNEEC (Best Available Technique Not Entailing Excessive Costs) standard which is implemented, for example, in UK domestic legislation under s 7(10) of the Environment Protection Act 1990.

Preventive principle

Broadly stated, the preventive principle requires that activity which does, or will, cause environmental pollution or damage is to be prohibited. The preventive principle therefore seeks to minimise environmental damage by requiring that action be taken at an early stage of the process and, where possible, before such damage has actually occurred. It has been noted that the preventive principle is now supported by an extensive body of State practice in the form of domestic environmental protection legislation and international treaty law in the form of multilateral environmental instruments. At the international level, this is especially significant because the acceptance of this principle means that States are actively constrained against allowing polluting activities within their own national jurisdictions, in addition to their international obligation not to allow activities which cause damage to territories of other States and areas beyond national jurisdiction (Principle 21 of Stockholm Declaration and Principle 2 of Rio Declaration). This general prohibition against polluting activities has only recently been included within multilateral treaties, a notable example being Art 194 of the 1982 UN Convention on the Law of the Sea (UNCLOS), which enjoins all States to prevent, reduce and control pollution of the marine environment as a whole, both within and without their national maritime zone jurisdictions. The preventive principle is now applied to a greater or lesser degree in most countries' domestic environmental legislation, and Scourge plc would do well to implement it as a standard requirement in its own activities throughout the world.

Precautionary principle

The precautionary principle has a much shorter history than the preventive principle. It has only recently appeared in binding international treaty law, as opposed to within declarations and other international instruments of a non-binding character. However, its potential impact on the development of environmental law is immense. In its most progressive (some would say, extreme) formulation, the precautionary principle may be utilised to overturn the traditional burden of proof and require any proposed activity to be guaranteed not to cause pollution before it is allowed to commence.

Therefore, legal formulations of the principle have tended to include a cost benefit element. For example, Principle 15 of the 1992 Rio Declaration provides that, where there are threats of serious or irreversible damage, lack of full scientific certainty shall not be used as a reason for postponing cost effective measures to prevent environmental degradation. The 1992 Framework Climate Change Convention incorporates a similar, cost benefit approach in its legal formulation of the precautionary principle (Art 3(3)). On the other hand, the 1992 Paris Convention for the Protection of the Marine Environment of the North Atlantic introduces a different formulation of the principle, linking it with the preventive principle: preventive measures are to be taken when there are reasonable grounds for concern even when there is no conclusive relationship between inputs into the environment and their alleged effects (Art 2(2)(a)). Thus, despite its less entrenched legal status at the present time, the precautionary principle may soon also be universally applicable, albeit in a restricted sense, and this possibility should galvanise Scourge plc into consideration of its application as best practice in its own activities in the near future.

Polluter pays principle

This principle provides that the costs of environmental pollution should be borne by the entity whose activities were responsible for causing such pollution. It is explicitly provided for in Principle 16 of the Rio Declaration on Environment and Development 1992. It is possible to consider the application of this principle at both the general and specific levels. At the specific level, it has been held that, where certain individual entities are responsible for polluting activities, they should be required to pay the full costs of the rectification of any environmental degradation that has occurred as a result of their activities. The application of the polluter pays principle in this manner is manifest in the rules governing civil and State liability for environmental damage due to hazardous activities. Examples at the international level include the 1992 Conventions on Civil Liability for Oil Pollution Damage and Establishment of an International Fund for Compensation for Oil Pollution Damage (replacing the 1969 and 1971 conventions of the same names) and the 1960 Convention on Third Party Liability in the Field of Nuclear Energy (Paris), with the 1963 Supplementary Convention (Brussels).

At the more general level, the polluter pays principle may be seen to act in such a way that all human economic activity which impinges upon the environment should be fully accounted for in the economic pricing system of the goods and services produced by such activity. In economic terms, this process is called 'the internalisation of environmental costs' and is potentially much more far reaching in its impact on our daily lives than the mere provision of full compensation for environmental damage as a result of defined polluting activities. It is significant, therefore, that it is this version of the polluter pays principle that is included within Principle 16 of the 1992 Rio Declaration.

Perhaps because of the uncertainty in the level of application of the polluter pays principle to be preferred and the obvious economic implications of its application, the polluter pays principle has not received the broad geographic and subject matter support over the long term accorded to the preventive principle, or the attention accorded to the precautionary principle in recent years. Thus, it is doubtful whether it has achieved the status of a generally applicable rule of customary international law, except, perhaps, in relation to the Member States in the EU, the UN ECE (Economic Commission for Europe) and the OECD (Organisation for Economic Co-operation and Development). Bearing in mind that its application presents a more truthful picture of the actual costs incurred in the environmental impact of certain economic activities that may involve Scourge plc, it is submitted here that this principle should also be incorporated into Scourge plc's statement of best practice.

Principle of citizen participation in environmental decision making

The successful implementation of this principle, which holds that, in order to ensure the effective implementation of environmental laws, particularly at the domestic level, individuals must be given legally enforceable rights to participate in the environmental decision making process, has great potential to exert a negative impact on Scourge plc's activities, especially if certain of these practices have already been criticised by NGOs representing citizens' interest groups. At the international level, such participatory rights are provided in Principle 10 of the 1992 Rio Declaration, but are noticeably less in evidence in other binding international instruments. By contrast, EU and UK domestic law may recognise such rights in specific circumstances. Thus, Scourge plc's project management teams should take into account the possibility that they will have to negotiate not only with the relevant regulatory authorities concerning the environmental impact of their activities, but also with representatives of the local communities, who may be able to exert considerable pressure over the entire process to the extent that domestic legislation and the courts allow them to do so. This is especially true in developed countries.

In conclusion, therefore, it may be seen that there are a number of important environmental principles that are at varying stages in terms of their legal status and implementation as applicable law within the countries in which Scourge plc are in fact operating or proposing to operate. In its statement of best practice for its range of activities around the globe, Scourge plc would be well advised to implement these principles to the greatest extent possible, bearing in mind the excessive cost factor, in order to ensure that it is able to operate in any country without the additional consideration of having to implement different environmental standards in its projects.

Question 40

The inability of States to develop rules of general, customary international law for the protection of the global environment means that progress on this issue is dependent solely on the progressive extension of treaty law to all parts of the globe, both in terms of the subject matter covered by these treaties and their geographical scope.

Discuss

Answer plan

This essay question invites the student to explore the limits of the development of rules of customary international law, through an examination of the relevant case law in this area, before going on to discuss the gradual evolution of international treaty law on global environmental issues.

Having discussed the case law and noted the paucity of specific rules of customary law on the environment, the essay can examine some of the initial international environmental instruments, which were non-legally binding but nevertheless global in the scope of their application.

Following this, the discussion can move on to the major treaty regimes on the environment, paying special attention to their progressive extension, both in terms of their subject matter and geographical scope. Conclusions can then drawn as to the viability of treaty law as opposed customary law for the future development of this branch of international law.

Answer

Among the rules of customary international law which have emerged from prior State practice, international case law, intergovernmental declarations and UN General Assembly resolutions concerning the protection of the environment are:

(a) no State can cause, or allow its territory to be used to cause damage to the environment of other states; and
(b) every State is under an obligation urgently to notify States at risk of having their environment adversely affected by any situation or event.

The first duty – that no State should allow its own territory to be used to cause damage to the environment of other States – is formulated in Principle 21 of the 1972 Stockholm Declaration and re-affirmed in Principle 2 of the 1992 Rio Declaration.

There are two main problems with the application of these general principles of international environmental law, First, the generality inherent in their wording makes it difficult to construe specific duties or obligations by which a State can be regarded as bound under international law. Secondly, the rules of international environmental law are largely founded on the traditional concept of prohibiting one State from causing harm to another, that is, they are predicated upon the regulation of bilateral relations between States.

What is required, however, are rules which are global in their scope in order to protect the biosphere from environmental harm. When the problems with the environment transcend national and international boundaries, the ability of traditional sources of international law to cope is limited. Furthermore, international environmental law has to protect, preserve, and regulate those areas of the world which are outside States' territorial jurisdiction, known as the global commons – that is, the high seas, deep sea bed, atmosphere, Antarctica, outer space, etc.

The traditional framework of transfrontier pollution merely focuses on acts which take place or originate within the territory of one State and give rise to conflict between the rights of the two States. The following cases chart the development of this doctrine: the *Corfu Channel* case (1949); the *Trail Smelter* arbitration

(1939–41); the *Lake Lanoux* arbitration (1957); and the *Nuclear Test* cases (1974).

In the *Corfu Channel* case, for example, it was held that every State has an obligation not knowingly to allow its territory to be used for acts contrary to the rights of other States. It is questionable, however, whether these 'rights' include environmental rights. In the *Trail Smelter* arbitration, this duty is stated more explicitly, in that no State has the right to use or permit the use of its territory in such a manner as to cause injury by fumes in or to the territory of another State.

In the *Lac Lanoux* case between Spain and France, allegations by Spain, the downstream State, that France the upstream State, had violated a treaty obligation by diverting the course of the waters of a shared transboundary river to the detriment of Spain, were ultimately found to be groundless. In the course of its judgment, the arbitral tribunal held that the applicable principle was that of the equitable utilisation of the various uses of a shared transboundary watercourse between the countries that shared it. Such equitable use therefore entailed that any activity to which the river or its waters were put to must not injure the interests of the other States sharing the river.

In the *Nuclear Test* cases (1974), an important question that was not answered by the court was whether or not the applicant countries had to show evidence that the extraterritorial effects of the nuclear testing had indeed caused harm before these effects could be deemed to have violated their territorial integrity. This question is related to another, very important issue concerning State responsibility – that is, whether material damage must be shown before the extraterritorial effects of a State's activity, which is lawful *per se*, can be said to be in breach of an international obligation. In other words, is a State's activity which is lawful *per se*, in the sense that it is a lawful exercise of sovereignty within its own territory, nevertheless in breach of international law, simply because it has extraterritorial effects? It would appear to be the case that, unless some form of material damage can be proven, the mere fact of a 'violation of territorial sovereignty or integrity' implicit in an action which has transfrontier effects is not sufficient to render State responsibility or liability for these extraterritorial effects (*Trail Smelter* arbitration between Canada and the United States).

It is clear from the above cases, however, that there is an inherent problem in public international law with respect to the imputation of an international obligation upon States to protect the environment, whether it is the environment of a neighbouring State or the environment as a whole, that is, the environment as an area of global commons. Principle 21 of the Stockholm Declaration on the Human Environment, for example, goes further than the above international case law; it notes that States have the responsibility to ensure that activities within their jurisdiction and control do not cause damage to the environment of other States, or to areas beyond the limits of national jurisdiction. The legal status of Principle 21, however, remains in doubt.

Given the vagaries of traditional sources of international law, with only treaties and custom said to be able to bind States to international legal obligations, and even then only if States have either signed and ratified the treaty concerned, or by way of State practice and *opinio juris*, it is perhaps no wonder that, in the field of the environment, these traditional sources of international law are being replaced by what may be called international environmental regulation. These normally take a written form. In its final form, international environmental regulation manifests itself in the form of environmental treaties. However, international environmental regulation also comes in the form of declarations of principles, guidelines, resolutions, action plans, etc, and are usually accompanied by forms of environmental institutions, whether they be bilateral joint commissions or multilateral commissions with executive bureaucracies. It can now be seen that the more successful of these principles are being put forward in the new treaties as binding obligations, thereby transcending their initial non-binding character and becoming part of international environmental law.

This is confirmed by the latest decision of the ICJ in the *Case Concerning the Gabcikovo-Nagymaros Project (Hungary v Slovakia)* (1997), where the court held, *inter alia*, that new environmental norms and standards had been developed and set forth in a great number of instruments during the last two decades. These new norms had to be taken into consideration not only when States contemplated new activities, but also when continuing with activities begun in the past. Unfortunately, this reference both to the need and acceptance of principles of environmental protection among States is somewhat undermined by the court's reluctance to provide an explicit statement of the applicable principles in this case, apart from vague allusions to the concept of sustainable development, to be achieved through (a) the integration of environmental considerations in development projects; (b) a precautionary approach based on the preventive principle, taking into account the often irreversible character of environmental damage; and (c) nature conservation.

The 1972 UN Conference on the Human Environment, which yielded, *inter alia*, the now famous set of principles known as the Stockholm Declaration, represents the first formal sign of increasing international concern for environmental degradation on a global scale. It has been noted that the 26 principles in the Stockholm Declaration reflected a compromise between those States which were concerned only to indicate their recognition and concern over the mounting problems affecting the global environment, and those that wanted the adoption of the declaration to act as a catalyst for specific international and domestic action, along the lines set down by the principles within it. Here we see another reason why international environmental 'soft' law, with its inherently non-binding character, is useful for the progressive development of the law on this subject. Although none of the principles in the Stockholm Declaration creates legally binding obligations, nevertheless these principles set down general guidelines for the behaviour of States.

The passage of time has seen many of these principles incorporated into international agreements addressing specific environmental problems and re-affirmed in global, regional and national policy statements, if not actual legislation.

The declaration therefore fulfils an inspirational purpose, even though it is not, in itself, a legalistic document, nor can its provisions be held to be binding upon States. Thus, only a handful are of special legal significance. From a legal perspective, the most relevant provisions are Principles 21 (see above and below), 22 (co-operation regarding liability and compensation for victims of pollution), and 24 (co-operation on international environmental matters). The other principles are generally couched in non-legal language, but here again it may be seen that recent history has shown their relevance in the progressive development of international environmental law. The Stockholm Declaration's principles, however, are weak on techniques for implementing environmental standards, such as environmental impact assessment, prior notification and consultation procedures, access to environmental information, participation in the formulation of environmental policies and the availability of administrative and judicial remedies. These procedural rules for ensuring the implementation and application of the environmental standards laid down are much more in evidence within later treaty instruments.

The most important of the Stockholm Declaration's principles, as noted above, is that enunciated by Principle 21. This is, in many respects, the 'golden' rule of international law for the protection of the environment, and may be described as the starting point for the subdiscipline of international environmental law. It has been called the fundamental principle of State responsibility for transboundary environmental harm, enshrining, as it does, the principle of national sovereignty while imposing limits on a State's activities where these inflict environmental damage to other States and to areas beyond national jurisdiction. Although worded in a general, even vague way, Principle 21 is clearly formulated as a legal principle which could be interpreted and applied in concrete situations through international mechanisms for dispute settlement. It is held by many writers to be representative of international law, and has subsequently been referred to as such in a number of multilateral environmental treaties. It also appears, although in a modified version, in Principle 2 of the 1992 Rio Declaration.

International environmental treaties, like other general treaties, can be bilateral or multilateral in nature, and general or particular in their remit. Most environmental treaties contain a mixture of mostly obligatory and sometimes hortatory language. For example, the word 'shall' in treaty articles connotes a legally enforceable obligation undertaken by the State concerned. A phrase such as 'shall endeavour', on the other hand, is less obligatory in character, more hortatory. Compare, for example, Art 207(1) of the 1982 Law of the Sea Convention: 'States shall adopt laws and regulations to prevent, reduce and control pollution of the marine environment from land based sources ...', with Art 207(3): 'States shall endeavour to harmonise their policies in this connection at the appropriate regional level.'

International environmental treaties, however, arguably contain several distinctive elements which serve to assist States in their efforts to prevent, control or mitigate the particular environmental threats that they address. These include implementation measures, supervisory and monitoring mechanisms, simplified treaty modification procedures, and action plans.

Implementation measures

The implementation of treaty obligations is usually left to the State party, and is mostly done by national, domestic legislation. Treaties regulating the protection of the environment often create a framework of obligations which require municipal legislation to implement.

Supervisory and monitoring mechanisms

There are two main methods of supervision exercised under international law. Generally, the State parties to a treaty supervise implementation of the treaty by other State parties. Environmental treaties, however, often establish additional supervisory organs, in the form of special institutions or organisations. This may be in the form of a secretariat, whose duty is merely to gather reports from all State parties and inform all other State parties of the alleged non-compliance of one party. An example of this is the 1989 Basel Convention on the Transboundary Movement of Hazardous and other Wastes. Or, it may be in the creation of a whole system for the observance and supervision of the implementation of a convention, as in the 1980 Canberra Convention on Antartic Marine Living Resources (CCAMLR). However, procedures that override the State parties' jurisdiction in respect of the implementation of international obligations remain rare. The most accepted supervisory technique remains that which is based on an individual State reporting system. Such reporting systems based on individual State compliance, however, are justifiably criticised as leading to impartial and therefore untrustworthy reporting that does not augur well for the overall effectiveness of an environmental treaty regime.

The acquisition of new knowledge, dissemination of information, and observation of the biosphere, for the purpose of noting environmental change, make international co-operation for the protection of the environment even more necessary and a permanent facet of international environmental law. Most environmental protection treaties therefore contain institutional provisions, granting more or less extensive competence to international organs. These international organs perform three main functions: managing the international convention concerned, gathering and distributing information, and supervising enforcement of the convention's norms by State parties.

Co-operative machinery can also be utilised to resolve differences between State parties to a convention. The favoured method of dispute settlement in environmental treaties is arbitration. This recourse to arbitration is often set out in an annex or protocol to the convention.

Simplified treaty modification procedures

In the usual case, the amendment of a treaty requires the consent of all the States party to that treaty. Such a procedure is time consuming, as it needs to reconvene, or at least officially inform, all the States which took part in the initial negotiation of the treaty and those which subsequently became parties. Furthermore, amendments usually require a two-thirds majority vote before coming into effect. Those States which are outvoted may not consider themselves to be bound by the amendment.

One method of avoiding these problems is through the use of framework style conventions, which set down general obligations, leaving the detailed obligations on particular issues or specific pollution standards to be included in protocols or annexes to the main body of convention. With respect to the framework convention and protocol method, this has the advantage of allowing more progressive State parties to agree on detailed obligations, while leaving other State parties to be bound by the general obligations of the convention, all these States still party to the same overall treaty regime. Good examples of treaties which utilise the convention and protocol approach are the UN Environment Programme (UNEP), regional seas treaties covering diverse marine regions such as the Mediterranean, the Red Sea, the Persian Gulf, the Caribbean, the south Pacific, and the southeast Pacific. The 1973 International Convention for the Prevention of Marine Pollution, as modified by a protocol in 1978 (MARPOL 1973/78) is another excellent example of this approach, with various annexes attached to the main body of the convention providing for specific obligations and standards on individual issues such as vessel source operational discharges causing marine oil pollution, sewage and garbage, and the carriage of noxious liquids and other hazardous cargoes.

The annex procedure allows detailed standards to be applied, and easier modification should higher standards be required in due course, without having to amend the general obligations of the multilateral treaty or convention, which remain in effect. A good example of such a treaty would be the 1972 Oslo and London Conventions on, respectively, the Prevention of Dumping of Wastes in the Northeast Atlantic and Global Marine Environments .

Another way in which the traditional amendment procedure may be facilitated is through the use of the tacit approval procedure. Thus, when a proposed amendment appears to command some support, it is held to come into effect after a certain period of time, unless certain State parties which have strong objections to the proposal notify the others. This tacit approval procedure has the merit of reversing the burden of proof, so that progressive States are not held back by recalcitrant ones.

Action plans

These are generally set out in hortatory language. They are programmes of action which States agree to undertake in order to be in a better position to comply with their obligations under the treaty. They are characteristic of environmental treaties, either as a precursor to a convention, or as part of the implementation of one. In the case of the UNEP Regional Seas Programmes, for example, action plans often precede the formal negotiations toward a draft convention.

In conclusion, it is submitted here that international environmental agreements contain several important aspects, as provided in the following, non-exhaustive list, which arguably aid States in their efforts to ensure the successful implementation and effectiveness of the environmental treaty regime they have established:

- definitions (of pollution or any other environmental interference);
- substantive obligations for environmental protection against the identified threat or pollution defined within the treaty;
- procedural obligations for consultation, exchange of information and research providing an objective standard for the due diligence test;
- provisions for monitoring the compliance, implementation and enforcement of the procedural and substantive obligations above;
- establishment of international institutions to govern the environmental treaty regime that has been set up;
- simplified treaty amendment procedures to aid progressive development of the regime;
- provisions for State responsibility and liability (if any) for non-compliance with the due diligence requirement resulting in pollution damage or harm to the interests of another State or the interests of all the States within a treaty regime;
- dispute settlement procedures for the resolution of interpretation and implementation issues; and
- proposals for future action in order to ensure continued protection environmental protection from the threats identified.

The progressive development of international environmental treaties incorporating these elements is arguably the main way forward for continuing efforts to establish a truly effective system of global environmental protection under public international law.

Question 41

States alone cannot be expected to be able to protect the global environment. To ensure such a goal, the participation of intergovernmental organisations (IGOs), non-governmental organisations (NGOs) and individuals is necessary. In particular, the recognition of a human right to a healthy environment is an essential requirement.

Discuss the proposed approach with respect to any problems it may face under the traditional doctrine of public international law.

Answer plan

This essay question incorporates two main issues concerning international environmental law:

- the need to extend the present customary regime of international environmental law to cover more than merely activities that may cause harm to the environment of States only, and include the development and implementation of international rules for the protection of the global environment, including areas beyond national jurisdiction, and
- the overlap between international environmental and human rights protection, notably through the possible provision of a human right to a healthy environment.

First, the lack of progressive development of customary rules of international law for environmental protection can be traced by recourse to the case law.

Secondly, the special problem presented by the global commons, such as the high seas or the atmosphere, in terms of their lack of protection from the polluting activities under the jurisdiction or control should be highlighted.

Thirdly, a number of treaties covering these global commons areas, for example, the high seas (Part VII of the 1982 UNCLOS), atmosphere (1987 Montreal Protocol to the 1985 Vienna Convention on Substances that Deplete the Ozone Layer), and climate (1992 Framework Convention on Climate Change) can be discussed.

Fourthly, the recognition of individual and community interests and possible rights in relation to their surrounding environment can be described and analysed.

Answer

This essay will focus on two main issues concerning international environmental law: first, the need to extend the present customary regime of international environmental law to cover more than merely activities that may cause harm to the environment of States only, and include the development and implementation of international rules for the protection of the global environment, including areas beyond national jurisdiction, and secondly, the overlap between international environmental and human rights protection, notably through the possible provision of a human right to a healthy environment.

Among the rules of customary international law which have emerged from prior State practice, international case law, intergovernmental declarations and UN General Assembly resolutions concerning the protection of the environment are: (a) no State can cause, or allow its territory to be used to cause, damage to the environment of other States; and (b) every State is under an obligation urgently to notify States at risk of having their environment adversely affected by any situation or event. The first duty – that no State should allow its own territory to be used to cause damage to the environment of other States – is formulated in Principle 21 of the 1972 Stockholm Declaration and re-affirmed in Principle 2 of the 1992 Rio Declaration.

There are two main problems with the application of these general principles of international environmental law. First, the generality inherent in their wording makes it difficult to construe specific duties and obligations by which a State can be regarded as bound under international law. Secondly, the rules of international environmental law are largely founded on the traditional concept of prohibiting one State from causing harm to another, that is, they are predicated upon the regulation of bilateral relations between States. The traditional framework of transfrontier pollution merely focuses on acts which take place or originate on the territory of one State and give rise to conflict between the rights of the two States. The following cases chart the development of this doctrine: the *Corfu Channel* case (1949) and the *Trail Smelter* arbitration (1939–41).

In the *Corfu Channel* case, for example, it was held that every State has an obligation not knowingly to allow its territory to be used for acts contrary to the rights of other States. It is questionable, however, whether these 'rights' include environmental rights. In the *Trail Smelter* arbitration, this duty is stated more explicitly, in that no State has the right to use or permit the use of its territory in such a manner as to cause injury by fumes in or to the territory of another State.

It is clear from the above cases, however, that there is an inherent problem in public international law with respect to the imputation of an international obligation upon States to protect the environment, whether it is the environment of a neighbouring State or the environment as a whole, that is, the environment as an area of global commons. Principle 21 of the Stockholm Declaration on the Human Environment, for example, goes further than the above international case law: it notes that States have the responsibility to ensure that activities within their jurisdiction and control do not cause damage to the environment of other States or to areas beyond the limits of national jurisdiction. The legal status of Principle 21, however, remains in doubt, although it is regarded by many states as reflective of customary international law on this matter. This principle has been reaffirmed by Principle 2 of the Rio Declaration on Environment and Development 1992.

What is required, however, are rules which are global in their scope in order to protect the biosphere from environmental harm. When the problems with the environment transcend national and international boundaries, the ability of traditional sources of international law to cope is limited. Furthermore, international environmental law has to protect, preserve, and regulate those areas of the world which are outside States' territorial jurisdiction, known as the global commons – that is, the high seas, deep sea bed, atmosphere, Antarctica, outer space, etc. There are now a number of multilateral treaties regulating environmental threats to these areas of global commons, such as Parts VII and XII of the 1982 UNCLOS (the high seas), the 1987 Montreal Protocol to the 1985 Vienna Convention on Substances that Deplete the Ozone Layer (global atmosphere), the 1992 Framework Convention on Climate Change (global climate change) and the 1991 Madrid Protocol to the Antarctic Treaty on Environmental Protection. While these treaty instruments provide obligations as between

State parties for the protection of these global commons areas, questions still abound as to whom these obligations are actually owed, whether they cover non-parties to the treaties under general or customary international law, and how a State party can make a claim under the terms of a treaty for environmental damage sustained in areas beyond its own national jurisdiction.

These structural problems faced by public international law in its attempts to regulate pollution in global commons areas are exacerbated by the transboundary activities of entities such as multinational or transnational companies, which are occasionally beyond the reach of both international and domestic law. Traditionally, it is well known that public international law is the system of law governing States alone, as the only entities capable of possessing international legal personality. The possession of international legal personality was, to a large extent, dependent upon the ability of a State to show evidence of its sovereignty over a specific piece of land territory and the human population within this territory. State sovereignty over territory and population, as well as the activities undertaken within the State, meant that States were the supreme entities under international law. However, in recent years, this paradigm has come under increasing pressure from a variety of new international factors, all of which play an increasingly important role in international affairs, but whose international legal status has not yet been clarified. Among these new international entities are global and regional IGOs, such as the United Nations and the European Union respectively; international NGOs in the fields of human rights and environmental protection (such as Amnesty International, Greenpeace, Friends of the Earth, World Wide Fund for Nature); and transnational or multinational companies (TNCs or MNCs), such as Royal Dutch Shell, Microsoft, Coca-Cola, Nestlé, Novartis, Unilever, etc.

While the IGOs have begun making inroads towards being accepted as having partial international legal personality, for example, in terms of their participation in multilateral conventions (with the acceptance of States), the other two types of international entities – the NGOs and TNCs/MNCs – have not yet been accorded such international legal status. Both these new types of international entities have important reasons for being given at least partial international legal personality. In the case of the human rights and environmental protection NGOs, this is in order to give the views of their constituencies an airing in the international arena, in order that the issues raised are accepted by States as requiring urgent action.

The last couple of decades have been marked by a proliferation of international environmental organisations (including those established by treaty) and greater efforts by existing institutions to address environmental issues; the development of new sources of international environmental obligation from acts of such organisations; new environmental norms established by treaty; the development of new techniques for implementing environmental standards, including environmental impact assessment and access to information; and the formal integration of environment and development, particularly in relation to international trade and development assistance. In this context, it is important to note, too, the rise of environmental NGOs, such as Greenpeace, Friends of the Earth and the World Wide Fund for Nature, and the consequent part they have played in raising public consciousness over environmental issues at the international, national and local levels. The importance of their role, both in terms of the issues they raise and the constituencies they represent, has been explicitly recognised in their success at gaining certain participatory (although not voting) rights at the negotiations and conferences of parties to international environmental treaties. Examples of these include the Convention on International Trade in Endangered Species (CITES) 1973 (Art XI(7)), the 1987 Montreal Protocol on Substances that Deplete the Ozone Layer (Art 11(5)), the 1989 Basel Convention on the Control of Transboundary Movements of Hazardous Wastes, and the 1992 Framework Convention on Climate Change.

Apart from the greater provision and recognition of the role of environmental and human rights NGOs on the international stage, there are two other main aspects to the issue of the provision of environmental information and consultation or participation in environmental decision making processes. First, at the interstate level, both general and specific international environmental instruments have laid down, in varying degrees of strictness, requirements to exchange relevant environmental information and consult each other on potentially hazardous activities conducted in their territorial jurisdictions or under their control. These obligations to notify and consult other States may be regarded as partly fulfilling a duty of due diligence under international law. Secondly, various international agreements have been arguably more progressive in their provision of environmental rights in one form or another by States to their citizens. This trend reflects that which is appearing at the domestic and regional levels, calling for greater provision of substantive and procedural rights to citizens for environmental protection.

Focusing on this second main strand of the evolving legal regime for ensuring environmental protection, this involves the recognition by States of a duty to inform, consult and possibly even allow certain rights of participation to their citizens in environmental policy decision making matters, especially when these involve their local environments. The overall scope of this duty is yet to be properly defined at the international level, but the range of possibilities that it encompasses is extremely wide. These include: the rights of individuals or local communities to be consulted within local environmental decision making processes (such as planning inquiries); their input in environmental impact assessment exercises; their rights of representation before courts of law in order to challenge environmental laws and policies which may affect them negatively; and the legal remedies they may be able to rely upon, ranging from injunctions against certain activities to damages for civil liability, and even criminal sanctions or penalties. The nature and extent of the recognition of this right at the international level is discussed below.

On an even broader front, the question of whether similar types of rights may be enjoyed by many other different constituencies, such as ethnic minority groups, indigenous peoples, future generations of peoples, animals, plants, and the natural environment *per se*, is one which will be noted but not discussed at length here due to constraints of space and time. Suffice to note, as publicists on this issue have done, that claims of this kind are usually intended to effect a reorientation of the relationship between man and the environment, through broader participation in the process of law enforcement, dispute resolution, and environmental guardianship.

It is clear from the above points that even an accepted definition of the term 'environmental rights' has yet to be recognised under international law. Among the many unanswered questions concerning this right are, *inter alia,* whether it is a substantive new right, or merely a re-interpretation of an existing right, or even a procedural rather than a substantive right; who has the right to exercise it; at what stage in any environmental decision making process they can exercise this right; and what remedies they can request in the exercise of this right. These issues have only recently been addressed by international lawyers as part of a general trend towards realising the extent of limitations placed upon the doctrine of State sovereignty by international human rights and environmental law.

Without needing to enter into a discussion on exactly what an 'environmental right' should entail and to whom it should be made available, the focus here will be on the extent to which certain formulations of it have been recognised already under international law, especially in the aftermath of the 1992 Rio 'Earth Summit'. The conclusion that may be arrived at through such an analysis is that autonomous and explicit environmental rights, which would legitimise international supervision of the whole range of a State's domestic environmental policies and allow individual claimants access to human rights or environmental institutions, are currently lacking in international law. Such environmental rights that do exist are either derived from other existing treaty rights – such as the right to life, health or ownership of property – or of a much more general nature, in the sense of the right to an environment of quality suitable for the enjoyment of all other human rights.

In the absence of a well defined and fully accepted catalogue of 'environmental rights' that States agree are owed to their citizens, this leaves environmental rights to be protected only in a procedural sense. In other words, this means that environmental protection can proceed only on the basis of an exercise of procedural rights in order to ensure access to environmental information, allow participation in environmental decision making, and provide administrative and judicial remedies for cases of environmental injustice.

The prevailing ambivalence among States to the provision of substantive, as opposed to procedural, rights to environmental protection may be discerned from an examination of the relevant provisions on this subject in the general standard setting international environmental instruments, such as the 1972 Stockholm Declaration on the Human Environment and the 1992 Rio Declaration on Environment and Development. Although Principle 1 of the Stockholm Declaration arguably provides for individual and collective rights to an environment of such quality as to permit a life of dignity and well being, it is significant that no other treaty refers explicitly in these terms to the right of a decent environment. Where environmental rights are mentioned at all, they are usually phrased in collective terms (peoples' as opposed to individual's rights), as in Art 24 of the African Charter on Human and Peoples' Rights, or as a right to a healthy, as opposed to decent, environment, such as in Art 12 of the 1966 UN Covenant on Economic and Social Rights. Even these weaker formulations of substantive environmental rights have yet to be fully accepted.

The 1992 Rio Declaration contains no explicit human right to a decent environment. Indeed, by placing human beings at the centre of concerns for sustainable development in Principle 1, albeit 'in harmony with nature', the declaration appears to have laid down an explicitly anthropocentric approach that views the environment and its natural resources as existing only for human benefit, with no intrinsic value in themselves. Principle 10 of the Rio Declaration, however, does give substantial support in mandatory language for participatory environmental rights of an individualistic and fairly comprehensive nature. This formulation of participatory rights is distinguishable from other such rights found in the context of human rights instruments due to its focus on environmental matters and its emphasis on participation rights throughout the environmental decision making process, from 'appropriate' access to information to effective access to administrative and judicial remedies. The accompanying paragraph in Chapter 23 of Agenda 21, elaborating upon this broad right of participation, also emphasises the need for individual, group and organisational inputs to the environmental impact assessment procedures (para 23.2).

Aspects of Principle 10 of the Rio Declaration can also be found in Principle 23 of the 1982 World Charter for Nature; Arts 2(6) and 3(8) of the 1991 Espoo ECE Convention on Environmental Impact Assessment; Art 14 of the 1992 Biodiversity Convention; and, in recent EU directives on these issues, namely, environmental impact assessment (1985) and access to environmental information (1990). The inclusion of provisions relating to participatory rights in environmental decision making processes within these global, as well as regional, instruments arguably reflects significant international support among States for procedural as opposed to substantive rights to a healthy environment.

CHAPTER 12

HUMAN RIGHTS

Introduction

Like the international law for the protection of the environment, public international law for the protection of human rights is a relatively recent, post-Second World War (1939–45), phenomenon. It is without doubt, however, one of the most significant advances of international law during this second half of the 20th century. Perhaps more important though is the fact that, also like international environmental law, the development of this new branch of public international law represents a clearly implied restriction on the hitherto unrivalled sovereignty under modern public international law of a nation State over activities and individuals within its own territory. The international protection of human rights can therefore be seen as presenting an implicit systemic or structural threat to the traditional notion of public international law as a system of binding rules which govern only other sovereign States and possibly certain well known global and regional intergovernmental organisations (IGOs) (see Chapters 4, 5 and 11 above).

Quite apart from the implied threat to the system of public international law itself, the international protection of human rights also presents sub-disciplinary problems of its own accord. Chief among them are: (1) the issues of the definition of fundamental individual and collective (or group) human rights that require universal legal protection; and (2) the exact nature in which they are to be legally protected within the domestic jurisdiction of a State which is deemed to be bound by these rights under public international law. Although some redress may be afforded within the system of public international law under the doctrine of state responsibility for the protection of foreign nationals and their property (see Chapter 10 above), the ill treatment of the nationals of a State within the confines of the territorial jurisdiction of the State itself has only recently been argued to amount to a possible breach of general or customary international law in its own right, aside from where it is explicitly provided for under international conventional or treaty law.

This expansion of the jurisdictional scope of public international law to include the protection of human rights, albeit through the provision and acceptance of a very limited type of individual legal personality, which is confined to the possibility of an individual making claims against the governmental institutions of a State, either in its own courts of law or in a supra-national court of human rights, is nevertheless a significant achievement in itself under public international law. Again along with international law for environmental protection, human rights protection is an area of public international law where States cannot anymore readily rely on the doctrine of domestic jurisdiction and the principle of non-interference in the internal matters of a State, as provided, for example, in Art 2(7) of the UN Charter 1945, in order to deny the application of binding international rules within a state's territorial jurisdiction.

Further problems of a substantive nature arise when determining the extent to which certain fundamental human rights are protected by the traditionally recognised sources of international law, namely customary international law or, more usually, conventional or treaty law which is the main source of the international law for human rights protection, again, not unlike the situation found in international environmental law. These substantive difficulties are coupled with procedural problems related to the actual implementation of recognised and accepted international human rights obligations in terms of the lack of compulsory enforcement mechanisms both at the supra-national and domestic levels of jurisdiction within the nation State. This has led to criticism of the apparent ineffectiveness of international human rights law, with the notable exception of the operation of the regionally applicable European Convention on Human Rights 1950.

At the global level, the UN Charter 1945 incorporates several provisions reaffirming, recognising and promoting the observance of human rights, from the second paragraph of its Preamble, through to Arts 1(3) and 55(c), with Art 56 of the Charter arguably placing States under an international legal obligation to take practical steps for the provision of legal remedies for the protection of human rights.

A substantive enumeration of civil, political, economic, social and cultural rights followed in the 1948 Universal Declaration of Human Rights, a UN General Assembly Resolution adopted without objection (and with only eight abstentions) which, though non-legally binding in itself, has nevertheless not been without legal effect, especially in terms of providing the impetus for the acceptance of these rights under customary international law and more specific international treaty regimes of global application, such as the UN Convention against Torture and Other Cruel, Inhuman or Degrading Treatment or Punishment1984. For example, in the case of *Filartiga v Peña-Irala* (1980), a US court held that the 1948 Universal Declaration of Human Rights provided evidence of the definition and acceptance under customary international law of certain basic or fundamental human rights, especially the right to be free from torture (Art 5).

In addition to the UN Charter 1945 and the 1948 Universal Declaration, two other global treaties, both in terms of their subject matter and geographical scope, must be highlighted here. These are respectively, the 1966 International Covenant on Civil and Political Rights (ICCPR) and the 1966 International Covenant on Economic, Social and Cultural Rights (ICESCR). Both these Covenants are legally binding instruments laying down, respectively, a reasonably comprehensive list of obligations providing for the protection of universally recognised (so called 'first generation' civil and political rights), as well as the rather more subjectively defined economic, social and cultural rights (so called 'second generation' rights). Although several commentators have warned of the rather dubious distinctions made between first and second generation human rights, it can readily be seen that both the definition (more amorphous) and enforcement (more flexible, less stringent) of these so called second generation rights are more uncertain in their legal nature and content than those of first generation rights. Indeed this distinction is perhaps the most important issue in respect of the legal protection of human rights under international law: exactly which human rights are susceptible to such protection and the extent to which these rights are in fact protected either by supra-national institutions or the State itself.

As with the other substantive areas of public international law, such as the international law of the sea and international environmental law, questions on human rights can be found in both essay and problem form. The essay questions usually invite the student to consider certain theoretical issues in relation to the international protection of human rights. The provision of treaty and case law examples is particularly important to illustrate any points made in relation to the issues raised in the essay.

In problem questions involving the alleged ill treatment of both nationals and foreigners, it is especially important not to neglect the fact that such ill treatment of foreigners can be considered a breach or violation of an international obligation possibly giving rise to state responsibility under general international law, quite apart from any claim as a result of a breach of an international obligation for the protection of human rights.

Checklist

When answering both essay and problem questions on the international protection of human rights, a number of points need to be borne in mind:
- the structural difficulty that human rights protection gives rise to within a system of public international law that ostensibly rests upon the exclusivity of Sovereign States within their own territorial jurisdictions;
- the extent of the recognition and acceptance of substantive international obligations for the protection of human rights by States under general or customary international law, as opposed to international treaty law which is both codified and predicated upon acceptance by the provision of explicit consent;
- the recognition, acceptance and provision of procedural rights in order to effectuate the substantive human rights obligations accepted by States in treaty or customary law, either through recourse to a supra-national institution or court or the requirement that national or domestic institutions implement these obligations as part of domestic law, or both;

- the nature and extent of the protection accorded by States to individuals within their internal legal systems for the adjudication and enforcement of certain accepted human rights obligations, whether under international customary or treaty law.

Question 42

Can it be argued that there is now an effective system for the universal protection of human rights under international law?
Discuss.

Answer plan

This essay question gives the student an opportunity to explore a number of theoretical and practical questions surrounding the protection of human rights under international law.

In answering this essay question, therefore, the student should be concerned first of all to be able to distinguish between the conceptual issues that need to be tackled before proceeding to an examination of the problems thrown up by the implementation of human rights obligations by nation States.

Some of the theoretical or conceptual points and practical issues that may be raised are as follows:
- what are the structural or systemic difficulties with respect to the recognition and acceptance of international obligations to protect human rights?
- what types of human rights may now be considered to have been accorded legal protection and why is this the case?
- are these rights protected under international law on a universal basis, or is their protection based on regional mechanisms?
- how exactly are these rights protected, for example, through supra-national institutions or domestic implementation through national institutions? And to what extent are these rights legally protected?
- since human rights obligations are owed by States to individuals (as well as to other States), in the absence of a

centralised system of enforcement at the global level, can the national or domestic implementation of these rights against the States themselves be successful?

Answer

There are a number of theoretical and practical questions surrounding the system for the protection of human rights under international law that need to be answered before it is possible to arrive at an estimation of its effectiveness. Indeed, the question of what is meant by 'an effective system' is in itself a difficult one to answer. For some, the effectiveness or otherwise of any particular system of rules is to be measured solely in terms of how far it is able to successfully change the behaviour of the individuals that are subject to this system of rules. Judged by this measure, it may be difficult to see how the system for the protection of human rights under international law can claim to be effective in the light of continuing abuses of human rights which are supposed to be legally protected in every country in the world. On the other hand, if the focus of attention is shifted to the issue of whether an adequate system is being established in a situation where there was no previous system for the protection of such rights, and the question is whether this system will eventually be effective in yielding a better record of human rights protection in different countries around the world, then it may be possible to state that a certain measure of effectiveness has already been achieved through the mere establishment of a system where previously there was none.

This latter view concerning the effectiveness of the international legal system for the protection of human rights takes into account the structural difficulties that are encountered when an international community composed of sovereign and equal States, a major characteristic of which suggests that these States have near total sovereignty over all activities and nationals within their territorial jurisdiction, is confronted with the international obligation to protect the human rights of their own nationals.

Another question arising from the issue of the effectiveness of international human rights law concerns whether in fact such effectiveness must necessarily always culminate in the acceptance and provision on the part of the nation State of legally enforceable human rights in a national or even supra-national court of law.

There can be no doubt however that a general international obligation for the protection of human rights of both nationals and aliens within the territorial jurisdiction of States does now exist both under treaty law and, even arguably, under customary international law. At the global level, the UN Charter 1945 incorporates several provisions reaffirming, recognising and promoting the observance of human rights, from the second paragraph of its Preamble, through to Arts 1(3) and 55(c), with Art 56 of the Charter arguably placing States under an international legal obligation to take practical steps for the provision of legal remedies for the protection of human rights.

Questions persist, however, as to the exact nature and extent of the specific human rights that States are obliged to accept, implement and enforce, and by the fact that their universal application is by no means uniform. These continuing questions raise the issue of effectiveness once again and it is not possible to state at the present time that there is an effective system for the universal protection of human rights under international law.

This admission of the general ineffectiveness of the universal system should not, however, be allowed to detract from the undoubted success of certain regional systems human rights enforcement, notably the European Convention on Human Rights 1950 which established supra-national regional institutions, namely the European Commission on Human Rights and the European Court of Human Rights to hear cases against the governments of States Parties where it is alleged that rights and freedoms provided under the Convention have been abused.

Having noted that a universal system for the legal protection of human rights exists but that it does not enforce a uniform standard of human rights effectively, the next issue we need to consider is the specific types of human rights that should be accorded legal protection. A substantive enumeration of civil, political, economic, social and cultural rights in of Human Rights followed the general obligations laid down by the provisions of the 1945 UN Charter.

The 1948 Universal Declaration is a UN General Assembly Resolution adopted without objection (and with only eight abstentions) which, though non-legally binding in itself, has nevertheless not been without legal effect, especially in terms of providing the impetus for the acceptance of these rights under customary international law and more specific international treaty regimes of global application, such as the UN Convention against Torture and Other Cruel, Inhuman or Degrading Treatment or Punishment 1984. For example, in the case of *Filartiga v Peña-Irala* (1980), a US court held that the 1948 Universal Declaration of Human Rights provided evidence and definition of the acceptance under customary international law of certain basic or fundamental human rights, especially the right to be free from torture (Art 5).

In addition to the UN Charter 1945 and the 1948 Universal Declaration, two other global treaties, both in terms of their subject matter and geographical scope, must be highlighted here. These are respectively, the 1966 International Covenant on Civil and Political Rights (ICCPR) and the 1966 International Covenant on Economic, Social and Cultural Rights (ICESCR). Both these Covenants are legally binding instruments laying down, respectively, a reasonably comprehensive list of obligations providing for the protection of universally recognised (so called 'first generation') civil and political rights, as well as the rather more subjectively defined economic, social and cultural rights (so called 'second generation' rights). Although several commentators have warned of the rather dubious distinctions made between first and second generation human rights, it can readily be seen that both the definition (more amorphous) and enforcement (more flexible, less stringent) of these so called second generation rights are more uncertain in their legal nature and content than those of first generation rights. Indeed, this distinction is perhaps the most important issue in respect of the legal protection of human rights under international law: exactly which human rights are susceptible to such protection and the extent to which these rights are in fact protected either by supra-national institutions or the state itself.

Returning to the issue of the establishment of institutions to ensure the international protection of human rights, it may be asked to what extent these rights are protected and how, exactly, are these rights protected, for example, by national institutions or supra-national institutions? In this respect, it is important to note that these institutions do not always manifest themselves in the form of supra-national courts of law, like the European Court of Human Rights.

For example, it is arguable that the 1966 International Covenant of Civil and Political Rights (ICCPR) mentioned above provides at least three different institutional means of obtaining changes in the otherwise abusive behaviour of a State Party in respect of its human rights violations. However only one of these may be held to provide a form of individual redress which approaches the notion of a legally enforceable right and it is not a compulsory requirement. These three methods of enforcement are respectively, the system of periodic reporting every five years by the State Party to the Human Rights Committee under Art 40 of the ICCPR 1966; the procedure established on a reciprocal basis under Art 41 for inter-State complaints, through the Human Rights Committee; and, finally, the possibility of utilising the optional individual complaints procedure under the 1966 Optional Protocol to the Covenant, again to the Human Right Committee for deliberation. Individual applications are subject to the rule requiring exhaustion of local remedies. Although this procedure is entirely optional and, in theory, the Human Rights Committee does not act judicially when considering complaints made by individuals, nevertheless it has been noted that the proceedings against State Parties before the Committee are becoming more 'judicial' in their character and approach. For example, in the case of *Bleir v Uruguay* (1982) the Committee established that the burden of proof in respect of individual complaints does not rest on the applicant alone, especially considering the obvious lack of equal access to vital evidential information on the part of the individual applicant as against the full apparatus of the State against which the complaint has been made.

The relative effectiveness of the optional system has also been enhanced recently by more widespread publication of the individual awards as a result of successful complaints, and the practice of the Committee to require States found responsible for a breach of the Covenant to submit information within a deadline on measures introduced in order to redress the violations found by the Committee.

Despite this limited progress on the effectiveness of the system established by the Covenant and its Optional Protocol, however, it is pertinent to ask whether, in the absence of a centralised system of enforcement at the global level, the national or domestic implementation of these rights against the States themselves can be successful? In this respect, it is important to note that, although the States Parties to the Optional Protocol are arguably under a specific duty to implement and enforce the obligations of the Covenant, the parties to the Covenant itself are not subject to a stringent requirement of enforcement and the possibility of continuing abuse is ever present.

Question 43

Diana is a Bognian national by birth, a nationality she retained after she married Charles, an Arcadian national, although she thereby obtained Arcadian nationality also. In February last year, whilst on holiday in Bognia, they were caught up in a demonstration mounted by opposition political parties to the cancellation of the planned and constitutionally required Arcadian national elections by the Arcadian government under the pretext of a national emergency due to the poor performance of the local economy. The police forces beat up Charles and Diana, along with scores of Bognian demonstrators and innocent bystanders and take them into custody. Charles and Diana were held in the same conditions as the Bognians, which is to say three to a prison cell intended for one, one mattress between three, no bedding, no heating and no light. They were denied access to any Arcadian consular official or a lawyer, having been told that they were not entitled to any special privileges and were to be treated just like everyone else. They were held for 30 days before being released without charge and summarily deported back to Arcadia.

Upon their return to Arcadia and after recovering from their ordeal, Charles and Diana contact the Arcadian Foreign Ministry requesting that some form of compensation be sought on their behalf. However, while Arcadia has ratified the 1966 International Covenant on Civil and Political Rights, Bognia has not done so.

Advise the Arcadian government.

Answer plan

Although this problem question raises several issues in respect of international human rights protection, particularly under the 1966 International Covenant on Civil and Political Rights (ICCPR), it is nevertheless important to begin the answer by considering the issue of State responsibility on behalf of Bognia for its ill treatment of foreign, namely Arcadian nationals, ie, Charles and, arguably, also Diana.

Having considered the issue of Bognian State responsibility for its abuse of Charles and, arguably, Diana's basic human rights, the student can then turn to the question as to whether there has also been a violation of an international human rights obligation, either under customary international law, or international treaty law, in this case the 1966 ICCPR.

After a discussion as to whether it may be assumed that the obligations (as opposed to the institutions and procedural rules) of the 1966 ICCPR are to be treated as forming part of customary international law, the student can then proceed to consider what action is available to Arcadia under the terms of the substantive obligations held to be indicative of accepted customary international law.

Answer

Although this problem raises several issues in respect of international human rights protection, particularly under the 1966 International Covenant on Civil and Political Rights (ICCPR), it is nevertheless important to begin by considering the issue of State responsibility on behalf of Bognia for its ill treatment of foreign, namely Arcadian nationals, ie, Charles and, arguably, also Diana.

The question to be answered here is as to whether Arcadia has a valid claim under international law against Bognia under State responsibility on behalf of Charles and Diana, both Arcadian citizens. The international law of State responsibility in its most basic version, which commands general agreement under customary international law, considers that if a State violates an international obligation, it bears responsibility for that obligation.

Where a State is deemed to have violated such an international legal obligation, this gives rise to apparently serious consequences for it under the international law of State responsibility. The ill treatment of foreign nationals within the territorial jurisdiction of a State constitutes such a violation giving rise to State responsibility. Another violation that may be alleged in this situation is the possible unlawful expulsion of Charles and Diana from Bognia. Thus, Arcadia can claim international responsibility on the part of Bognia if Arcadia is able to show that Bognia has acted or omitted to act in breach of its international obligations towards Arcadia, at least in respect of the ill treatment and injuries that Charles and Diana suffered while they were in Bognia.

An important criterion that needs to be fulfilled is the requirement that the nationality of the individuals concerned be the same as the State claiming on their behalf. Arguably, Charles will be able to show this relationship easily, being an Arcadian national but the situation may be more complicated for Diana as she obtained Arcadian nationality by her marriage to Charles, and was originally Bognian. The *Nottebohm* case (1955) appears to lay down a rule requiring a genuine link between the person and the nationality she espouses, although this rather strict requirement has been toned down in other cases such as the *Flegenheimer Claim* (1958).

Assuming Charles and Diana are able to provide evidence of their Arcadian nationality in order to fulfil the requirement of nationality for the purpose of Arcadia making a claim under the doctrine of State responsibility on their behalf, it is important to note that the rules of public international law on this issue have moved away from a historical requirement (pre-World War II) to prove fault as a basis for international responsibility, to the position (for example, under the Draft Articles on State Responsibility submitted by the International Law Commission (ILC)) that States should be responsible for their actions independently of fault; the main reason for dispensing with the need to prove fault being the absence of adequate procedures to establish it. Thus, increasingly, responsibility for result became the accepted form of responsibility for wrongful actions, although not for omissions. Adopting this test in relation to Charles' and Diana's injuries and ill treatment by the Bognian police, it may be possible to impute international responsibility on the part of

Bognia without needing to show fault on the part of any of the Bognian authorities actually responsible for their ill treatment.

Yet another complication which may arise in relation to claims made under State responsibility is the standard of protection that both Charles and Diana would have been entitled to receive while they were in Bognia. In this respect, also, recent trends in the adjudication of State responsibility have moved away from the acceptance of a national standard in favour of an international minimum standard of treatment so that it is not a valid defence to claim that Charles and Diana were not treated any worse than a Bognian citizen as a result of the Bognian police action. Last, but not least, any claim for State responsibility by Arcadia against Bognia on behalf of Charles and Diana must first ensure that both of them have exhausted all local remedies within Bognia for redress against their ill treatment and injuries before proceedings can begin on the international plane.

Quite apart from the possibility of claims made under the international law of State responsibility by Arcadia on behalf of Charles and, arguably, Diana too, Arcadia may be able to make a claim under the international law of human rights protection for breach of their rights by the Bognian authorities. Unlike the international law on State responsibility, however, human rights obligations either owed between States or between a State and its nationals within its territorial jurisdiction is a relatively recent phenomenon and their acceptance by any State is still subject to specific requirements of proof under conventional or customary international law.

Aside from the implied threat to the system of public international law itself, that the latter proposition may hold, the international protection of human rights also presents sub-disciplinary problems of its own accord. Chief among them are the issues of the definition of fundamental individual and collective (or group) human rights that require universal legal protection and the exact nature in which they are to be legally protected within the domestic jurisdiction of a State which is deemed to be bound by these rights under public international law. Although, as we have seen above, some redress may be afforded within the system of public international law under the doctrine of State responsibility for the protection of foreign nationals and their property, the ill treatment of the nationals of a State within the confines of the territorial jurisdiction of the State itself has only recently been argued to amount to a possible breach of general or customary international law in its own right, aside from where it is explicitly provided for under international conventional or treaty law.

In particular, as in the situation before us where one State (Bognia) is not party to the relevant multilateral convention governing issues of ill treatment and abuses of certain human rights, then it is incumbent upon the other State (Arcadia) to show that these substantive obligations are nevertheless binding upon it (Bognia) under customary international law. In this respect there are strong arguments for assuming that the obligations (as opposed to the institutions and procedural rules) of the 1966 ICCPR are to be treated as forming part of customary international law.

First, the Covenant has now gained acceptance among the vast majority of the international community of States and more importantly is regarded by the international community as a whole as a statement of certain basic and fundamental rights that all States should uphold both within and without the treaty regime itself. Secondly, many of the fundamental rights that are included within this treaty have now also been incorporated into regional treaties, national constitutions and re-affirmed in all manner of Declarations and Resolutions. There can be little doubt therefore that Bognia is bound to uphold the rights contained in the 1966 ICCPR, in respect of all individuals within its jurisdiction.

The question arises however as to the means of redress available to Arcadia in respect of the alleged violations of these rights, in particular Art 7 (the right to be free from torture or cruel, inhuman or degrading treatment or punishment), Art 9 (right of liberty and security of person and to be free from arbitrary arrest or detention) and Art 10 (right to be treated with humanity when lawfully deprived of their liberty) in respect of Charles and Diana. Even within the institutions that treaty regime has set out, involving possible recourse to a State application to the Human Rights Committee under the procedure laid down in Art 41, the prospects for redress are limited and the report of the Committee is in any case non-binding upon the State Party concerned. The relative ineffectiveness of this procedure is highlighted by the fact that, to date, no State applications have been received against another State Party to the Covenant. As Bognia is not even a party to the 1966 ICCPR, it would appear that Arcadia's only option is again under the doctrine of State responsibility in terms of a claim of ill treatment, injury and abuse of the relevant substantive obligations provided in the Covenant that can now be argued to be part of customary international law binding upon all States and Bognia in particular in this case. A possible Bognia defence of a state of public emergency can be discounted as it does not fulfil the definition under Art 4 of the 1966 ICCPR as threatening the life of the Bognian nation.

Question 44

Does the development of international human rights law mean that individuals are now subjects of international law?

Discuss.

Answer plan

This essay question focuses on the issue of the implementation of human rights protection under international law and its implications for the system of public international law generally. It allows the student to discuss the various supervision, monitoring and implementation mechanisms developed by both global and regional treaty regimes.

Within these treaty implementation regimes, however, emphasis should be placed on the recognition and acceptance to different degrees of the partial legal personality accorded to individuals and even certain interest groups in order to ensure the application of the substantive legal obligations that States have entered into.

To this extent, examples can be drawn from various treaties and case law to show the extent of this acceptance of partial legal personality at the international level.

Answer

Like the international law for the protection of the environment, public international law for the protection of human rights is a relatively recent, post-Second World War (1939–45), phenomenon. It is without doubt, however, one of the most significant advances of international law during this second half of the 20th century. Perhaps more important, though, is the fact that, also like international environmental law, the development of this new branch of public international law represents a clearly implied restriction on the hitherto unrivalled sovereignty under modern public international law of a nation State over activities and individuals within its own territory. The international protection of human rights can therefore be seen as presenting an implicit systemic or structural threat to the traditional notion of public international law as a system of binding rules which govern only other sovereign states and possibly certain well known global and regional intergovernmental organisations (IGOs).

Such partial acceptance of international legal personality as manifested by the right to make a claim under State responsibility on behalf of harm suffered by employees has been accorded to intergovernmental organisations such as the UN under international law. This acceptance of partial personality was highlighted in the *Reparation for Injuries Suffered in the Service of the United Nations* case (1949), where an Advisory Opinion of the ICJ held that the Member States of the UN had brought into being an entity possessing objective international personality, which included the capacity to bring international claims against any UN Member State in respect of injuries suffered by individuals in the course their service with the UN.

This essay will focus on the issue of the implementation of human rights protection under international law and its implications for the system of public international law generally. It will discuss the various supervision, monitoring and implementation mechanisms developed by both global and regional treaty regimes. Within these treaty implementation regimes, emphasis will be placed on the recognition and acceptance to different degrees of the partial legal personality accorded to individuals and even certain interest groups in order to ensure the application of the substantive legal obligations that states have entered into.

This expansion of the jurisdictional scope of public international law to include the protection of human rights, albeit through the provision and acceptance of a very limited type of individual legal personality, which is confined to the possibility of an individual making claims against the governmental institutions of a State, either in its own courts of law or in a supra-national court of human rights, is nevertheless a significant achievement in itself under public international law.

Along with the international law for environmental protection, human rights protection is arguably an area of public international law where States cannot anymore rely on the doctrine of domestic jurisdiction and the principle of non-interference in the internal matters of a State, as provided, for example, in Art 2(7) of the UN Charter 1945, in order to deny the application of binding international rules within a State's territorial jurisdiction. To this extent, examples can be drawn from various treaties and case law to show the extent of this acceptance of partial legal personality at the international level.

At this point it is also important to draw a distinction between (1) the recognition of the rights of an individual as a possible subject of international law under customary international law; as opposed to (2) where recognition is accepted by explicit agreement on the part of the traditional subjects of international law, namely States. There are now many instances where individuals have been granted partial personality at the international level, by way of explicit provision to that effect under bilateral and multilateral treaties entered into by the States, and/or other individual parties, involved. Partial personality has been granted, not merely in relation to the legal protection of human rights, but also in areas such as State responsibility for the ill treatment of foreign nationals (both individual and corporate), and the internationalisation of certain contracts under international law between governments and multinational companies.

In terms of the recognition, acceptance and enforcement of human rights under customary international law, however, there are very few examples, if at all, where individuals have been allowed to make claims as against their governments or government officials, aside from constitutional provisions laying down such rights for enforcement within the domestic legal system. A related but not applicable example in this respect, because it did not involve a claim by an individual against a government, is the case of *Filartiga v Peña-Irala* (1980), where a US court held that the 1948 Universal Declaration of Human Rights provided evidence of the definition and acceptance under customary international law of certain basic or fundamental human rights, especially the right to be free from torture (Art 5).

Returning to the acceptance under international treaty law of such partial personality on the international plane in the implementation and enforcement of human rights obligations by individuals, it is also important to note that such acceptance has not necessarily involved the legal enforcement of these human rights in national or supra-national courts of law, like the European Court of Human Rights.

For example, it is arguable that the 1966 International Covenant of Civil and Political Rights (ICCPR) mentioned above provides at least three different institutional means of obtaining changes in the otherwise abusive behaviour of a State Party in respect of its human rights violations. These three methods of enforcement are respectively, the system of periodic reporting every five years by the State Party to the Human Rights Committee under Art 40 of the ICCPR 1966; the procedure established on a reciprocal basis under Art 41 for inter-State complaints, through the Human Rights Committee; and finally, the possibility of utilising the optional individual complaints procedure under the 1966 Optional Protocol to the Covenant, again to the Human Right Committee for deliberation. However only the last of these may be held to provide a form of individual redress which approaches the notion of a legally enforceable right and it is not a compulsory requirement. Individual applications are also subject to the rule requiring exhaustion of local remedies.

Although this procedure is entirely optional and, in theory, the Human Rights Committee does not act judicially when considering complaints made by individuals, nevertheless, it has been noted that the proceedings against State Parties before the Committee are becoming more 'judicial' in their character and approach. For example, in the case of *Bleir v Uruguay* (1982), the

Committee established that the burden of proof in respect of individual complaints does not rest on the applicant alone, especially considering the obvious lack of equal access to vital evidential information on the part of the individual applicant as against the full apparatus of the State against which the complaint has been made. The relative effectiveness of the optional system has also been enhanced recently by more widespread publication of the individual awards as a result of successful complaints, and the practice of the Committee to require States found responsible for a breach of the Covenant to submit information within a deadline on measures introduced in order to redress the violations found by the Committee.

Another example of an international mechanism which was established to contribute to the supervision, monitoring and reporting process in respect of gross human rights abuses is the Human Rights Commission, set up by the UN Economic and Social Council (ECOSOC). This Commission, although a primarily political rather than judicial body, has potentially wide powers to oversee the development of the human rights objectives of the UN Charter 1945. It has jurisdiction to investigate allegations of widespread violations of human rights. However, the reports of the Commission are not legally binding and there is no enforcement mechanism to ensure that abuses, even of a gross or widespread nature, will be redressed or at least not repeated.

Since 1970, the Commission has altered its procedure so as to enable it to investigate individual complaints submitted to it under the auspices of the Sub-Commission on Prevention and Discrimination of Minorities, which is in turn empowered to make recommendations to the Human Rights Commission, which may then instigate an investigation, with the consent of the State. Again, however, the results of any such investigation are not legally binding upon the State concerned. Also the Sub-Commission may only take action in respect of allegations that reveal a consistent pattern of gross human rights violations.

At the regional level, the outstanding example of the provision of legally enforceable rights for individuals either at the level of national or domestic courts of law or through recourse to a supranational court is the 1950 European Convention on Human Rights, which has created a set of international institutions that accept, hear and pass judgment upon individual applications against the governments of States parties to the Convention, alleging human rights abuses. Although many States parties have formally incorporated the Convention into their domestic law, the European Court of Human Rights continues to act as the final, supra-national court of appeal for applicants from these States, as well as those States that have yet to incorporate the Convention into domestic law such as the UK, at least until the Human Rights Bill currently before Parliament is passed into effect.

Therefore, it may be concluded that individuals are still not to be regarded as fully-fledged subjects of international law in the sense of possessing complete international legal personality. However, under certain circumstances, mainly when explicitly provided for in treaty obligations accepted by States, they have been granted partial legal personality for the purpose of enforcing their rights under the human rights treaty concerned. It is important to note that the provision of such a right of enforcement is usually dependent upon the express consent of the State party concerned.

A related development which augurs well for the promotion of greater access to justice on the part of individuals, is the increasing acceptance, in certain jurisdictions, of public interest groups as fulfilling the requirement of *locus standi*. For example, in the UK environmental non-governmental organisations, such as Greenpeace, are becoming more able to bring claims before courts on issues affecting their individual members.

CHAPTER 13

PEACEFUL SETTLEMENT OF DISPUTES

Introduction

In this book, we have already dealt with questions concerning the law making process in international law. What happens, however, when a dispute arises over the application or interpretation of that law? This chapter is dedicated to the adjudication processes which attempt to resolve such disputes as arise. The student should never lose sight of the fact that the vast majority of disputes that arise over international law are decided quietly through diplomatic channels. In the same way, the vast majority of potentially litigious municipal disputes are settled by a communication between solicitors. When such methods fail, the international community has developed a number of mechanisms for conflict resolution.

Chapter VI of the UN Charter provides that parties shall first seek a solution by 'negotiation ... arbitration, judicial settlement, resort to regional agencies or arrangements, or any other means of their own choice'. Resort to the International Court of Justice (ICJ) at the Hague (and its predecessor, the Permanent Court of International Justice (PCIJ)) is easily the most conspicuous method conflict resolution. It is to be recalled, however, that, in the 52 year history of the ICJ, it has so far only heard 67 contentious cases and 22 advisory cases. Thus, since 1946, the World Court has, on average, had to deal with 1.7 cases per year: hardly an overwhelming work load for any court.

As well as examining the structure of the ICJ and the way in which it gains jurisdiction in contentious and advisory opinions, the student will also be called upon to examine arbitration (which is not dealt with in this chapter) and methods of alternative dispute resolution.

In answering a problem question, for example, the following issues should frequently arise:

- the competence of the World Court and the access contentious parties have to it;
- the way in which, if the case is before the ICJ, that court has the necessary jurisdiction to hear the case on its merits;
- contentious litigation and third States;
- the availability of provisional measures in contentious litigation;
- advisory jurisdiction of the World Court;
- the legal relationship between the World Court and the Security Council; and
- methods of alternative dispute resolution

A common essay question on this topic is a variation of the following: Is there a future for the ICJ? Discuss.

Checklist

Students should be familiar with the following areas:
- arbitration;
- alternative dispute resolution;
- the nature of the International Court of Justice;
- the way in which the International Court of Justice can obtain jurisdiction;
- the effectiveness of the International Court of Justice;
- the relationship between other UN organs and the International Court of Justice; and
- other international courts.

Question 45

What mechanisms exist for dispute resolution as alternatives to decisions by the International Court of Justice or arbitration? Discuss.

Answer plan

There are currently 185 Member States of the United Nations. There is an ever growing struggle between those States for scarce economic resources. Communication links are now vastly superior to those at any prior time in human history. These factors combined mean that disputes between States are becoming, and will become, commoner and commoner. Article 2(4) of the UN Charter states that the use of force to resolve such disputes is now illegal under international law. Consequently, States must resolve other methods to remedy problems that might at one time only have been settled by force. They could utilise the formal structure of the International Court of Justice or resort to arbitration. However, these methods are very expensive and notoriously time consuming. As a consequence, the international community has developed alternative methods of dispute resolution.

In the following essay, the student will need to discuss these methods, and consideration should be given to:

- negotiation as a means of alternative dispute resolution: its definition and its nature;
- mediation as a means of alternative dispute resolution: its definition and its nature;
- conciliation as a means of alternative dispute resolution: its definition and its nature; and
- inquiry as a means of alternative dispute resolution: its definition and its nature; the *Dogger Bank* incident.

If the student has sufficient time and space, consideration might also be given to commenting upon the general effectiveness of such methods.

Answer

Less formal in its means and methods than reference to the International Court of Justice or arbitration is that form of 'peacemaking' known as alternative dispute resolution. This is primarily based upon the disputing parties settling their dispute based upon diplomatic, consensual agreement rather than dispute settlement through judicial decision making (that is, resort to arbitration or the ICJ). Such alternative means of dispute resolution to be discussed in this essay include: negotiation, mediation, conciliation, and an inquiry.[1]

Negotiation, unlike all other methods of alternative dispute resolution, is a matter entirely left in the hands of the parties to that dispute. Negotiations, handled through diplomatic channels, leave open the possibility of concessions being made that would prove satisfactory to both parties. It equally creates the possibility of third States intervening as friendly mediators between the disputants. As a consequence, negotiation has become the first and primary form of dispute settlement in the international community, and any other form is seen as a secondary resort. The Hague Convention on the Pacific Settlement of Disputes of 1899, although recognising that arbitration is the most effective and equitable means of settlement of international disputes, states that it is necessary only to those disputes which diplomacy has failed to settle.

Article 2(3) of the UN Charter, read along with the UN Resolution 2625 (XXV),[2] places a clear duty on the parties to a dispute to seek an early and just settlement of their international disputes by negotiation. In seeking such a settlement, the parties 'shall agree upon such peaceful means as may be appropriate to the circumstances and nature of the dispute'. In the *North Sea Continental Shelf* case (1969), the ICJ judgment stated that the disputing parties could even be obliged 'to conduct themselves [so] that the negotiations [they engage in] are meaningful'.

Negotiation between the disputing parties can also be resorted to when both anticipate a conflict arising in the future. This may have the effect of allowing both parties to achieve the same ends but in such a way that the negative impact upon the rival party will be reduced as far as is possible. After the 1982 Falkland Island dispute between Argentina and the UK, these States hoped to avoid unnecessary military confrontations due to the presence of their respective military forces in the south Atlantic. In 1990, they entered into an Interim Reciprocal Information and Consultation System. This agreement provided for a consultation system which will govern 'movements of united of their Armed Forces in Areas of the South West Atlantic. The aims of this [conciliation] system are to increase confidence between Argentina and the United

Kingdom and to contribute to achieving a more normal situation in the region [including a direct communications link]'.

There are, however, problems that arise through solving international disputes by leaving the disputing parties to negotiate a diplomatic settlement. It can only work where both parties are willing to compromise. It will only prove effective where both parties recognised that a dispute exists on a particular problem. It also can break down where there is a great disparity between the relative powers of the parties and/or in which one of the parties believe that they can only achieve their goals by means of military force. An illustration of this latter point was the ultimatum that Austria-Hungary sent to Serbia in 1914, which closed negotiations before they had begun.

One advantage of negotiations is that it gives third States (or persons or organisations) a chance to intervene in a potentially dangerous situation. This is particularly important when the dispute appears to be beyond the ability of the disputing parties to settle by peaceful means. This third party can use its good offices in order to start or restart negotiations between the disputing parties. When such parties begin to negotiate, the third party can then withdraw. Alternatively, the third party could act as a mediator in the dispute. A mediator attempts to perform the role of a catalyst for dispute resolution, both as an individual and as a State. The mediator makes his or her proposals informally and not based upon treaty provisions. Any information used is that provided by the parties to the dispute. Unlike in a commission of inquiry, the mediator does not undertake an independent investigation. Where negotiations are deadlocked, the mediator can attempt to persuade the parties to try to consider a proposal that both sides might find accommodating. Such proceedings are normally held informally and out of the public eye, in contrast to arbitral or judicial proceedings with their formalised procedures for taking evidence from witnesses in an open hearing. There is no prior commitment by the parties to accept the mediator's proposal.

The individual mediator might devise his or her own proposals which, it is believed, following consultation with both parties, both sides will accept. In 1885, when a dispute between Germany and Spain over the Caroline Islands threatened to result in war, that matter was settled under the personal mediation of Pope Leo XIII. In a dispute between Chile and Argentina over the Beagle Channel award, both parties agreed to have Cardinal Antionio Samor as mediator, following the intervention of the Pope. In February 1998, the UN Secretary General, in order to persuade Iraq to comply with UN Security Council Resolutions, in effect, succeeded in brokering a peace between the United States, the UK and Iraq.

On a State level, one can note the mediating role played by Germany (regarding the Balkan dispute) at the Congress of Berlin 1878; by the former Soviet Union in a conflict between India and Pakistan in 1966; Algeria served in the capacity of mediator during the Iran/US hostages crisis in 1979–80; and perhaps most famously, the mediating role played by the US with regard to Israel and Egypt in 1977 and Israel and Palestine in 1993. Switzerland and the International Committee of the Red Cross are frequently used in mediatory capacities in those conflicts where the parties are unlikely to negotiate directly.

Treaties can also provide for mediation as a resort should dispute arise over the terms or application of a treaty. In 1856, the Treaty of Paris (which brought about peace following the Crimean War) bound the signatory powers, in the event of a dispute between themselves and the Sultan of the Ottoman Empire, or amongst themselves, to have recourse to the mediatory action of the whole body of signatories (Art VIII).[3]

Superficially, there seems to be little practical difference between a mediator and a conciliator. A conciliator is designated by the potential disputants to help reconcile their differences. Judge Manley O Hudson described conciliation as 'a process of formulating proposals of settlement after an investigation of the facts and an effort to reconcile opposing contentions, the parties to the dispute being left free to accept or reject the proposals formulated'.[4] The key distinction between conciliation and arbitration is that, if a report is arrived at by a conciliator, both parties are free to accept or reject it findings. Unlike negotiation or mediation, conciliation, because it is based upon either bilateral or multilateral treaty provisions, places third party dispute resolution assistance in a more formalised setting. Like the commission of inquiry, a conciliation commission can engage in a fact finding role. However, the conciliating body normally attempts to promote a resolution to the dispute.

The Hague Conventions of 1899 and 1907 provided for the creation of conciliation commissions, which could be set up by treaty between the disputing parties. They were factually to investigate the matter in question and produce a report on the situation, the understanding being that no party was bound by the results of that report. Following the First World War, the League of Nations General Assembly recommended that States should conclude bilateral treaties requiring the submission of disputes to special conciliation commissions. If the commission failed to resolve the dispute, the parties in question could only then submit their case to the Council of the League. Around 20 treaties were concluded containing such conciliation agreements. These included the Locarno Treaties between Germany, France, Belgium, Czechoslovakia, and Poland. The Locarno Treaties were followed by the League's 1928 General Act for the Pacific Settlement of Disputes.[5] The first chapter of this Act dealt with the procedures and terms under which conciliation was carried out. Under its provision, League Member States established either *ad hoc* or permanent conciliation commissions to act, unless they submitted their disputes to the PCIJ or to a binding arbitration procedure. Almost 200 such treaties were concluded between 1918 and 1939.

Conciliation procedures can now be found within a number of multilateral treaties. These include: 1957 European Convention on the Peaceful Settlement of Disputes;[6] 1963 Charter of the Organisation of African Unity; 1975 Convention on the Representation of States in Their Relations with International Organisations of a Universal Character; 1978 Vienna Convention on the Succession of States in Respect of Treaties; 1981 treaty establishing the Organisation of Caribbean States: moreover, special procedures and arrangements for conciliation are contained within the 1990 UN Draft Rules on Conciliation of Disputes between States and the 1992 Convention on Conciliation and Arbitration Convention within the Conference on Security and Co-operation with Europe (CSCE).

Another form of alternative dispute settlement is that of inquiry. This occurs when a neutral party attempts to provide the disputing parties with an objective assessment. The presence of this third party may bring about the introduction of a better balanced approach to resolving the dispute before it erupts into open conflict. This has proven to be particularly useful with regard to disputed boundaries. Here, the commission of inquiry may be established to search into the historical, geopolitical facts of a given situation and clarify the issues at stake. Note that this would only be a matter of clarification and not recommendation, although, as will be seen below, there has been an occasion when a commission has accorded blame and responsibility.

Commissions of inquiry were first formally created by the convention produced by the Hague Peace Conference of 1899. The role of the commission, which formulated the Convention for the Pacific Settlement of International Disputes 1899, was to outline the procedures which, being limited to the discovery of the facts of an incident, might be resorted to in cases in which the contending parties might be unwilling to submit the entire dispute, involving highly sensitive question of State pride, security and general political interest, to the procedure of arbitration. Article 14 stipulated that the inquiry's report should in no sense have the character of an arbitral award. It should leave the respective parties entirely free to give whatever effect they wished to the given finding.

The first great test of this Hague procedure resulted from the *Dogger Bank* incident of 1904. In October 1904, during the Russo-Japanese War, the Russian Baltic Squadron, at that time on its journey east, encountered, off the Dogger Bank in the North Sea, a fleet of British fishing vessels steaming out of Hull. Troubled by rumours of the schemes of Japanese agents, and fearing an attack by torpedo boats, Admiral Rojdestvensky ordered his fleet to open fire upon the vessels. This resulted in the sinking of one British fishing steamer and damage to others, causing death and injury amongst their crews. The Russian fleet then proceeded on its voyage, without notifying the disaster until it put into the port of Vigo in Spain. British feeling was incensed by this outrage. The British fleet was mobilised, and war seemed a highly probable outcome. Following French diplomatic intervention, prompting negotiation between the British and Russian governments, it was agreed to refer the matter to an international commission of inquiry. Both governments signed a treaty setting up a five member inquiry that met in Paris and would inquire into, and report on, all the circumstances relating the incident, particularly as to the allocation of blame and responsibility to the respective parties. It can be seen that in, respect to the scope of its jurisdiction, the treaty between the parties that set up the inquiry went further than that of the Hague Convention provisions. Thus, in effect, the established commission carried out the functions of an arbitral tribunal. The inquiry found that there were no torpedo boats of any State among the British fishing fleet on the night in question. Further, there was no real justification for the order from Admiral Rojdestvensky to open fire on the fishing fleet. As a result, the sum of £65,000 sterling was paid in 1905 by Russia to the United Kingdom by way of indemnity.

The success of this commission in resolving a very dangerous international situation greatly enhanced the prestige of inquiry as a means of settling disputes. Based on the experience of the *Dogger Bank* case, a large number of additional regulations were made with respect to procedure at the Second Hague Conference of 1907.[7] In particular, it was established that there were to be three neutrals on the commission instead of one. This was hoped to secure a greater degree of impartiality in the decisions finally reached.

Since 1945, the UN has become increasingly involved in fact finding missions as a means of bringing peaceful ends to disputes. For example, a Panel for Inquiry and Conciliation was set up by the General Assembly in 1949; the Geneva Convention of 1949 and the Additional Protocol I set up provisions for inquiries for alleged violations of humanitarian law.[8] Article 5, Annex VII of the 1982 Law of the Sea Convention also allows for the use of fact finding commissions of inquiry. Further, in accordance with a UN resolution of 1967, nominations of experts were requested and received for a register that might investigate matters of controversy.

In conclusion, it can be seen that there are, in international law, a number of alternative dispute mechanisms to arbitration and judicial decision. However, they all have one factor in common: their effectiveness depends upon the how far the parties concerned actually want them to be effective.

Notes

1 See Chapter VI of the UN Charter entitled Pacific Settlement of Disputes, especially Art 33 for the list of methods.
2 Declaration on Principles of International Law Concerning Friendly Relations and Co-operation among States in Accordance with the Charter of the UN.
3 Unfortunately, a restrictive clause in the protocol to the treaty which stated that mediation should be resorted to only 'as far as circumstances permit' rendered the Article ineffective.
4 Hudson, *International Tribunals*, 1944, p 223.
5 The General Act for the Pacific Settlement of International Disputes, Adopted by the Ninth Assembly of the League of Nations, September 1928, Chapter I, 'Conciliation'. See Wheeler-Bennett, JW (ed), *Documents on International Affairs*, 1928, p 15.
6 The 1957 European Convention for the Peaceful Settlement of Disputes has not as yet come into force due to the fact that the required number of States have yet to ratify it.
7 See Arts 10–36 of the Convention for the Pacific Settlement of International Disputes.
8 First Convention, Art 52; Second Convention, Art 53; Third Convention, Art 132; Fourth Convention, Art 149; Additional Protocol I, Art 90.

Question 46

Johnonia and Paulania are both Member States of the United Nations. Johnonia loaned to Paulania $50 m on condition that the money was to be spent only on environmental projects within that country. This provision was contained within a treaty between the two States. Another provision of the treaty specified that in no circumstances could the money be spent on weapons of war. The treaty was silent as to what body should arbitrate should there arise a dispute over the terms of the treaty.

Paulania spent the entire $50 m loan on purchasing a Skulking bomber from the Federal States.

Johnonia, outraged by this violation of the treaty, wished to have the matter resolved through arbitration. Paulania refused on the grounds that this was a matter that could be resolved entirely by the Paulanian municipal courts. Johnonia then turned to the ICJ for redress.

Johnonia's declaration of acceptance of compulsory jurisdiction by the ICJ reads as follows:

> On behalf of the government of Johnonia, I declare that I recognise as compulsory *ipso facto* and without special agreement, on condition of reciprocity, the jurisdiction of the International Court of Justice for all disputes which may arise unless the parties may have agreed or may agree to have recourse to another method of peaceful settlement. This declaration does not apply to differences relating to matters which are essentially within the national jurisdiction of Johnonia as understood by the government of the Johnonian Republic.

The Paulanian declaration recognising the compulsory jurisdiction of the ICJ reads:

> I declare on behalf the Paulanian government that Paulania recognises as compulsory *ipso facto* and without special agreement the jurisdiction of the International Court of Justice on condition of reciprocity in conformity with Art 36(2) of the statute of that court.

In such circumstances, would the ICJ have sufficient jurisdiction to hear the merits of Johnonia's case? Does Johnonia's declaration amount, in effect, to a rejection of the compulsory jurisdiction of the ICJ?

Answer plan

Questions on the peaceful settlement of disputes commonly involve a discussion upon the jurisdiction of the International Court of Justice. States, unlike individuals in municipal law, have a choice as to whether they allow the World Court to adjudicate a dispute. Politicians are notoriously loathe to lose full control over a contentious matter and allow neutral parties to intercede on behalf of the international community. This is even more likely to be the case with regard to issues of public international law, because of that law's very vagueness. Parties to any dispute want to be able to make a reasonably accurate prediction of their chances of success in litigation. Such calculations are far harder to make when the law concerned depends upon the establishment of customary rules, the general principles of law recognised by civilised nations, the writings of publicists or rules of *jus cogens*.

The drafters of the ICJ statute (which mirrored that of the earlier PCIJ) were well aware of this reluctance of States to give up an element of their sovereignty. It became apparent that, if the jurisdiction of the ICJ had been genuinely compulsory, very few States indeed would accept such jurisdiction, with the consequence that the World Court would have been rendered ineffective at birth. The solution was the options clause, which allowed States voluntarily to give the court jurisdiction to decide certain issues. This acceptance can be *ad hoc*, once the dispute has come about. It may also be declared *post hoc* by a party to a dispute when the other party has filed its application with the Registry of the ICJ. Finally, such consent may be expressed *anti hoc*, that is, in advance and in anticipation of all disputes that might be submitted to the court. It is this last *anti hoc* expression of consent that is the main topic of discussion in the question below. It will be noted that, in giving such *ad hoc* consent, a State may also attach a reservation to the declaration of consent. What, then, happens in a contentious case when the declarations of consent to jurisdiction are different? What happens when the reservations differ in their breadth?

In order to answer this question, the student will need to discuss:
- the nature of the so called optional clause;
- reservations that have been made to the optional clause;
- the effect of the Johnonian and Paulanian reservations;
- the *Norwegian Loans* case (1957);
- the minority judgment of Judge Lauterpacht in the *Norwegian Loans* case: was the French reservation void *ab initio*? and
- The current standing of the Lauterpacht view.

Answer

In this essay, it will be contended that, firstly, because of the requirement for reciprocity, and secondly, because of the nature of the narrower Johnonian reservation to compulsory jurisdiction, the case against Paulonia would not be heard upon its merits by the International Court of Justice.

As Johnonia and Paulania are both Member States of the UN, they will automatically be parties to the Statute of the International Court of Justice and consequently be bound by its terms. Under this statute, there are a number of different ways in which the court can gain jurisdiction over an issue. Article 36(2) of the statute reads:

> The States parties to the present statute may at any time declare that they recognise as compulsory *ipso facto* and without special agreement, in relation to any other States accepting the same obligation, the jurisdiction of the court in all legal disputes concerning: (a) the interpretation of a treaty; (b) any question of international law; (c) the existence of any fact which, if established, would constitute a breach of an international obligation; (d) the nature and extent of the reparation to be made for the breach of an international obligation.'

Article 36(2) is known as the 'optional clause' of the statute. Under its terms, States can choose whether they recognise the jurisdiction of the ICJ or not. It is noted that both Johnonia and Paulania have made such declarations accepting the jurisdiction of the court.

However, these declarations of acceptance contain reservations to the compulsory jurisdiction of the ICJ. This is a common practice amongst 62 States that have thus far declared their recognition of the jurisdiction of the court in disputes which concern them. In effect, this means that the potential defendant could ultimately choose for itself whether it is willing to face judicial proceedings or not. Some States have tendered very narrowly drawn declarations. For example, Egypt's declaration of 1957 only accepts the jurisdiction of the ICJ should a dispute arise involving the Egyptian control and management of the Suez Canal. Some declarations are very broad in nature. The Nicaraguan declaration allows for jurisdiction in any dispute to which Nicaragua is a party. In the instant case, both parties have devised reservations. However, it is to be noted that the Johnonian reservation is far wider in scope than that of Paulania, for the Johnonian declaration contains a so called self-judging reservation. It can refuse to allow the dispute to be submitted to the ICJ if it believed that it related to matters which are essentially within the national jurisdiction of Johnonia as understood by the government of the Johnonian Republic. It is also noteworthy that Paulania makes its declaration of compulsory jurisdiction conditional upon reciprocity by the other party. In this regard, it is to be noted that Art 36(3) of the Statute of the International Court of Justice states that: 'The Declaration referred to above [36(2)] may be made unconditionally or on condition of reciprocity ...' The question therefore arises: can Paulania successfully argue that the jurisdiction of the ICJ has been ousted in this instance? Paulania claims that resolution of this dispute should be left to the Paulanian municipal courts. Can Paulania, which wishes to avoid the action before the ICJ, invoke Johnonia's narrower declaration as the one upon which jurisdiction should be determined. If reciprocity was to be genuine, it might argue, it should only permit jurisdiction to be based upon the narrower declaration rather than that of the wider.

Such a view was adopted by the majority of the ICJ in the *Norwegian Loans* case (1957). Between the 1885 and 1909, the State of Norway had gained considerable loans from France. Such loans, it had been agreed, were to be repaid in gold by the Norwegian government on the demand of the French creditors. Following the outbreak of the First World War, the Norwegian government, in an effort to maintain its current gold reserves, passed legislation which withdrew the convertibility of the Krone to equivalent value in gold. Further, if requests were made by the French creditors for payment in gold rather than in the Krone, Norway could make immediate payment of their loans in gold.

The French government wished this matter to be settled by international arbitration or by an international judicial body. Norway, however, believed it to be a matter that could be settled entirely by Norwegian municipal courts. The matter was to be governed by Norwegian contract law and nothing more. The French government filed in the Registry of the ICJ an application instituting proceedings against Norway before the ICJ. The World Court never heard the French case on its merits, for the whole action foundered on the court's want of jurisdiction. France had included a self-judging clause in its declaration accepting the compulsory jurisdiction of the ICJ. Norway had a reservation requiring reciprocity. In the judgment of the majority of the ICJ, Norway was entitled to rely on the narrowness of the French declaration in order to avoid the jurisdiction of the court. If the French were to be able to refuse the ICJ jurisdiction if the matter was, in their belief, one confined to French national jurisdiction, this reservation should be reciprocated. Such reciprocation would enable Norway to place reliance on the terms of the French reservation and hence determine for themselves whether they would allow this matter to be resolved by the ICJ. As Norway believed resolution of the dispute was a matter for its municipal courts, it could therefore reject the jurisdiction of the World Court. In the words of the majority judgment: 'In accordance with the condition of reciprocity to which acceptance of the compulsory jurisdiction is made subject in both declarations, and which is provided for in Art 36, para 3, of the Statute, Norway, equally with France, is entitled to except from the compulsory jurisdiction of the court disputes understood by Norway to be essentially within its national jurisdiction.'

Could it be argued in this instance, and with regard to the Johnonian declaration, that, in effect, its declarations have the real effect of ousting the compulsory jurisdiction of the ICJ entirely? As such, should these declarations be declared void? The majority of the court in the *Norwegian Loans* case determined that it had no need to examine this matter.[1] However, Sir Hersch Lauterpacht, in his minority opinion, did examine the matter. He referred to Art 36(6) of the Statute of the International Court of Justice, which allowed the court, in the case of dispute, to determine its own jurisdiction. He considered that the French reservation is not one that is contrary to some merely procedural aspect of the statute: it is contrary to one its basic features and is at variance with the principal safeguard of the system of the compulsory jurisdiction of the court. Without it, the compulsory jurisdiction 'being dependent upon the will of the defendant party ... has no meaning'. As a consequence, Judge Lauterpacht treated the French declaration as devoid of legal effects and as incapable of providing a basis for the jurisdiction of the court: 'It is for that reason that, in my view, the court has no jurisdiction over the dispute.'

What is the current standing of such a view, a view elaborated upon by Judge Lauterpacht two years later in the *Interhandel* case (1959)? In the *Nicaragua* case (1986), Judge Schwebel, although according 'great force' to the view expressed by Lauterpacht, states that, 'since declarations incorporating self-judging provisions apparently have been treated as valid, certainly by the declarants, for many years, the passage of time may have rendered Judge Lauterpacht's analysis less compelling today'.

Thus, it can be seen that because of the requirement for reciprocity and the nature of the narrower Johnonian reservation to compulsory jurisdiction, it could be contended that the case against Paulonia would not be heard upon its merits by the ICJ.

Notes

1   'The court does not consider that it should examine whether the French reservation is consistent with the undertaking of a legal obligation and is compatible with Art 36, para 6, of the Statute which provides: In the event of a dispute as to whether the court has jurisdiction, the matter shall be settled by the decision of the court. The validity of the [French] reservation has not been questioned by the Parties.'

Question 47

The year is 2020. There is unity amongst the permanent Members of the Security Council on one issue: each is in desperate need of an oil supply, and there is now only one State that produces oil, Austranglia.

An airliner is destroyed over the Great Sea on 1 January 2020. This resulted in the death of all the passengers, many of whom were from the Federated States. A grand jury in the Federated States brings charges against Bruce, an Austranglian citizen. The Federated States seek custody of Bruce so that he might stand trial for his crime. Both States are parties to the Montreal Convention for the Suppression of Unlawful Acts against the Safety of Civil Aviation 1971. Article 14(1) of that convention states that:

> Any dispute between two or more Contracting States concerning the interpretation or application of this convention which cannot be settled through negotiation, shall, at the request of one of them, be submitted to arbitration. If, within six months from the date of the request for arbitration, the parties are unable to agree on the organisation of the arbitration, any one of those parties may refer

the dispute to the International Court of Justice by request and in conformity with the statute of that court.

Austranglia, wishing to comply with the terms of the Montreal Convention, exercises its own criminal jurisdiction over Bruce.

On 21 January 2020, the UN Security Council passed Resolution 200 urging Austranglia to respond to the request of the Federated States to extradite Bruce so that he might stand trial in the Federated States.

On 3 March 2020, Austranglia filed in the Registry of the ICJ an application instituting proceedings against the Federated States. In the memorial submitted, the Austranglians declare (a) that the terms of the Montreal Convention alone shall govern the dispute; and (b) that the Federated States is under a legal obligation to respect Austranglia's right not to have the convention set aside by means which would be in variance with the UN Charter.

On 4 March, the Security Council adopts Resolution 201 which, under Chapter VII of the UN Charter, requires Austranglia to extradite Bruce to the Federated States, and imposes economic sanctions against Austranglia if the terms of the resolution fail to be complied with.

Austranglia ignores Resolution 201. The Security Council then adopts Resolution 202, authorising, under Chapter VII of the UN Charter, use of force by the Security Council power.

Forces from each of the permanent Security Council Member States then invade Austranglia and divide that territory into zones of occupation. These zones then subsequently become annexed to their own States through the adopted of Security Council Resolution 203.

The General Assembly requests that the ICJ deliver an advisory opinion on the matter.

Discuss.

Answer plan

This question raises, arguably, the most topical question discussed in this book. Put bluntly, it is the age old question first known to be put by Juvenal thus: *Sed quis custodiet ipsos Custodes*? (But who is to guard the guards themselves?). We recognise that the Security Council is to be the international policeman. We further recognise that, as a body, it has signally failed to perform that role during the Cold War. In the 1990s, however, we see that policeman intervening in a way unseen since the Korean War. Can this body be constrained, or even criticised, by the judicial organ of the United Nations? Who or what is to perform the function of forcing the Security Council, and, in particular, the permanent Member States of the Security Council, to abide strictly by the terms of the UN Charter. For example, Art 2(7) states clearly that:

> Nothing contained in the present Charter shall authorise the United Nations to intervene in matters which are essentially within the domestic jurisdiction of any State or shall require Members to submit such matters to settlement under the present Charter; but this principle shall not prejudice the application of enforcement measures under Chapter VII.

Such enforcement measures were organised to be used against Iraq during the Gulf War of 1990–91. Once Kuwait had been liberated, actions carried out under that mandate ceased. Yet we see, with the adoption of Security Council Resolution 688 (1991), the setting up of 'safe havens' in northern Iraq. There were, no doubt, perfectly valid, humanitarian reasons for acting in this way. Yet a lawyer must surely ask: was it not a clear breach of Art 2(7) of the UN Charter? One of the most significant questions facing international law in the future might prove to be: can the Security Council, through its State practice, make nugatory some parts of the UN Charter, and totally remodify the meaning of others? If so, can any body act to restrain it?

In answering this question, students should consider the following:

- the nature of advisory opinions;
- whether Security Council resolutions supersede the parties' commitments to the Montreal Convention; and
- whether it is possible for the ICJ to invalidate Security Council resolutions that appear to contravene the outlined purposes of the UN Charter.

Answer

In this essay, two key issues will be addressed: first, the effect of the Security Council resolutions upon the terms of the Montreal Convention; and secondly, the possibility of the World Court being able to review the way in which the Security Council exercised its powers under Chapter VII with regard to the invasion and annexation of Austranglia.

Under Art 65 of the Statute of the International Court of Justice, the court may give an advisory opinion 'on any [international] legal question at the request of whatever body may be authorised by, or in accordance with, the Charter of the United Nations to make such a request'. The General Assembly would be legally capable of making such a request (Art 961 of the Charter) and, upon receiving the request, the ICJ would be competent to give such an advisory opinion (Arts 65–68 of the Statute of the ICJ). It should be noted, however, that advisory opinions are not binding in law on the requesting body, nor, indeed, upon any other international entity. They are to be considered as highly respected analyses of international law of great weight. The Federated States and other Members of the Security Council may well attempt to block the court giving such an opinion. However, as was stated by the court in their *Advisory Opinion in Interpretation of Peace Treaties with Bulgaria, Hungary and Romania* (1950):

> It follows that no State, whether a Member of the United Nations or not, can prevent the giving of an advisory opinion which the United Nations considers to be desirable in order to obtain enlightenment as to the course of action it should take. The court's [advisory] opinion is given not to the States, but to the organ which is entitled to request it ...

In giving its advisory opinion, the ICJ would be faced with two key questions. First, do the Security Council resolutions that have been adopted supersede the parties' commitment to terms of the Montreal Convention? Secondly, is it possible for the ICJ to invalidate Security Council resolutions that appear to contravene the outlined purposes of the UN Charter?

The events in the question concerned bear a strong resemblance to those concerning the Lockerbie bombing. On the night of 21 December 1988, over Lockerbie, Scotland, Pan Am flight 103 was destroyed by a terrorist bomb, killing all the passengers. Charges were brought by the Lord Advocate for Scotland in November 1991 against two Libyan nationals suspected of having caused a bomb to be placed aboard the aircraft. The majority of the dead were US citizens. Later, a grand jury in the USA also brought charges against the two Libyans thought to have planted the bomb. Libya, the UK and the US were all parties to the Montreal Convention.

On 21 January 1992, the Security Council made a recommendation under Resolution 731 that Libya should respond to the request of those States which wished for the extradition of the two suspected Libyan terrorists so that they might stand trial in Scotland. On 3 March 1992, Libya filed in the Registry of the World Court an application instituting proceedings against the UK and the USA in respect of a dispute concerning the interpretation or application of the Montreal Convention.[1] Libya filed two memorials[2] which requested the court to adjudge and declare: (a) that the Montreal Convention is applicable to this dispute; (b) that Libya has fully complied with all of its obligations under the Montreal Convention and is justified in exercising the criminal jurisdiction provided for by that convention; (c) that the UK and the USA had breached, and were continuing to breach, their legal obligations to Libya under paras 2 and 3 of Art 5, Art 7, para 3 of Art 8, and Art 11 of the Montreal Convention; and (d) that the UK and the USA were under a legal obligation to respect Libya's right not to have the convention set aside by means which would, in any case, be at variance with the principles of the UN Charter and with the mandatory rules of general international law prohibiting the use of force and the violation of the sovereignty, territorial integrity, sovereign equality and political independence of States. It is to be noted that, under Art 7 of the Montreal Convention, Libya had the choice of whether it would extradite the terrorist suspects or not. They wished to exercise this power under the applicable treaty and put the suspects on trial within Libya. Likewise, in the question asked, Austranglia wished to exercise sole criminal jurisdiction over Bruce.

The Security Council subsequently adopted Resolutions 748 (1992) and 883 (1993), which were not recommendatory in nature, but mandatory under Art 25 of the Charter. These resolutions, under Chapter VII of the Charter, required Libya to return the alleged offenders and imposed sanctions upon Libya for not doing so.

Libyan Arab Jamahiriya v United Kingdom (1998) and *Libyan Arab Jamahiriya v United States* (1998)[3] considered the merits of the Libyan contention. Could subsequent Security Council resolutions supersede the terms of the Montreal Convention? If this were so, it would mean, first, that the jurisdiction given to the ICJ by Art 14(1) of the Montreal Convention would be made nugatory, and secondly, that the choice given to Libya of whether to extradite the suspects given to it under Art 7 of the Montreal Convention would likewise be made nugatory. In response to the argument ousting ICJ jurisdiction, the court rejected the UK and US submission. The court found that the date (3 March 1992) on which Libya filed its application, is, in fact, the only relevant date for determining the admissibility of the application. Security Council Resolutions 748 (1992) and 883 (1993) cannot be taken into consideration in this regard since they were adopted at a later date. Security Council Resolution 731 (1992), adopted before the filing of the application, could not form a legal impediment to the admissibility of the Libyan action because it was a mere recommendation without binding effect (as was recognised, moreover, by the UK itself). Consequently, Libya's application could not be held inadmissible on these grounds.[4]

Was Art 7 of the Montreal Convention superseded by the UN resolutions? Once again, the ICJ examined the UK and US contention that, even if the Montreal Convention did confer on Libya the rights it claims, these rights could not be exercised in the instant case because they were superseded by Security Council Resolutions 748 (1992) and 883 (1993) which, by virtue of Arts 25 and 103 of the UN Charter, have priority over all rights and obligations arising out of the Montreal Convention. Further, because of the adoption of those resolutions, the only dispute which existed after such resolutions was between Libya and the Security Council. This, clearly, would not be a dispute falling within the terms of Art 14, para 1, of the Montreal Convention (that is, between two or more Contracting States) and thus not one which the court could entertain.[5]

The court found that it could not uphold this line of argument. Again, because the relevant mandatory Security Council resolutions had been adopted after the filing of the application on 3 March 1992, if the court had jurisdiction on that date, it would continue to do so; the subsequent coming into existence of the above mentioned resolutions cannot affect its jurisdiction once it had been established.

Thus, it is contended that, in the ICJ's advisory opinion, the court would recommend that the Federal States could not force the extradition of Bruce from Austranglia. What, though, of the subsequent use of force against Austranglia, authorised by Security Council Resolution 202. What of the annexation of Austranglian territory? It is certainly the case that, under Chapter VII of the UN Charter, the Security Council is given powers to authorise the use of force 'to maintain or restore international peace and security.' Indeed, it was under Art 39 that the Security Council based its decision to enforce sanctions against Libya. However, what if, as is contended here, Austranglia in fact poses no threat to international peace and security; that, in truth, the Security Council powers are in reality seeking a pretext in order to legitimise their conquest of the oil rich Austranglia.

Judge Fitzmaurice, in his dissenting opinion in the *Legal Consequences* case (1971), specifically referred to Art 25 of the UN Charter, which compels States to carry out the decisions of the Security Council in accordance with the present charter. He stated:

> If the effect of [Art 24] were automatically to make all decisions of the Security Council binding, then the words 'in accordance with the present Charter' [Art 25] would be quite superfluous'.

He proceeded by stating further:

> There is more. Even when acting under Chapter VII of the charter itself, the Security Council has no power to abrogate or alter territorial rights, whether of sovereignty or administration. Even a wartime occupation of a country or territory cannot operate to do that. It must await the peace settlement.[6]

Such words suggest that, in its advisory opinion in the question before us, the ICJ could critically review the actions of the Security Council.

Such a matter was raised by Judge Weeramantry, in his dissenting opinion, in the *Case Concerning questions of interpretation and application of the Montreal Convention arising out the aerial incident at Lockerbie (Provisional Measures)* (1992). He, however, rejected the contention that the court could review Security Council action taken under Chapter VII. 'It would appear,' he stated, 'that the Council and no other is the judge of the existence of the state of affairs which brings Chapter VII into operation'. It could be argued that a distinction can be made between taking initial action under Art 39 and attempting to annex territory. There is no provision for this under Chapter VII. Whether such an annexation could be reviewed by the Security Council is still a moot point.

In conclusion, it is contended that, in its advisory opinion, the ICJ, when reviewing would the effect of the Security Council resolutions upon the terms of the Montreal Convention, would uphold the terms of the latter convention in the face of such resolutions. Further, there is likelihood that the court would be unable to review the way in which the Security Council exercised its powers under Chapter VII with regard to the invasion and annexation of Austranglia. One should not forget, however, that, no matter what the decision given by the ICJ, as an advisory opinion, it is in no sense binding upon any party to the dispute.

Notes

1 *Case Concerning questions of interpretation and application of the Montreal Convention arising out the aerial incident at Lockerbie (Provisional Measures)* (1992).
2 One in which the UK was the respondent, in the other the US was the respondent. It is to be noted that Libya also requested the ICJ to grant provisional measures on 3 March. This the ICJ refused to do on account of Security Council Resolution 748.
3 See ICJ website on http:/wwwicj-cij.org
4 Paragraphs 40–45 of the *Libya v UK* judgment; paras 39–44 of *Libya v US* judgment.
5 Paragraphs 37–38 of the *Libya v UK* judgment; paras 36–37 of *Libya v US* judgment.
6 With regard to the annexation of Austranglian territory, note that General Assembly Resolution 3314 Art 53 states that: 'No

territorial acquisition or special advantage resulting from aggression is or shall be recognised as lawful.' This view is supported by State practice. In response to Iraq's declaration of a 'comprehensive and internal merger' with Kuwait, the Security Council in 1990 adopted Resolution 662 which stated that the annexation of Kuwait had no legal validity and was to be considered null and void. It further called upon State and international organisations not to recognise the annexation.

CHAPTER 14

USE OF FORCE

Introduction

Two key elements are necessary for a grasp of this subject. First, the student should become well acquainted with Chapter VII of the UN Charter, which is entitled: 'Action with respect to threats to the peace, breaches of the peace, and acts of aggression', and contains Arts 30–51. Students will discover that the chapter is set out in a logical way, beginning with the Security Council recognising that a threat to the peace exists, making recommendations accordingly or deciding whether UN sanctions or force should be authorised (Art 39). Under Art 40, the Security Council can adopt provisional measures before the Security Council makes the necessary recommendations or decides upon measures (for example, sanctions and force) provided for in Art 39. Such recommendations by the Security Council will be in the form of resolutions. Articles 41 and 42 authorise the Security Council to enforce sanctions in order to gain compliance to its decisions (Art 41) and, should sanctions be sure to fail or are failing, to make the peccant State(s) obey such decisions by way of UN 'enforcement action' (Art 42). Articles 43–47 deal with the responsibility of Member States contributing troops to UN actions (Arts 43 and 45), the degree of control that contributing State has over those troops (Art 44), and the Military Staff Committee which is to command such troops (Arts 46 and 47). Articles 48–50 deal with the co-operation expected from other UN Member States regarding actions undertaken under Chapter VII (Arts 48 and 49) and financial assistance that can be given to States that suffer economically as an indirect result of Chapter VII actions (Art 50). Article 51 (along with Art 2(4)) is the article that will be most often referred to by the student answering a question on use of force. For Art 51 preserves the inherent right to self-defence. It would be difficult to think of many acts of aggression in which the aggressor has not argued that its actions are justified by self-defence.

315

The second key element in answering questions of use of force concerns State practice. The terms of articles in Chapter VII are inevitably vague. It was a rule of customary international law, and is now stated in Art 31(3) of the Vienna Convention on the Law of Treaties 1969, that, when interpreting treaty provisions, account should be taken of State practice and General Assembly resolutions. It is therefore necessary that the student should have an understanding of the legal justifications and defences States have used for their military actions. Have these justifications and defences been accepted?

In answering a question, the following issues should normally be considered:

- what justification might exist for the military action undertaken by the party;
- whether such action was in breach of Art 2(4) of the UN Charter;
- whether it is self-defence under Art 51;
- whether it could have been an action in self-defence under customary international law;
- whether it was an action in anticipatory self-defence and, if so, whether it was justified; and
- whether the action amounted to enforcement action under Chapter VII of the charter.

Checklist

Students should be familiar with the following areas:
- Article 2(4) of the UN Charter;
- Chapter VII of the UN Charter;
- anticipatory self-defence;
- the Caroline criteria; and
- Collective self-defence under the UN Charter.

Question 48

Is it still legally true to say that war is the continuation of politics by other means?

(*Von Clausewitz On War*, 1832.)

Answer plan

This question requires a knowledge of the history of the development of the law on conflict. It begins by showing that the notion of the illegality of warfare is a relatively modern concept. The student will need to consider:

- the traditional view of the legality of conflict;
- the Hague Conventions;
- the League of Nations and the Covenant of the League;
- Art 2(4) of the UN Charter;
- General Assembly resolutions;
- the role of the Security Council;
- the role of the Secretary General;
- judicial decisions; and
- whether Von Clausewitz is still correct.

Potential writers of such an essay should try to confine themselves as firmly as possible to the formal structure. So often, essays of this type turn into rambling monologues about the sorry state of the world.

Answer

This essay will outline the ways in which the international community has attempted to make illegal the use of force as a means exerting pressure upon other States.

If one looks at a work on international law prior to 1945, it is noticeable that war, as a means of executing State policy, is viewed with a degree of inevitability. Further, any attempt by the international community to make such actions illegal would be futile. In a community of equal States, no one State could be deprived of seeking its best ultimate interest by means of a treaty commitment. This is illustrated by Hall in *A Treatise on International Law*, 1898:

> As international law is destitute of any judicial or administrative machinery, it leaves States, which think themselves aggrieved, and which have exhausted all peaceful methods of obtaining satisfaction, to exact redress for themselves by force. It thus

recognises war as a permitted mode of giving effect to its decisions.

Prior to 1914, in an attempt to remedy this deficiency, methods were attempted to reduce the possibility of war. A first step was taken in 1899, completed in 1907, when the Hague Conference established the rules by which disputes might be arbitrated and established the Permanent Court of Arbitration. This curiously named body was neither 'a court' nor 'permanent'. In order to solve a dispute between two States, the court will act according to a special compromise (arbitration agreement), which specified the area of dispute and defined the body's jurisdiction. Tragically, none of the efforts succeeded in preventing the conflict produced a had been made prior to the conflict that broke out in 1914. The convention also set up procedural mechanisms to enable conflict to be averted. War was to subject to embargo if it were not preceded by a declaration of war or an ultimatum. The true test of the court's capacity came in 1914, when both the Serbians and the Russians wished the issue of the issue of the assassination of Archduke Franz Ferdinand and its consequences to be settled by the Permanent Court. Germany and Austria-Hungary refused to be party to the arbitration.

However, following both the world wars of the 20th century, the victors have attempted to create a legal regime which would legalise war in a very narrow set of circumstances. In such a way, so called 'aggressive war' would become illegal. When viewed together, the effect of the preambular *consideratum* to the Covenant of the League and Art 10 of that document was that contracting States were, implicitly, bound to adjure war. Moreover, the way in which war could be eliminated, or contained, was by a policy of 'collective security'. Article 11(1) of the Covenant stated that: 'any war or threat of war [is] a matter of concern to the whole League, and the League shall take any action that may be deemed wise and effectual to safeguard the peace of nations.' Just as, prior to the Great War, procedural formalities acted as hurdles to the resort to conflict, so the covenant did likewise (see Arts 12 and 13 of the Covenant). However, despite these procedural hurdles, Von Clausewitz's statement would still have had validity following the covenant, for, if negotiations and other means proved of no avail, Art 15(7) stated that Member States could 'take such action as they consider necessary for the maintenance of right and justice'. Clearly, aggressive war was still legitimate in certain circumstances. An attempt to plug this loophole was made by the Pact of Paris of 1928.[1] Under Art 1 of this treaty, the Contracting Parties stated their rejection of the recourse to war for the solution of international controversies. More significantly, Von Clausewitz's maxim was, for the first time, legally condemned. The Contracting Parties rejected recourse to war as an instrument of national policy. Article 2 of the pact established that resolution of disputes amongst the signatory parties could only be brought by peaceful means.

The League failed in its central purpose of maintaining peace. In its stead, the provisions of the United Nations Charter were seen as an attempt to resurrect both the notion of the illegality of force as a means of State self-interest and the concept of world policing through collective security. Under Art 2(4) of the UN Charter, there was an attempt to avoid States arguing that the aggressive measures they were undertaking were not war (and thus not governed by its constraints) but some form of lesser action. Now:

> All Members shall refrain in their international relations from the threat or *use of force* against the territorial integrity or political independence of any State, or in any other manner inconsistent with the purposes of the United Nations [emphasis supplied].

As to the purposes of the new organisation, these are set out in Art 1, para 1, which states that the UN is intended to maintain international peace and security, and to that end:

> ... to take effective *collective measures* for the prevention and removal of threats to the peace ... and in conformity with the principles of justice and international law, adjustment or settlement of international disputes or situations which might lead to a breach of the peace [emphasis supplied].

Such provisions of the charter have since been restated, amplified and clarified. Perhaps the most authoritative is the 1970 Declaration on the Principles of International Law Concerning Friendly Relations and Co-operation Among States in Accordance with the Charter of the United Nations (Friendly Relations Declaration). The declaration further provides that no State shall 'organise, assist, foment, finance, incite or tolerate subversive, terrorist or armed activities directed towards the violent overthrow of the regime of another State, or interfere in civil strife in another State'. Although disputes have arisen regarding the precise legal status of the declaration, it is generally viewed as an authoritative interpretation of broad principles of international law expressed in the charter.

Whilst collective security, governed by Security Council control, is responsible for maintaining international peace, there are parameters, delineated by the charter, outlining the limits of those powers. Under Art 2(7), it precludes the organisation itself from intervening in matters which are essentially within the domestic jurisdiction of any State. Hence the General Assembly's Declaration on the Inadmissibility of Intervention in the Domestic Affairs of States and the Protection of Their Independence and Sovereignty, takes on special significance. The declaration, *inter alia*, provides that no State has the right to intervene, directly or indirectly, for any reason whatever, in the internal or external affairs of any other State. Consequently, armed intervention and all other forms of interference or attempted threats against the personality of the State or against its political, economic and cultural elements are condemned. This provision was severely compromised by Security Council Resolution 688, which established the so called 'safe havens' in northern Iraq for the persecuted Kurds.[2]

The Security Council and the General Assembly are the primary organs of the United Nations. They have the key responsibility under the UN Charter to regulate the use of force. However, it was evident that the five permanent Members of the Security Council, when drafting the text at the San Francisco Conference in 1945, attempted, through the provisions of the charter, to monopolise control over the UN's policing function. Under Chapter VII of the charter, it is the Security Council alone which can determine the existence of any threat to the peace (Art 39). It is the Security Council alone which, under Art 42, could take such actions by air, sea or land forces as may be necessary to maintain or restore international peace and security. Such action may include demonstrations, blockade, and other operations by air, sea or land forces of Members of the United Nations. Hence, use of force was, post 1945, illegal unless it was an enforcement action legitimised and organised by the Security Council.

In addition to an enforcement action under Art 42, there was an additional way, under Chapter VII, in which use of force could be seen as legitimate. Use of force is permitted under the final article of the chapter (Art 51) as a means of self-defence. It was noticeable that, at the time of the Gulf War in 1991, the Security Council made no attempt to demonstrate whether the action it took against Iraq was carried out as an enforcement action or by way of self-defence. It was merely described as 'an action carried out under Chapter VII powers'.

The Cold War stalemate on the Security Council fuelled the debate that had arisen over the precise allocation of authority in this area between the Security Council and the General Assembly, and a focal point of this debate has been the General Assembly's 'Uniting for Peace' resolution.[3] Under this resolution, the General Assembly claimed the authority to recommend collective measures in situations where the Security Council is unable to deal with a breach of the peace or act of aggression because of a veto by one of the five permanent Members. The decision of the International Court of Justice in the *Certain Expenses* case (1962), though it did not directly address the legality of the Uniting for Peace resolution, contained *obiter dicta* on the charter's allocation of powers between the Security Council and the General Assembly. Equally, the ICJ's advisory opinion in the *Namibia* case (1971) clarifies the scope of the both the main UN organs. Though Security Council and General Assembly decisions are not regarded as conclusively binding, they may be regarded as interpretations of the charter entitled to a degree of authority.

Interpretations or legal opinions by the Secretary General on the use of force may also be regarded as having some authority in the attempt to invalidate the claim of Von Clausewitz in contemporary international law. The Secretary General is the chief administrative officer of the United Nations (see Art 97 of the UN Charter). As such, he is required to carry out functions assigned to him by the principal organs of the organisation, including the General Assembly and the Security Council (see Art 98 of the UN Charter). He is deprived of any independent law making authority. As the recent events regarding Iraq have demonstrated, the key responsibility of the Secretary General has been that of brokering peace.

There are also other means by which the UN can restrain conflict as a means by which States can pursue their ends. There are a number ICJ decisions and advisory opinions which bear on the use of force. The doctrine of *stare decisis* does not apply to ICJ decisions, and such decisions do not create law in the way that common law decisions do. Despite this, they are viewed as authoritative statements of the law and have a highly important role in shaping the international legal process. The leading decision in this area is the *Nicaragua* case (1986).

In conclusion, it can be seen that, in a legal sense, the statement made by Von Clausewitz would now be untrue. However, a sceptic might respond by commenting on the superficiality of such a response. For in a real sense, the law on the use of force has been determined by the politics of the Security Council.

Notes
1 Treaty on the Renunciation of War as an Instrument of National Policy 94 League of Nations Treaty Series, p 54.
2 This resolution was adopted by 10 votes to 3 (Cuba, Yemen and Zimbabwe), with two abstentions (China and India). Upon reading UN Doc S/PV (1982) it is clear that the resolution had been heavily criticised for being in violation of Art 2(7) of the UN Charter.
3 GA RES/337A, UN GOAR, 5th Sess, Supp No 20, at 10, UN Doc A/1775 (1951).

Question 49

Ufasia has declared a holy war against the Federal States. Ufasia State Radio broadcast that it would encourage any acts of violence carried out anywhere in the world against the Federal States. There is evidence that the Ufasian secret service agents were sending funds and supplying arms to those groups that were determined to use violent means against the Federal States.

On 10 May 1998, a bomb exploded in a public house in Liguria. The public house was often frequented by Federal State soldiers stationed in Liguria. Five of the soldiers were killed. The Federal States then launched, on 20 May, an aerial attack upon Ufasia. They bomb military bases and the residence of the Ufasian leader. Over 100 civilians are killed in the air raids. The aircraft took off from Albino, an ally of the Federal States.

Discuss.

Answer plan

To answer the following question, the student will need to know about the key terms of the UN Charter, General Assembly resolutions and State practice involving use of force.

Key issues include:
- whether the sponsoring of terrorism amounts, in this instance, to an armed attack upon the Federal States;
- whether an attack upon Federal States citizens abroad amounts to an armed attack;
- whether an act of retribution is illegal under international law;
- what is an act of anticipatory self-defence (the Caroline criteria);
- whether an attack upon the Ufasian leader would be legal under international law; and
- what responsibility Albino might incur for allowing the Federal States to launch the attack from its territory.

The student will note the importance in this and the subsequent question of the interpretative role of General Assembly resolutions.

Answer

This essay will address the following question: can the Federal States justify is action on the basis of self-defence?

Article 2(4) of the United Nations Charter binds Member States 'to refrain in their international relations from the threat or use of force against the territorial integrity or political independence of any State, or in any other manner inconsistent with the purposes of the United Nations'. There are, however, a number of significant exceptions to Art 2(4), one of which is contained within Art 51 of the charter. This article states that:

> Nothing in the present Charter shall impair the inherent right of individual or collective self-defence if an armed attack occurs against a Member of the United Nations, until the Security Council has taken measures necessary to maintain international peace and security.

Do the sponsorship of terrorist activities by Ufasia amount to an 'armed attack' that would allow the Federal States to resort to force as a means of self-defence? This issue arose in the case of *Nicaragua v United States* (1986). The United States had armed and trained contra rebels in the hope that they would bring down the regime in that State. The US had also provided the rebels with training in logistics and funding. The ICJ, in its majority judgments, stated: 'In the case of individual self-defence, the exercise of this right is subject to the State concerned having been the victim of an armed attack.' The court then examined Art 3(g) of the Declaration of Aggression (General Assembly Resolution 3314 (XXIX)), which it took to reflect customary international law. This article states that an armed attack must be understood as including not merely actions carried out by regular armed forces across an international border but also the sending by, or on behalf of, a State of armed bands, groups, irregulars or mercenaries, which carry out acts of armed force against another State of such gravity as to amount to (*inter alia*) the equivalent of an armed attack by a regular force. In the question asked, however, Ufasia has not sent armed bands against the Federal States, but has only provided funds and logistics. The ICJ also considered this matter. But the court does not believe that the concept of 'armed attack' includes 'also assistance to rebels in the form of the provision of weapons or logistical or other support. Such assistance may be regarded as a threat or use of force, or amount to intervention in the internal or external affairs of other States'. Thus, arguably, the Ufasian activity would not permit the Federal States to resort to use of force in self-defence.[1]

A further consideration is whether the attack on citizens of the Federal States abroad constitutes an armed attack on the Federal

States itself. Whilst there has been little argument as to whether an armed attack against the territory, the aircraft and ship of a State constitutes an armed attack, the position of an armed attack upon its citizens abroad is more controversial. The better view is that it does so. First, because Art 51 refers to an attack launched 'against Member States'. Article 1 of the Montevideo Convention on Rights and Duties of States 1933 states that population is one of the key elements of statehood. Consequently, an attack upon the citizens of the Federal States should be just as much an attack on the Federal States as it would have been if the attack had been launched against its territory. Secondly, the attack launched in this instance was launched against symbols of the Federal States' sovereignty; those attacked were Federal State troops. Thirdly, State practice demonstrates that such activity would be regarded as an armed attack. This proved to be one of the justifications for UK intervention in Egypt (1956), US intervention in the Dominican Republic (1965), Grenada (1983) and Panama (1989), and of Israeli intervention in Uganda (1976).

Even if it had been established that the act of terrorism did amount to an armed attack against the Federal States, it is important to note that a distinction should be made between self-defence and mere retribution. Whilst traditional international law allowed an individual State to use force as a reprisal for a prior wrong committed against it, in certain circumstances,[2] modern international law only permits such actions to be authorised by the Security Council under Chapter VII of the Charter. The United Nations General Assembly Declaration on Principles of International Law concerning Friendly Relations and Co-operation among States 1970 states that 'States ... have a duty to refrain from acts of reprisal involving the use of force'.[3] Consequently, it is incumbent upon the Federal States to show that it acted to prevent further attacks that it had anticipated. Under pre-charter customary law, a State could use force by way of self-defence not only in a direct response to an armed attack, but also in anticipation of an armed attack. It will be noted that Art 51 preserved the inherent right to armed attack. Consequently, rather than superseding pre-charter customary international law, Art 51 preserved it. Even if one accepts its existence, it should also be acknowledged that, under customary international law, it can only be exercised in a narrow set of circumstances. These circumstances were most famously stated by the US Secretary of State Daniel Webster to the British government following the Caroline incident. The use of force was to be based upon whether the necessity of that self-defence is 'instant, overwhelming, and leaving no choice of means, and no moment for deliberation'. Moreover, in an earlier letter based upon the same incident, Webster wrote of the requirement of proportionality. He wrote that 'the act justified by the necessity of self-defence must be limited by the necessity, and kept clearly within it.' Arguably, the right of anticipatory self-defence can only be triggered when these criteria are met.

Could it be stated that, in carrying out its bombing raid, the Federal States' response met the requirement of necessity? Was there no other path by which it might gain redress? Did it act instantly? This proves to be problematic, because, to a large extent, it depends upon the knowledge of the Federal States' intelligence network.[4] If they have proof that another attack will take place in the future, arguably, sanctions would not prove to be method that would avert the attack. The bombing of Ufasia must be the only way in which the Federal States believes it can avert the future attacks. Further, such attacks must be imminent. It would not be enough for the Federal States to argue that it had intelligence that Ufasia had orchestrated terrorist attacks at some unspecified future time. Evidence of this can be seen in State practice, most notably the condemnation by the Security Council of the UK following the *Harib Fort Incident* (1964). Further, there was a 10 day interval between the terrorist attack and the bombing of Ufasia. As a result, it could not be argued that the Federal States acted instantly.

If the criterion of proportionality is to be truly met, the Federal States intelligence network would not only need to be exceptionally well informed, it would need the power of foreseeing the future. For it would have to establish that, in the future attack, it had anticipated 100 individuals, or thereabouts, would have been killed. Despite being difficult, if not impossible, to meet in these circumstances, the requirements outlined by Webster have to be met if the Federal States is legitimately to claim that it is acting in self-defence. In the *Legality of the Threat or Use of Nuclear Weapons* case (1996), it was emphasised by the ICJ, in its advisory opinion, that the submission of the exercise of the right of self-defence to the conditions of necessity and proportionality is a rule of customary international law. The court also emphasised that the same rules applied to a claim made under Art 51 directly as to the preserved rules of customary international law.

It also seems apparent from the question that attempts were made to kill the Ufasian leader in this bombing raid. Retaliation against a national leader would be a direct violation of the Convention on the Prevention and Punishment of Crimes Against Internationally Protected Persons 1973.[5] Thus, even if the leader in question had been directly responsible for sponsoring the terrorist act, an attack upon him in response would not be legal under international law.

Lastly, it should be noted that Albino, the State from which the air strike was launched, also has, arguably, breached international law. If the action undertaken by the Federal States cannot be categorised as an action in self-defence (and thus is, therefore, a breach of Art 2(4)), Albino can be held to be in breach of General Assembly Resolution 3314 (XXIX), entitled the 'Resolution on the Definition of Aggression 1974'. Article 3(f) of this resolution states that acts which shall qualify as aggressive shall include the '... action of a State in allowing its territory, which it has placed at the disposal of another State, to be used by that other State for perpetrating an act of aggression against a third State'. As such, the State of Albino would incur international responsibility for its actions.[6]

In conclusion, it can be seen that for the Federal States to make out its case that it was acting in self-defence would require intelligence information of extraordinarily, perhaps impossibly, high quality. If the case was to come within the pale of Art 51 (and self-defence in customary international law), the Federal States would need to show that the attack was imminent; that it did constitute an armed attack on the Federal States; that the violent remedy it pursued was the only that was capable of averting the future attack; and that it predicts that the use of force directed at the target was proportionate to the use of force that would immanently be brought to bare against it. Arguably, if the above could not be established, then the action taken by the Federal States was a breach of Art 2(4) of the UN Charter.

Notes

1. It has been noted that Art 2(4) refers to the illegality of force used against the 'territorial integrity or political independence' of other States. The Federated States might argue that their military action was not against the territorial or political independence of Ufasia but, rather, it was a direct response to their knowledge of imminent acts of terrorism that had been orchestrated by Ufasia. Bowett, DW, in *Self-Defence in International Law*, 1958, seems to argue that any illegal act, regardless of its nature, which is proven to threaten the major security interests of the victimised state legitimates a military response. That response is to protect the territorial independence and political integrity of the victimised State.
   It is contended that in these circumstances the above position is untenable. Note should be made of Art 3(b) of the United Nations General Assembly Resolution on the Definition of Aggression 1974 which states that 'bombardment by the armed forces of a State against the territory of another State or the use of weapons by a State against the territory of another State' would amount to a *prima facie* act of aggression.
2. See the *Naulilaa Arbitration* 2 RIAA 1011 (1928).
3. SC Res 188. Note also that Security Council has adopted a similar line. In response to the Harib Fort incident the Council condemned 'reprisals as incompatible with the purposes and principles of the United Nations'.
4. The situation in the question is reminiscent of the US bombing of Libya in 1986. At the time of the bombing US Ambassador Walters issued a statement to the UN Security Council on 5 April 1986 in which he announced that US intelligence had succeeded in gaining irrefutable proof of Libyan involvement in the bombing of the La Belle discotheque in Berlin. Moreover, they had proof of imminent terrorist attacks upon other US targets. At the time the veracity of these reports could not be examined because it might compromise US Security.
5. 28 UST 1975 TIAS No 8534.
6. When the United Kingdom permitted US airbases to launch attacks on Libya in 1986 the representative of the United Arab Emirates raised this point in the Security Council debate on the attack. See UN Doc S/PV 2674, p 6 (1986).

USE OF FORCE

Question 50

Poltova was in dispute with its small neighbour, Kantuvo. Kantuvo was, at one time, a part of Poltova until it was colonised by Imperia. Kantuvo gained its independence from Imperia in 1963. Poltova wishes to compel Kantuvo to raise the price of the oil that it produces in order to raise the world price of the product. This would benefit Poltova which is an oil producing nation. When Kantuvo refused to comply with its demands, Poltova placed a blockade around Kantuvo and, by so doing, prevented 80% of all Kantuvo's imports and exports.

Despite the severe economic pressure Kantuvo suffered, it still refused to raise the price of its oil. Poltova then invades Kantuvo and annexes it to its own State.

The Security Council, in an attempt to restore the peace and force the withdrawal of the Poltovan forces, proceeded to impose economic sanctions on that State. The sanctions failed to achieve their objective within six months of the initial attack.

Lenora, a permanent Member of the Security Council, proposes a Security Council resolution which would authorise the collective use of force against Poltova. This resolution was vetoed by Cantata, another permanent Member of the Security Council.

Lenora, deciding to act alone, then launches an attack against Poltova in an attempt to liberate Kantuvo.

Discuss.

Answer plan

Yet again, this is a question in which a good knowledge of Chapter VII of the UN Charter will be required. One hopes that the student will make obvious comparisons between the action taken by Poltova and the action taken by Iraq in 1990. It will be noted, however, that Iraq's initial justification for its attack upon Kuwait was that its forces had been requested to intervene by opposition groups to restore order within the country.

The following factors need to be considered:
- whether economic measures can amount to an armed attack;

329

- whether the economic blockade imposed by Poltova amounts to an armed attack;
- Poltova's argument that Art 2(4) does not forbid a State from using military force to redress grievances that took place before the UN Charter was created;
- the legality of the action taken by the Security Council; and
- the legality of the action taken by Lenora.

The action taken by Lenora in this question clearly has similarities to the position in which the United States and the United Kingdom would have been placed with regard to Iraq in February 1998 if peace had not been brokered by the UN Secretary General.

Answer

This essay will examine the legality of the following acts by the following parties: Poltova in implementing its blockade and, subsequently, in its military action and annexation; the Security Council in imposing sanctions upon the invader; and the independent military action of Lenora.

Article 2(4) of the UN Charter states that:

> All Members shall refrain in their international relations from the threat or use of force against the territorial integrity or political independence of any state, or in any other manner inconsistent with the purposes of the United Nations.

Would a blockade constitute 'force' and thus mean that Poltova was in breach of Art 2(4) of the UN Charter? Poltova might argue that the refusal of Kantuvo to increase its oil price was the equivalent to a use of force for which it had the right to use measures such as a blockade or an armed attack in self-defence. Article 51 of the UN Charter states that:

> Nothing in the present charter shall impair the inherent right of individual or collective self-defence if an armed attack occurs against a Member of the United Nations ...

Further, the ICJ in the *Nicaragua v United States* (1986) stated that: 'In the case of individual self-defence, the exercise of this right is subject to the State concerned having been the victim of an armed attack' (see also Art 51 of the UN Charter). Could economic action amount to a type of armed force? Harris argues that the scope of Art 2(4) probably does not prohibit 'pressure ... or economic pressure (for example, a trade boycott or the blocking of a bank account)'. He then proceeds to note that, during the drafting of Art 2(4), Brazil had proposed that States should also be required to 'refrain from economic measures' This proposal was rejected. The matter was not clarified by the General Assembly's 1970 Declaration on Principles of International Law Concerning Friendly Relations and Co-operation among States in Accordance with the Charter of the UN (2625 (XXV)), primarily because of disagreements between the western and eastern blocks. However, Art 5(1) of the General Assembly Resolution on the Definition of Aggression (3314(XXIX)) 1974 states that: 'No consideration of whatever nature, whether political, economic, military or otherwise, may serve as a justification for aggression.'[1] Thus, it is contended that Poltova could not legitimise its actions, either the blockade or the use of force, on the basis of self-defence.

Kantuvo could argue that the imposition of the blockade amounted to an armed attack upon it. This was the response of Israel in 1967 when Egypt blockaded the Gulf of Aqaba in 1967. Israel's delegate to the UN thought that such an action justified an armed response by Israel by way of self-defence. He stated that: 'Blockades have traditionally been regarded as acts of war. To blockade, after all, is to attempt strangulation, and sovereign States are entitled not to have their trade strangled'. Further, despite Art 5(1) of Resolution 3314 and inconsistent State practice, it could be contended that the blockade could be viewed as an act of aggression. Article 3 of Resolution 3314 states that: 'Any of the following acts, regardless of a declaration of war, shall, subject to and in accordance with the provisions of Art 2, qualify as an act of aggression ... (c) The blockade of the ports or coasts of a State by the armed forces of another State.' This aggression is exacerbated by the fact that it deprives Kantuvo of 80% of all its imports and exports.[2]

Poltova might argue that its intervention in Kantuvo was not in breach of Arts 2(3) and 2(4) of the UN Charter on the basis that Kantuvo had been taken away from it by force by Imperia. Such an argument was put forward by the Argentinian delegate at the

UN following the invasion of the Falkland Islands in 1982. Representing Argentina, Mr Costa Mendez stated that:

No provision of the charter can be taken to mean the legitimisation of situations which have their origin in wrongful acts, in acts carried out before the charter was adopted and which subsisted during its prevailing force. Today, in 1982, the purposes of the organisation cannot be invoked to justify acts carried out in the last century in flagrant violation of principles that are today embodied in international law.

It is contended that this view would run counter to the objectives of the charter (see the *Corfu Channel* case (1947)). After 1945, a State has to use peaceful means for resolving a territorial dispute, however valid its claim to that disputed territory might be. As Harris points out, the only exception to this would be if the action were taken in self-defence. As stated above, Poltova would be unlikely to succeed in establishing that it was acting upon this basis. In addition, Poltova's annexation of Kantuvo would also be viewed as an illegitimate act. Article 5(3) of General Assembly Resolution 3314 states that: 'No territorial acquisition or special advantage resulting from aggression is or shall be recognised as lawful.' This view is supported by State practice. In response to Iraq's declaration of a 'comprehensive and internal merger' with Kuwait, the Security Council in 1990 adopted Resolution 662, which stated that the annexation of Kuwait had no legal validity and was to be considered null and void. It further called upon State and international organisations not to recognise the annexation.[3]

Acting under Arts 39 and 40 of Chapter VII of the Charter, the Security Council can determine that the invasion constituted a breach of international peace and security. It can then demand that Poltova withdraw immediately and unconditionally from Kantuvo and call upon the parties to resolve their dispute through negotiation. The Security Council acted in this way with regard to the North Korean invasion of South Korea (1950)[4] and the Argentinian invasion of the Falkland Islands (1982)[5] and the Iraqi invasion of Kuwait (1990).[6] Article 41 of the charter would allow the Security Council to impose economic sanctions upon Poltova in an attempt to achieve its withdrawal from Kantuvo. Security Council Resolution 661[7] was an attempt peacefully to secure Iraqi withdrawal from Kuwait in 1990. It imposed a financial and trade embargo on Iraq and occupied Kuwait and established a sanctions committee (composed of Security Council Members) to observe and monitor the implementation of the sanctions. Should sanctions fail to work, resort may be had to collective force (an enforcement action) under Art 42 or an action in collective self-defence under Art 51 of the Charter.[8]

The sanctions imposed by the Security Council produce no withdrawal of Poltovan forces from Kantuvo. Further, the veto on military action in the Security Council prevents military action under Chapter VII being taken (see Art 27 of the Charter on Security Council voting). Lenora thus proceeded to act alone by taking its own military measures to liberate Kantuvo. Can there be a legal basis for these actions? First, if there are Lenoran citizens in Kantuvo, Lenora might justify its actions upon the basis of self-defence under Art 51 or under customary international law. It might be argued that an armed attack (or threat of such an attack) on Lenoran citizens anywhere in the world is an armed attack on Lenora. Such a controversial approach, with its very broad interpretation of self-defence, has been supported by State practice.

Secondly, Lenora may claim that it is acting by way of self-help (protecting its citizens in Lenora) or in order to protect the rights of the international community. The argument would run that, following the failure of the Security Council to carry out its enforcement role, States, such as Lenora, retain the right to maintain international law and order themselves. This argument was tested and rejected by the ICJ in the *Corfu Channel* case (1949). It was further rejected by the Security Council when submitted by the United Kingdom as a justification for its invasion of Egypt in 1956. Arguably, with the exception of humanitarian intervention, such actions have no support in State practice.[9]

In conclusion, it is contended that the blockade of Kantuvo and the military actions which followed, both Poltovan and Lenoran, are illegal under international law.

Notes
1 GA Res 3314 (XXIX) GAOR 29th Session, Supp 21; (1975) 69 AJIL 480.

2   With regard to the position of Israel and the matter of blockade, see Rostow, EV, 'Legal Aspects of the Search for Peace' (1970) Proc ASIL, Vol 64, pp 127, 131–34.
3   SC Res 662 (9 Aug 1990); 29 ILM 1327.
4   SC Res (25 June 1950).
5   SC Res 502 UN Doc S/PV 2346, p 6
6   SC Res 660 (2 Aug 1990); 29 ILM 1325.
7   SC Res 661 (9 Aug 1990); 29 ILM 1325.
8   The latter seems to have been the legal basis for the UN military action which sought the liberation of Kuwait in 1990–91. The legal basis for the operation is unclear because, of all the Security Council resolutions made concerning Kuwait, only two referred to specific articles under Chapter VII. In the Resolution leading up to the military action the Council employed the policy of simply referring generally to Chapter VII powers or, alternatively, making no reference to provisions within the Charter at all. Schachter argues (in 'United Nations Law in the Gulf Conflict' 85 AJIL 452, pp 457–63), that it would be more accurate to classify the military action as one of collective self-defence (Art 51) rather than an enforcement action (Art 42) because the Security Council did not set up a centralised UN command or utilise the Military Staff Committee (Arts 43, 46, 47).
    The controversial action in Korea was said to have had Art 39 as the source of its authority.
9   This proved to be one of the justifications for UK intervention in Egypt (1956), US intervention in the Dominican Republic (1965), Grenada (1983) and Panama (1989) and of Israeli intervention in Uganda (1976).

INDEX

Accretion, 111
Acquiescence, 110
Acquisition of territory, 107–29
Alternative dispute resolution, 293–99
Arbitration, 4, 292–306, 318
Archipelagic States, 188–93
Austin, John, 5–9, 62
Aviation
  accidents, 27, 29–30
  compensation, 27, 29–30
  custom, 27
  dispute settlement, 306–14
  seizure, 173–78
  treaties and conventions, 306–14

BATNEEC, 248
Bentham, Jeremy, 14
Bilateral treaties, 39, 68
Blockades, 330
Broadcasting, 145–47
Brundtland Report, 247

CITES, 41–42
Coastal States, 182, 185–86, 192, 193–203
Codification, 33–34
Colonialism, 88–94, 109–11, 116–17, 128
Comity, 154, 157

Commission of Inquiry, 298–99
Compensation
  aviation accidents, 27, 29–30
  State responsibility, 211–12, 214–16
Conciliation, 296–97
Conquest, 111, 114, 118–20, 126, 128
Conservation, 186, 196, 229, 232
Contiguous zones, 195
Continental shelf, 190, 192, 201
Contracts of employment, 168–70
Conventions
  See Treaties and conventions
Criminal law
  diplomatic immunity, 164, 166–73
  extradition, 148, 307, 310
  extraterritoriality, 134–39, 142, 147
  genocide, 21, 26, 137
  jurisdiction, 131–32, 134–39, 151
  slavery, 145, 147–49
  treason, 141–42
Custody, 131, 145, 148
Custom, 15, 18–21, 27–32
  aviation accidents, 27
  diplomatic representatives, 22–26, 160
  environment, 236–39, 245, 252–61, 263–64
  evidence, 19, 23
  genocide, 26

human rights, 272–75, 278, 281, 283–84, 287
International
    Court of Justice, 17, 23–24
    jurisdiction, 134
    law of the sea, 180–86, 188–91, 198–200, 203
municipal law, 59–66, 68, 72–78
objections, 26, 30
opinio juris, 19, 21, 25, 28, 35
sources of law, 23–24
State practice, 18–20, 28–29, 32
State responsibility, 219–20
treaties and
    conventions, 39, 40–41, 430–44, 55, 56
use of force, 325, 327, 333
war criminals, 25

Digests, 20
Diplomatic representatives
    commercial activities, 167–73
    contracts of
        employment, 168–70
    criminal law, 164, 166–73
    custom, 22–26, 160
    extraterritoriality, 160–61
    immunity, 73–74, 76, 158–65
    International
        Court of Justice, 24
    Libyan People's Bureau, 163
    missions, 160–65
    municipal law, 73–74, 76
    Teheran hostage crisis, 162
    treaties and
        conventions, 159–73
Discrimination
    foreign nationals, 216, 221

State responsibility, 215
Dispute settlement, 291–314
    alternative dispute
        resolution, 293–99
    arbitration, 292–306
    aviation, 306–07, 308–14
    conciliation, 296–97
    enforcement, 308
    extradition, 307, 310
    inquiries, 297–99
    International
        Court of Justice, 291–314
    jurisdiction, 301–06
    jus cogens, 302
    mediation, 295–96
    negotiations, 293–95
    State practice, 314
    treaties and
        conventions, 294, 296–307
    United Nations, 291, 293, 294, 296, 299–300, 307–14
    use of force, 293
    war, 319
Dualism, 61
Dumping at sea, 260

Emergencies, 221
Endangered species, 41–42
Enforcement, 9
    dispute settlement, 308
    environment, 245, 268
    human rights, 276–77, 288, 290
    jurisdiction, 131, 133, 136
    law of the sea, 203
    municipal law, 61
    use of force, 315
Environment, 229–70
    BATNEEC, 248
    Brundtland Report, 247
    conservation, 229, 232

INDEX

custom, 233, 236, 237–39, 245–61, 263–64
decision making, 251–52, 266–68
dispute resolution, 231
due diligence, 231, 235, 267
dumping at sea, 260
enforcement, 268
European Union, 251
extraterritoriality, 242, 254
human rights, 262–63, 268, 269
individuals, 251–52, 267
information, 231, 267, 268
intergovernmental organisations, 245, 262–70
International Court of Justice, 232, 236, 255
International Law Commission, 238
law of the sea, 248–49, 257–58, 264–65
monitoring, 258–59
non-governmental organisations, 245, 246, 251, 262–70
nuclear tests, 242
oil pollution, 250
opinio juris, 230, 239, 243
personality, 245, 246, 265
polluter pays, 231, 250–51
precautionary principle, 232, 249
preventive principle, 232, 248–49
Rio Summit 19, 92, 232, 238–40, 246–50, 253, 256–57, 264, 268–70
sovereignty, 242, 245, 254, 268
State practice, 243, 253, 263
State responsibility, 20, 231, 235, 242, 261

Stockholm Declaration 1972, 229, 232, 238–41, 248, 253, 255, 257, 264, 269
supervision, 258–59
sustainable development, 231, 237, 239, 243, 247–48, 256, 269
treaties and conventions, 229–31, 233–34, 236, 249–50, 258–62, 265–66, 269
United Nations, 235, 238–39, 251, 260–61, 263
European Convention on Human Rights, 65, 71, 99, 272, 277, 288–90
European Union
EC law, 65, 71
environment, 251
extraterritoriality, 150–51, 154–55
jurisdiction, 150–51, 154–55
Exclusive economic zones, 185–86, 190–92, 196–203
Executive agreements, 59, 67–71
Exhaustion of local remedies, 214–16
Expropriation, 208–13, 217
Extradition, 148, 307, 310
Extraterritoriality, 131–42, 147, 150–56, 160–61, 254

Fisheries, 185–86, 190–92, 196–203

337

Flag States, 193–97
Force majeure, 222
Foreign investment, 214–17
Foreign nationals, 208–28

Genocide, 21, 27, 137
General principles of law, 24
Government
  exiled, 100–05
  locus standi, 82
  recognition, 79–88, 100–05
Grotius, 4, 13, 19–20

Hart, HLA, 7
History of public
  international law, 2, 12–14
Human rights, 65, 71, 271–90
  custom, 272–75, 278, 281, 283–84, 287
  enforcement, 276–77, 288, 290
  environment, 262–63, 268–69
  European Convention
    on Human Rights, 272, 277, 288–90
  individuals, 272, 285–90
  intergovernmental
    organisations, 271, 286
  International Covenant
    on Civil and Political
    Rights, 273, 278–81, 284–85, 288
  International Covenant
    on Economic, Social
    and Cultural Rights, 273, 278
  International Law
    Commission, 282
  jurisdiction, 287

law of the sea, 180, 202
locus standi, 290
non-governmental
  organisations, 290
personality, 99, 285–87, 290
slavery, 147
sovereignty, 286
State responsibility, 271, 282, 283, 286
treaties and
  conventions, 97–98, 272, 277–78, 284–85, 287–90
United Nations, 272–73, 277–78, 286, 289
Universal Declaration
  of Human Rights, 273, 288

Immunity from
  jurisdiction, 157–78
  comity, 157
  diplomatic, 73–74, 76, 158–65
  stare decisis, 157–58
  State, 157–58, 173–78
  treaties and
    conventions, 157–58, 174
Innocent passage, 184–85
Individuals
  environment, 251–52, 267
  human rights, 272, 285–90
  personality, 95–99
Inquiries, 298–99
Intergovernmental
  organisations, 245, 262–71, 286
International
  Court of Justice, 4, 15, 291–314
  advisory opinions, 308–14

338

custom,	17, 23–24	definition,	133
diplomatic representatives,	24	enforcement,	131, 133, 136
environment,	232, 236, 255	European Union,	150–51, 154–55
jurisdiction, 301–06		extradition,	148
recognition,	91, 92	extraterritoriality,	131–42, 147, 150–56
stare decisis,	322		
State responsibility,	206	genocide,	137
Statute,	17, 34, 38	Harvard Study,	134–37
treaties and conventions,	38	human rights, International	287
use of force,	322, 324, 326–27, 330–31	Court of Justice, law of the sea,	301–06 140–41, 144–50
International Covenant on Civil and Political Rights,	273, 279–81, 285, 288	nationality, personality, prescription, slavery,	141–42 136, 137, 140, 143 131, 133 145, 147–49
International Covenant on Economic, Social and Cultural Rights,	273	sovereignty, State practice, territorial sea,	133–34, 144–50 134 145–46
International Law Commission,	33, 205–06, 210, 222, 225–26, 238, 282	treason, United Nations, United States, *Jus cogens*,	141–42 148 147–56 47, 53, 302
International organisations, *See also* Particular organisations	91	*Jus gentium*, Law of the sea,	13 11, 140–41, 179–203
Intertemporal law doctrine,	114–18, 125	League of Nations,	318–19
Investments,	11	Mediation,	295–96
Jurisdiction,	131–55	Multinational enterprises,	95–99
See also Immunity from jurisdiction		Municipal laws conflicts,	67–71
broadcasting,	145–47	custom,	59–66, 68, 72–78
civil,	131–32, 150–56	diplomatic	
comity,	154	immunity,	73–74, 76
criminal,	131–2, 134–49, 151	Dualism, EC law,	61 65, 71
custody,	145, 148	enforcement,	61
custom,	134		

339

European Convention on
    Human Rights, 65, 71
  executive agreements, 59, 67–71
  incorporationism, 72–78
  public international law,
    relationship between, 59–78
  stare decisis, 65, 75–76
  State immunity, 75
  State practice, 75–76
  statutory interpretation, 63
  treaties and
    conventions, 59, 68–71
  United States, 69–71

Nation States, 3
National law
  See Municipal laws
Nationalisation, 208–13
Nationality, 141–42, 200
Natural law, 12, 15
Negotiations, 294–95
Nietzsche, Friedrich, 14
Non-governmental
  organisations, 245–46, 251, 262–70, 290
Novation, 111
Nuclear tests, 242

Occupation, 116, 128–29
OECD, 96–97
Opinio juris, 19, 21, 24, 25, 28, 35, 230, 239, 243

Permanent Court of
  Arbitration, 4, 318
Permanent Court of
  International Justice, 4, 15, 291

Personality
  environment, 245–46, 265
  human rights, 99, 285–87, 290
  jurisdiction, 136, 137, 140, 143
  multinational
    enterprises, 95–99
  recognition, 89, 92, 95–99
  States, 81, 89, 92
  United Nations, 96
Pirate radio stations, 145–46
Pollock, Frederick, 8
Polluter pays, 231, 250–51
Pollution, 186, 250
Positivism, 11–16
Precautionary principle, 232, 249
Precedent, 65, 75–76
Prescription, 110–11, 117, 123, 126–27, 131, 133
Preventive principle, 232, 248–49

Recognition, 79–105
  colonialism, 88–94
  de facto, 83, 85–88, 101–05
  de jure, 83–86, 101–04
  exiled governments, 100–05
  governments, 79–88, 100–05
  individuals, 95–99
  International
    Court of Justice, 91, 92
  international organisations, 91
  locus standi, 82
  multinational
    companies, 95–99
  non-recognition, 83–4
  personality, 89, 92, 95–99

340

INDEX

retroactive, 104
self-determination, 93
standards, 94
State practice, 92
States, 81, 88–94
United Nations, 90–91
United States, 83
Retribution, 323–28
Rio Summit 1992, 232, 238–40, 246–50, 253, 257, 264–65, 268–70
Roman law, 12–13
Russell, Lord, 10
Sanctions, 54, 315, 333
Self-defence
  acquisition of territory, 120–21
  State responsibility, 222
  use of force, 315, 321, 323–28, 330–33
Self-determination, 93, 112, 117–18
Self-help, 5, 333
Shareholders, 217
Slavery, 145, 147–49
Sources of public international law, 17–36
Sovereignty
  acquisition of territory, 110, 115, 128
  environment, 242, 245, 254, 268
  human rights, 286
  jurisdiction, 133–34, 144–50
  law of the sea, 181, 185, 191–92, 200–01
  States, 3–4
Stare decisis, 75, 157–58, 322
State practice, 4, 13–15
  codification, 33–34
  custom, 18–20, 28–29, 32

dispute settlement, 314
environment, 243, 253, 263
evidence, 19, 23
information, 20
jurisdiction, 134
law of the sea, 184–85, 193, 194
municipal law, 75–76
recognition, 92
treaties and conventions, 33
use of force, 316, 323–28, 332
State responsibility, 20, 205–28, 231, 235, 242, 261, 271, 282–83, 286
States
  See also State practice, State responsibility
  comity, 157
  immunity, 157–59, 172–78
  national, 3
  personality, 81, 89, 92
  recognition, 81, 88–94
  relations, between, 3
  seizure of assets, 173–78
  sovereignty, 3–4
  succession, 56–57
  treaties and conventions, 174
  war, 4
Stockholm
  Declaration 1972, 229, 232, 238–41, 248, 253, 255, 257, 264, 269
Straits, 184, 195, 197
Subjugation, 119–20
Sustainable development, 231, 237, 239, 243, 247–48, 256

341

Terra nullius,	108–11, 114–18, 120, 125–28	incorporationism,	72–78
Territorial sea,	140, 145–46, 191, 195, 197	International Court of Justice,	38
		interpretation,	43–47
Territory		investment disputes,	11
See Acquisition of territory		*jus cogens*,	47, 53
		law making,	39–40
Terrorism,	323–28	law, of,	37–57
Transnational corporations,	95–99	law of the sea,	179–203
travaux preparatoires,	46	mediation,	296
Treason,	141–42	multilateral,	39
Treaties and conventions,	7–8	municipal law,	59, 68–71
acquisition of		ratification,	25
territory,	110, 114, 116, 121–23	role,	32–36
		sanctions,	54
amending,	49–51	self-executing,	66, 70
aviation,	306–14	severance,	49
bilateral,	39, 68	sources of law,	30, 38–38
binding effect, of,	40–41, 52–57	State immunity,	174
conciliation,	297	State practice,	33
custom,	39, 40–41, 43–44, 55, 56	status,	9–10
		successor States,	56–57
definition,	53	termination,	49–51
denunciation,	50–51	*travaux preparatoires*,	46
diplomatic immunity,	159–73	United Nations,	33, 35, 39–40, 54
dispute settlement,	294, 296–314	use of force,	54, 316, 325
duress,	53–54	Vienna Convention,	34, 37–38, 43–44, 49–50, 53–55, 316
endangered species,	41–42		
environment,	229–30, 233–34, 236, 250, 258–62, 265–66	war,	49, 317
		withdrawal,	50–51
genocide,	21	United Nations	
guidelines,	9	acquisition of	
human rights,	97–98, 272, 277, 284–85, 287–90	territory,	111, 117, 119–21
		Charter,	6, 10, 31, 90, 272–73, 277, 289, 291, 294, 300, 307, 315, 319, 323–34
immunity from jurisdiction,	157–58		
importance,	38–42		

INDEX

dispute settlement, 291, 293–94, 296, 299–300, 307–14
environment, 235, 238–39, 251, 256, 260–61, 263
General Assembly, 6, 27–32, 323–28
genocide, 21
human rights, 272–73, 277–78, 286, 289
jurisdiction, 148
mental health, 35
personality, 96
recognition, 90–91
resolutions, 27–32
Security Council, 5, 296, 307–14, 320–34
slavery, 147
State responsibility, 212
treaties and conventions, 33, 35, 39–40, 54
use of force, 4, 315, 320–34
war, 6, 319–20, 323–28

United States
acquisition of territory, 118–23
extraterritoriality, 147–56
jurisdiction, 147–56
law of the sea, 180, 183
multinational enterprises, 97
municipal law, 69–71
recognition, 83
Universal Declaration of Human Rights, 273, 288

Use of force, 315–34
See also War
dispute settlement, 293
enforcement, 315, 321
illegality, 320–21, 328
International Court of Justice, 322
retribution, 323–28
sanctions, 315, 333
self-defence, 315, 321, 323–28
self-help, 5
State practice, 316, 323–28
terrorism, 323–28
treaties and conventions, 54, 316
United Nations, 4, 315, 321–34

War, 316–22, 317–22
crimes, 25
dispute resolution, 318–19
enforcement, 321
holy, 322–28
illegality, 5, 317–18
League of Nations, 318–19
Permanent Court of Arbitration, 318
procedural law, 4
ships, 184–85, 195
States, 4
treaties and conventions, 49, 317
United Nations, 6, 319–21, 323–38

World Court
See International Court of Justice

343